Along the Ramparts of the Tetons

Along the Ramparts of the Tetons

THE SAGA OF JACKSON HOLE, WYOMING

By Robert B. Betts

COLORADO ASSOCIATED UNIVERSITY PRESS BOULDER COLORADO

Copyright © 1978 by Robert B. Betts
International Standard Book Numbers 0-87081-113-4 (cloth edition)
and 0-87081-117-7 (paper edition)
Library of Congress Card Catalog Number 77-94083
Printed in the United States of America
Designed by Bruce Campbell

For my wife, Emmie.
Except for her, I would never have gone to
Jackson Hole to visit.
Except for her, I would never have had so
many kids to take to Jackson Hole.
Except for her, I would never have put down some roots
in Jackson Hole and become fascinated
with its past.

Contents

List of Illustrations

Introduction

For a century and a half men and women of record have fallen in love with Jackson Hole and stood in awe before the stunning up-thrust of the Teton Range.

Photographers have taken good pictures of these mountains, artists have painted them well, writers have set down good words—but there, not to be captured, stand the Tetons. They defy lens, pencil and brush and, most of all, language. Words like beauty, magnificence and majesty are only frail nouns that fall before the incredible fact.

There are a good many printed works, scientific and impressionable, about the mountains, the valley and the hub town of Jackson, but each is only a piece of the whole. Until now, so far as I know, the full story has not been told, certainly never as Robert B. Betts tells it.

He fills the vacancy. He begins with the geology of the Teton range and the valley, proceeds to prehistoric man, goes on to early and later Indians, to the mountain men, to first settlement and, finally, to dude ranching and tourists, to the valley as it is now.

He takes time along the way for brief sketches of noted mountain men, whose essential character, he believes, accounts for the present local live-and-let-live attitude, to the toleration of eccentricity, to the individualism and self-reliance that led residents to refuse a government grant for a swimming pool. He tells the John Colter story, deals with the fur trade, with the reclusive and strange early and later settlers, with cattle ranching, with trophy hunters aiming for elk, with the slaughter of elk for the tusks that used to adorn watch fobs and cuff links, with cattle-versus-sheep conflict, with bad men such as they were and with the establishment of the National Elk Refuge, winter feeding ground of the world's largest herd of elk.

In a chapter called *The Angry Years* he relates the long and bitter controversy about the future of Jackson Hole. Should the Tetons—the word is embrasive—be made a part of Yellowstone

National Park? What about a park separate and distinct? Should nothing be done, and the valley and its lakes be left to the natural and destructive ways of an unstructured society?

The differences were settled, finally, through a bold stroke by Franklin D. Roosevelt. Using presidential prerogative, he named the region a national monument in 1943. But that was after a long period of strife in which John D. Rockefeller, Jr., Horace Albright, Struthers Burt, numerous politicians and all the local inhabitants took their differing stands. Betts' sympathies, be it said, are on the side of salvation.

The author's interests are so many and varied as to put his book beyond easy classification. Pre-history, geological, animal and human, gets his attention. So does society. So do economics. So does the future. But he is curious about the individual in his own right, be the person of real importance or not, so long as he has some cachet.

It is a temptation to call this work scholarly, it is documented so well, but the adjective may suggest dullness, and dull this book is not. It is a temptation to call it chatty, but the word is cheapening. It might be called a history if it didn't poke into so many places that the academic historian would ignore.

But all right. Call it scholarly. Call it chatty. Say it is a history. The terms don't matter. What matters is that we have the story of Jackson Hole now.

A. B. Guthrie, Jr.

Preface

A man named Struthers Burt once wrote, "You must search for the loveliness of America; it is not obvious; it is scattered; but when you find it, it touches you and binds you to it like a great secret oath taken in silence."[1] My family and I were lucky. We found in Jackson Hole that piece of America which touches us and binds us to it. What brought it all about started in the summer of 1964, when my wife wanted the family to see the Tetons and spend some time on a dude ranch.

As Easterners who had never been to the Rocky Mountains, we had no idea of what to expect, so we were completely unprepared for our introduction to this country. And what a dramatic introduction it turned out to be. When the plane from Salt Lake City dropped through the clouds and began its steep descent into the valley of Jackson Hole, suddenly the Tetons were there, mountains unlike any other mountains we had ever seen—sheer, without foothills, a massive forty-mile parade of snow-draped peaks and pinnacles. Then, just as suddenly, the Tetons were above us and rising higher as the plane skimmed down past their enormous canyons to the small airport at their feet, until, at the moment of touchdown, we had to crane our necks to see up to the peaks rising more than a mile into the blue Wyoming sky.

But this was only the beginning of our introduction to this country and its people. Before the day was out, we had settled in at the Turner family's Triangle X Ranch, had taken a supper ride down to the Snake River, had sat around a campfire as cowboys strummed guitars and sang old Western songs, and had gone to bed to the sound of coyotes howling in the hills. In a matter of hours, we had been transported from the frantic pace of New York City into a land of wild beauty and friendly people, and our lives have never been the same since.

After coming back year after year to shed our city clothes and tensions, after making a number of friends whose ranks continue to grow, and after finding that our children had developed a deep attachment to this valley and its way of life, we finally built a home here, to which we one day hope to retire. It stands on a bluff on the eastern side of Jackson Hole, and from it we can see the entire Teton Range, the full spread of the fifty-mile valley and, far to the north, Yellowstone National Park. There are few, if any, more spectacular or famous landscapes on this third planet from the sun, so when the house was finished we were not surprised to learn that many of our Eastern friends planned to "drop by to catch the view," although it meant a trip of several thousand miles. And they are the reason this book came to be written.

At first, I had nothing more in mind than to compile a set of notes to help give our friends some understanding of how the Tetons were formed and some feeling for what I thought would be the relatively recent history of the men and women who have lived out their lives here. However, the more I delved into the subject the more it opened up into a view as vast and varied as the one from our front deck, a view which goes back almost to the beginning of time and encompasses a remarkable series of events and an equally remarkable cast of players. So the notes slowly grew into chapters and the chapters slowly grew into a book—not a formal, year-by-year history, to be sure, but rather an attempt to trace the primary forces and personalities that shaped the special character of this valley.

My favorite time of day in Jackson Hole is when the sun begins to slip over the Tetons and the temperature drops quickly. This is when the light, which is such an integral part of this indescribably beautiful landscape, does magical things to the mountains and the valley they shadow. Part of the magic, at least for me, is to look out upon this darkening sea of space and try to see it as a stage on which scenes but dimly remembered are once more acted out by the original players, now ghosts. It is a pastime I enjoy, and I can only hope that you, the reader, will also enjoy peering back into Jackson Hole's long and colorful history.

Jackson Hole, Wyoming   R. B. B.
October, 1977

Acknowledgments

As this book slowly evolved and one difficulty after another arose, I was reminded more than once of a cowboy named Bill Howard who years ago lived in Jackson Hole. Tired of having to be outdoors on horseback in all kinds of bad weather, Bill decided to move indoors and make his living by writing books. His reason for believing there was nothing to it was beautifully simple. "There isn't one single word in any of these books that isn't in the dictionary," he said. "All I need is a dictionary." [1] So Bill bought a dictionary, moved indoors and went to work. First, he spelled out the title of the novel-to-be, *Breathless Love,* then he opened the dictionary and began reading it. But the task turned out to be more than he had bargained for. Two weeks and two painfully written pages later, Bill said the hell with it and went back to riding in the rain and snow.

Many times I felt like doing what Bill did, saying the hell with it and going back to the trade I know. And I probably would have if I had been all on my own as he was. I was, however, more fortunate than he; I had far more than just a dictionary to draw on. I had a number of institutions and people who kept me going with their generous support in terms of information, advice, technical assistance and encouragement, the last being perhaps the most important contribution of all.

For out-of-print books, old magazine articles, obscure monographs, microfilms of early documents and photocopies of diaries and letters, I am especially indebted to the Western History Research Center of the University of Wyoming, the Yale University Library, the Teton County Library, the Grand Teton National Park Library and the New York Public Library.

The list of people to whom thanks are due is not as easy to compile, because along the way there were more than I can possibly name who contributed an item here or a point of view there, all of which helped. Principally, they are Dr. Gene Gressley of the University of Wyoming, who has been a staunch supporter of the project and a primary supplier of materials to it almost from its inception; Dr. Elizabeth R. Brownell, who has assembled and maintained the files of the Teton County Chapter of the Wyoming State Historical Society, and who kindly took the time to read the original manuscript and set me straight on a number of my "facts"; W. C. "Slim" Lawrence, who shared his endless knowledge of and enthusiasm for Jackson Hole's history with me; Dr. Gary Wright, Department of Anthropology, State University of New York at Albany, who most considerately allowed me to read his excellent work on the early peoples of Jackson Hole while it was still in manuscript form; Almer Nelson, former manager of the National Elk Refuge for more than thirty years, who went over the chapter on the elk herd; Conrad Schwiering, eminent artist of the Tetons and the West, who at just the right moment said just the right thing to rekindle my then almost extinguished interest; Joan Morcerf, who tirelessly and always with a smile typed revision after revision, giving more of her time than I had any right to ask; and my friend and business colleague John Peace and his son Bill, both of whom understood what I was trying to do and cheered me on in the belief that the job undertaken would somehow, someday turn into a book. To them all I owe much, but there is one matter for which I insist on taking sole credit: whatever errors that may have crept into the text.

Along the Ramparts of the Tetons

The feeling of emptiness one gets in Wyoming—the ache of vast-ness and of solitude—is not because it has no past. It is rather because the signs and monuments of the past are so meager and so few. The characters in its cavalcade—the Indians, the trappers, the miners, the scouts, the bullwhackers, the mule skinners, and the cowboys—left hardly a trace in their passing. They came, they did, and they went. The decaying logs of an old fur press, rotting sluice boxes, the stone abutments of a railroad trestle, a rusty beaver trap lying in the weeds along a river, a broken arrowhead kicked up in a field—these are the relics of Wyoming's history. Nearly everything else is scenery, emptiness, and the ever-enduring grass.[1]

—Hamilton Basso

1

Chartres Multiplied by Six

One of the great legends of the West is that in 1807 a young man named John Colter roamed by himself across many miles of what is now northwestern Wyoming. In the course of his epic journey, the legend says, he was the first white man to come upon what is today acclaimed to be one of the earth's most magnificent landscapes— the sky-piercing Tetons extending for a distance of more than forty miles along the serene and lovely valley of Jackson Hole. If the legend is true, then Colter in all likelihood made still another discovery. When he returned to civilization, he was probably the first to discover the frustration thousands of others have since experienced when they tried to convey in words or pictures the magnitude and beauty of this land.

While painters may suggest the dramatic size of some of the Tetons' thrusting peaks and plunging canyons, there is simply no way their brushes can wrestle the full immensity of this range down to a canvas. And photographers, no matter how wide their lenses, also go away knowing they have captured but a part of the whole, a fragment of a vista so vast it refuses to be reduced to a small rectangle of film. Nor do those who try to put this landscape into words have it any easier. Theodore Roosevelt, who could turn a phrase, was so overwhelmed the best he could do was call it "the most beautiful country in the world."[1] Bernard DeVoto, a virtuoso with words, did not even attempt to describe what he had seen. "There are no adjectives," he wrote, "adequate to express the beauty and sublimity of this, the Jackson's Hole—Teton Hole—Snake River country."*[2]

---

* Named in 1829 for David E. Jackson, a prominent member of the fur trade, the valley was long called Jackson's Hole, a hole being in the terminology of the early West a large, open valley encircled by high mountains. Around the turn of the century, local officials decided to shorten the name because "The term Jackson's Hole gives rise to ribald remarks not in keeping with the dignity of this beautiful valley." (Donald Hough, *The Cocktail Hour in Jackson Hole*, p. 169) Over the years, the more refined spelling has gradually become the accepted form.

There is, however, one word that many people turn to when they look out upon the sweep of the Tetons and Jackson Hole for the first time: "Shangri-la!" Trite? Perhaps. But it does convey the feeling this mountain-engirded valley evokes, although it falls far short as an accurate description of the terrain. Whereas the imaginary Shangri-la of *Lost Horizon* was a circular, verdant valley surrounded by towering, perpetually snow-capped mountains, Jackson Hole is an elongated, semiarid valley surrounded by mountains which are truly towering and perpetually snow-capped on only one side. Still, the word stands up. It catches the spirit of the place—the grandeur of the Tetons, the tranquillity of the valley and, perhaps more than anything else, the sense of remoteness one feels here that makes the outside world and all its turmoil seem far away, almost unreal.

Although it is true there are no adjectives adequate to express the beauty of the Tetons and Jackson Hole, a few facts and figures may help give some idea of the size of this land, which lies just west of the Continental Divide, just south of Yellowstone National Park, just east of Idaho and just north of the Snake River Canyon. This is big country, even by Western standards, with the Tetons and the valley alone taking up more than six hundred square miles, or about half the size of Rhode Island. Add onto this the enormous Teton National Forest adjoining the valley on the east, and the immediate area becomes as large as Rhode Island and Delaware combined. This is also high country, even by Rocky Mountain standards, with its lower elevations lying for the most part well over a mile above sea level. But as big and as high as this country is, the Tetons totally dominate it. Giants astride the horizon, their hulks loom over the valley and their glistening peaks can be seen from great distances across the wild and largely uninhabited region extending for many miles around them.

Running north and south through Grand Teton National Park, the Teton Range rises like a tidal wave of stone that has rolled in from the west, has crested and is about to come crashing down into Jackson Hole. And there they stand, frozen in place, shining mountains containing seven peaks ascending to altitudes of more than 12,000 feet above sea level, while still another nine peaks exceed 11,000 feet. The tallest of them all, the Grand Teton, measures in at 13,770 feet—or, put another way, just to match the 7,000 feet of its height that can be seen, from its massive base on the valley floor to its Matterhorn-like summit, would take five Empire

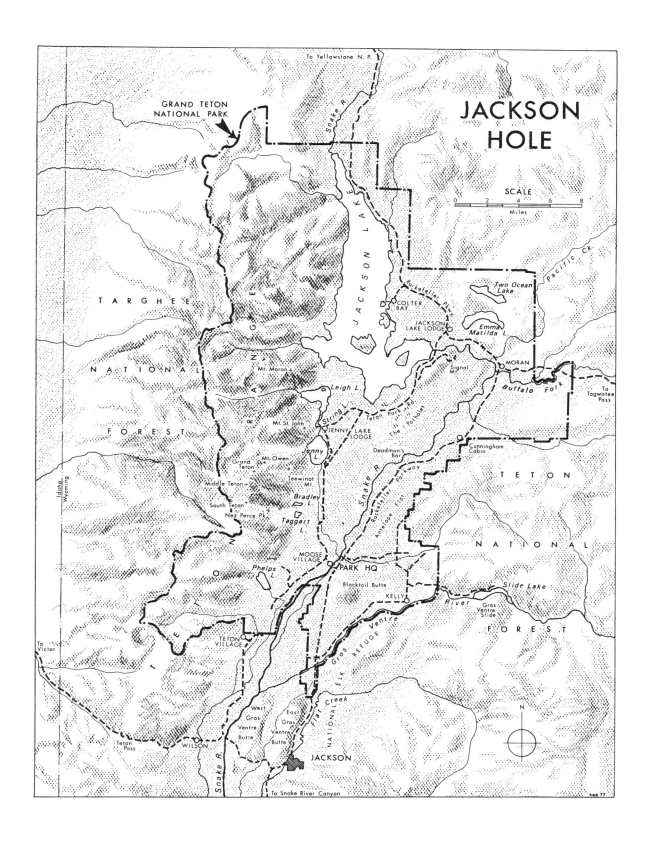

JACKSON HOLE

To Yellowstone N. P.

GRAND TETON
NATIONAL PARK

TARGHEE

SCALE
0   2   4   6   8
Miles

Pacific Ck.

Two Ocean
Lake

NATIONAL

JACKSON LAKE

COLTER
BAY

JACKSON
LAKE LODGE

Emma
Matilda L.

Rockefeller Pkwy.

MORAN

Mt. Moran

Buffalo Fork

To Togwotee
Pass

FOREST

Leigh L.

Signal Mt.

String L.

Teton Park Rd.

The Potholes

Mt. St. John

JENNY LAKE
LODGE

Jenny L.

Deadman's Bar

Cunningham
Cabin

Mt. Owen

Grand Teton

Teewinot Mt.

Middle Teton

Snake R.

TETON

Bradley L.

South Teton

Nez Perce Pk.

Taggart L.

Rockefeller Parkway

Antelope Flat

NATIONAL

Idaho
Wyoming

MOOSE
VILLAGE

Phelps L.

PARK HQ

Blacktail Butte

KELLY

Slide Lake

Gros
Ventre
Slide

Gros Ventre River

FOREST

T E T O N

NATIONAL ELK REFUGE

TETON
VILLAGE

Flat Creek

West
Gros
Ventre
Butte

East
Gros
Ventre
Butte

Snake R.

To Victor

Teton Pass

WILSON

N

JACKSON

To Snake River Canyon

kae 77

State Buildings stacked one on top of the other. In the same terms, for the skyline of Manhattan to begin to rival the dimensions of the entire Teton Range, it would have to be at least five times longer than it is and rise more than a mile into the sky.

As impressive as these figures are, the fact remains that the Tetons are not statistically of true championship class, for there are fifty mountains in the lower forty-eight states and eighteen mountains in Alaska whose peaks top 14,000 feet. Nevertheless, as high as these other mountains may be, they are not built in a way to deliver the visual impact of the Tetons. What makes the Tetons so spectacularly different from other mountains is that they have no foothills, no gently rising uplifts to blend in and soften the view, no subtle introductory passages leading to the main symphonic theme. Suddenly, like an unexpected clash of cymbals, the Tetons are there, sheer against the sky. This is the perspective, the optical trick the Tetons play to make themselves appear to rise higher than they actually do. And because of their jagged, uninterrupted outline, children often greet them with cries of delight as "fairy tale mountains" come true.

One of the principal features of the Tetons is a four-mile concentration of many of the tallest peaks and pinnacles. Composed mainly of the Grand Teton, Middle Teton, South Teton, Mount Owen, Mount Teewinot and Nez Percé Peak, this cluster is called the Cathedral Group, and it takes only one look to see why it was given this name: Chartres multiplied by six, a choir of shimmering granite spires soaring high above the nave and transept of the valley below. The name of the three Tetons themselves has a more worldly derivation, going back to the early nineteenth century when French-speaking trappers from Canada, far from home and womanless, saw them as *les Trois Tetons*, the three breasts. From a similar masculine viewpoint, an old Hudson's Bay Company map identified them as the Three Paps, and they were also called the Pilot Knobs by the Astorians, those first, ill-fated proconsuls of John Jacob Astor's western fur empire. The Indians, on the other hand, saw no Freudian symbols in these mountains. They knew them simply as the Hoary-headed Fathers, the Three Brothers and Teewinot, the pinnacles.

Above the timberline, all is a world of horned peaks, serrated ridges and wind-swept solitude. It is a world both serene and savage, where in summer fields of perpetual snow sparkle in the sun, and from which in winter avalanches are unleashed, without a

Sunset from the Snake River overlook. *Photo by Bob Clemenz.*

Winter morning along the Snake River. *Photo by A. Garaman.*

A bull elk, one of the thousands in the Jackson Hole herd. *Photo by Dick Cunningham.*

Indian paintbrush, Wyoming's state flower. *Photo by Richard Murphy.*

Trumpeter swan and cygnet. *Photo by William Fraser.*

whisper of warning, to thunder into the lower regions. Here, fed by snowmelt, hidden streams are formed that grow in size and gather momentum until they leap into view as waterfalls and cataracts. Here, too, are glaciers, vestigial reminders of the time when the upper rim of the Northern Hemisphere wore a cap of ice. Of the dozen or so small glaciers remaining in the Tetons, the largest is Teton Glacier, about 3,500 feet long and 1,100 feet wide, a miniature working model of the masses of ice which once carved the many peaks and canyons.

Farther down, the panorama broadens as the Tetons' shoulders slope steeply to the valley floor. Now comes the main phalanx of the range: deep and mysteriously shadowed canyons; blue-green forests of spruce, pine and fir; rock outcroppings shining as though a light glows from within them; and lush mountain meadows that dance in summer with the brazen colors only uninhibited Rocky Mountain wild flowers would dare to flaunt. It is an extraordinary scene made even more so by a phenomenon which occurs at this altitude, where the brilliance of the sun combines with the thinness of the air to make distances deceptive. One can look across the valley from eight or even more miles away and see so clearly that individual trees stand out on the distant mountains, an illusion like looking through binoculars without having the field of vision restricted by the tunneled sides. And just as we today are intrigued by this magnification of the far-off, so were the settlers of the West when their wagon trains began to climb up into the high country. One of them, Jessy Quinn Thornton, who was on the Oregon Trail in 1846, noted in his journal "a remarkable peculiarity in the atmosphere, which made it impossible for me to judge with any tolerable degree of accuracy as to the distance of objects."[3]

Strung out along the base of the Tetons are seven lovely alpine lakes, the largest of which is Jackson Lake. Seventeen miles long and at one point eight miles wide, it is big enough to kick up dangerous whitecaps in a storm, but when placid it innocently reflects the peaks rising directly above it. The other lakes are smaller and more jewel-like, also reflecting the peaks above them, and their water is so clear and pure it can astonish those who have forgotten, or never knew, how water is supposed to look and taste. Each of these lakes was custom-tailored by its own glacier that long ago crawled down from an adjacent canyon in the Tetons and, as a geologist put it more picturesquely than scientifically, "for a time rested its cold snout upon the floor of Jackson Hole."[4] One of these glaciers left its calling card in the southern end of Leigh Lake to let us know it was once here, moving with the power to change the surface of the earth. Before retreating into the Tetons, it deposited a boulder it had carried on its back all the way from Paintbrush Canyon—not a run-of-the-mill boulder, by any means, but one so large it forms an island almost half a city block long and as high as a five-story building. What is more, as it stands there in the water up to what may be only its chest or shoulders, these are just the dimensions which can be seen.

The mountains and highlands enclosing Jackson Hole on three sides are all quite different from the Tetons. To the south are the sharp-spined Hoback and Snake River ranges, to the north is the rolling Yellowstone Plateau and to the east are the foothills of the Gros Ventre and Washakie ranges, their gradually ascending slopes, covered with forests of lodgepole pine and groves of quaking aspen, offering a gentle counterpoint to the starkness of the Tetons opposite them. Although all of these mountains were molded into their present forms many thousands of years ago, one landscape-shaping event of immense proportions did occur on the eastern side of the valley as recently as the spring of 1925. As the result of unusually heavy rains and an earth tremor, a mile-long section of the north face of Sheep Mountain gave way, plunging down into the canyon of the Gros Ventre River below it. In less than three minutes, one of the largest landslides ever recorded took place as fifty million cubic yards of shale, sandstone and limestone roared into the canyon and dashed four hundred feet up the other side, damming the river and creating a lake where none had been before—a displacement of earth so large and so swift that if the Panama Canal had been excavated at the same rate it would have been completed in under an hour. Needless to say, the face of Sheep Mountain still wears the scar.*

Jackson Hole, the valley itself, is about sixty miles long and of irregular width, varying from six to twelve miles, and there are

* Not long after the landslide, a Gros Ventre Indian living on a reservation was shown a photograph of it, and not only did he recognize Sheep Mountain, but he also gave an unusual explanation as to why the slide had taken place. According to a tribal legend he recounted, since ancient times a party of Gros Ventre hunters and a herd of buffalo have been sealed within the mountain, the interior of which is hollow and contains a fertile valley. When the Indians are asleep, the mountain does not move. But when the Indians mount their horses and chase the buffalo, the hooves of the running animals shake the mountain and landslides occur. As quaint as the legend is, it reveals that at some time in the distant past the Gros Ventres recognized what geologists have since confirmed: the earth's crust in and near Jackson Hole is very unstable.

many places from which its entire extent can be seen. The effect is one of space on an oceanic scale, an effect heightened by one's first impression that the valley floor is absolutely flat, as flat as though a gargantuan bulldozer had scraped it to balance the bubble in a carpenter's level. But this is not so, and a more discerning look reveals the valley floor to be composed of many planes and elevations, all so skillfully constructed they blend together to give the appearance of being horizontal. This seemingly endless expanse is a restful landscape of sagebrush flats, river terraces, dark evergreen forests and gravel outwash plains, with here and there a few small mountains and buttes rising to give relief to the perspective. The most prominent of these are gracefully contoured Signal Mountain in the north, whale-shaped Blacktail Butte in the center and East Gros Ventre Butte and West Gros Ventre Butte standing like two sentries at attention in the south. Also in the south, on the eastern side of the valley, is the 23,754-acre National Elk Refuge, the main winter feeding ground of the largest elk herd in the world. Consisting at times of as many as fifteen thousand elk, the great herd of the Jackson Hole area summers in the surrounding high country, primarily Yellowstone, then migrates back to the valley and its environs when the first heavy snows begin to fall.

The last major feature of the Jackson Hole landscape is the Snake River, whose waters have flowed through the valley since time immemorial. Rising near the southern boundary of Yellowstone National Park, this turbulent river curves west, then south, passes through Jackson Lake, rushes down the valley through many twisting channels and exits from the local scene with the roar of white water between the narrow walls of the Snake River Canyon. While it is only natural to assume that this coiling, slithering ribbon of water was named for the reptile its path describes, this is not the case. The name comes from a major Indian tribe of the region, the Shoshonis, who were known to other tribes as the Snakes and to the French as *Gens du Serpent*, although not because they were of unsavory character or because they employed any unusually underhanded tactics in war. Instead, ethnologists believe they were called Snakes because of a misinterpretation of their tribal symbol, which in sign language was a sinuous, back-and-forth movement of the hand simulating the motion their ancestors had used to weave grass shelters in pre-tipi times.

As beautiful as Jackson Hole is, people do not journey from the far corners of the world solely to see its scenic wonders. Grand

Teton National Park, Yellowstone National Park and the wilderness areas bordering on them are also one of the last great sanctuaries for big game, in a way a Serengeti Plain of North America. Here many of the hounded and some of the endangered species can be seen living in a spacious natural environment which has changed but little with the arrival of man. In Jackson Hole, for example, when the elk come and go with the seasons, it is not unusual to see them moving across the valley by the hundreds, often in long, breathtaking lines. It is also not unusual, when taking a walk, to see a solitary bull moose browsing in a thicket of willows, or to witness the quiet domestic drama of a cow moose coaxing her calf to swim a river. Delicate pronghorns, resembling antelope but a species of their own, and long-eared mule deer can suddenly flit across one's path at dusk, phantoms in the gloaming, while at night, when the coyotes are yipping at the stars, black bears have been known to add to the din by turning over ranch garbage cans. Although grizzly bears seldom venture down into the valley itself, they are sometimes sighted along its outer edges, and high in the mountains close to Jackson Hole there are still bighorn sheep and occasional mountain lions. Even a small herd of buffalo lives here, offspring of a few adventurous bulls and cows who wandered away from a preserve in the upper end of the valley some years ago and proved to be too cantankerous to be driven back. (At one point, the herd discovered that the sand traps of the Jackson Hole golf course made delightful places in which to wallow, and by stubbornly refusing to leave added to the normal hazards golfers must overcome.)

Not only big game, but many different kinds of smaller animals and birds are to be found in Jackson Hole. The badger, porcupine, marten, ground squirrel, marmot, pocket gopher, otter, mink, coney, snowshoe hare, red-tailed hawk, sage grouse, osprey, sandhill crane—they and others too numerous to name are all here, with the full list naturalists have drawn up reading like a bill of lading for an American Noah's Ark. Like the ark itself, this country is also a refuge from a storm, a haven for wildlife standing high above the rising flood of civilization. It is to be hoped that it will stay this way, with man encroaching no farther than he already has, and that those who come here in the future will be able to experience the same enchanted moments we do now when a bald eagle wheels in lazy circles far above the valley, or a trumpeter swan and his mate glide regally across a pond, or a beaver family enjoys a playful sunset swim. At times like these the words written by a young woman many years ago become especially poignant for those who cherish this gifted land. Just before she lost her life in the Tetons, she made this final entry in her diary: "God Bless Wyoming and Keep it Wild."[5]

2
In the Beginning

Many of the tourists who drive through Jackson Hole are in such a hurry they pull off the highway for only several minutes to glimpse the view and snap a picture before moving on. They must get up to Yellowstone Park to see Old Faithful perform, or to the next motel so the kids can have a swim. Ask them, "Why the rush?" and they are likely to answer, "Because we're pressed for time." In those few words, they come close to summing up the human view of time—urgent, harassed, and understandably so, for we are given so little of it. But to nature time is inexhaustible, without a beginning or an end, an infinite river rising out of nowhere and flowing into nothing. This concept is almost impossible to comprehend, yet if we are to have some idea of how the Tetons and Jackson Hole were formed, we must look beyond their three dimensions and back into time on a colossal scale. In order to do this, time has to be reduced to the simplest ABC's our minds can grasp.

Imagine time as an encyclopedia, a single page of which represents the passing of 100,000 years. For the encyclopedia to cover all of the time that has elapsed from the first sunrise on earth to the one this morning, it would have to consist of 100 volumes, each 500 pages thick, or a total of 50,000 pages. The thought is staggering, especially when we consider how recent a development man is. All of his history, the entire sweep from Neanderthal man to the astronauts, is written on the very last page, page 50,000.

Some rainy afternoon when you have nothing better to do, fill out that last page. Take a sheet of paper and jot down all the important names and events of history that come to mind offhand. The planting of the first crop, the turning of the first wheel. Egypt, the pyramid of Cheops, India, Buddha, the Great Wall of China. Socrates, Aristotle, Plato. Caesar in Gaul, the Roman Empire's rise and fall. Christ, the Dark Ages, Mohammed, the Crusades. Renaissance and Reformation. Michelangelo, Leonardo, Gutenberg. Magna Charta, Columbus, the Armada. Will Shakespeare, good Queen Bess. The Aztecs in Mexico, the Incas in Peru. The French

Revolution, the Declaration of Independence, the Constitution. Napoleon at Waterloo, Lincoln at Gettysburg. Darwin, Marx, Edison, Einstein, Freud. Kitty Hawk, Ford's Model T, television, computers. And so on, down to the splitting of the atom and man clumping clumsily on the moon. You will probably find that you have easily filled the page, yet merely skimmed the surface of man's history. You will also probably find that just the list of achievements you have jotted down is so seemingly impressive it reinforces the natural inclination of our species to regard itself as something special indeed, central and vital to the order of things. But as busy as we have been and as much as we may think we have left a mark, this globe has spun around very nicely without us for five *billion* years—a disquieting reminder that humans are not one of creation's irreplaceable components.

Nor are mountains irreplaceable components. Although poets may write of them as being eternal, geologists know better. They know that even a range as mighty as the Tetons is only a passing phase in the ever-changing appearance of the earth's surface. Actually, the Tetons are latecomers as mountains go, the youngest of the Rocky Mountains and still growing at a rate estimated to be about a foot a century. They first appear in the 50,000-page encyclopedia only some eighty pages from the end, or less than nine million years ago, although many of the rocks they contain are truly ancient, dating back almost three billion years into Precambrian time, the earliest era in the earth's history.

By studying the layers of the different rocks in the Tetons and Jackson Hole, geologists have reconstructed a view, dim at some moments, brilliantly clear at others, of what this landscape looked like as it shifted and altered in the course of millions and millions of years. With their help, it is possible to peer back along the great arc of time, back through the darkness almost to the moment when the earth's geological clock first began to tick, and what we see is fascinating. It is as though we are in a theater watching the land of the Tetons unfold in the flickering light of a speeded-up motion picture.[1]

Earth time begins. The planet is formed of cosmic dust and revolves in darkness. Then titanic atomic engines within the sun ignite and there is light. The earth's surface is boiling hot and all the water drifts as vapor in the atmosphere. As the surface cools, the vapor condenses and torrential rains pour down to create the primordial sea. The continents are flat, plastic forms not even remotely resembling the shapes they will become, while just below the earth's thin crust all is a seething mass of molten matter. Eons pass. Under intense heat and pressure, the first metamorphic rocks are formed. Called gneisses and schists, they will become the core rocks of the Tetons, among the oldest rocks in North America. More eons pass. The granite is formed which will eventually be uplifted and exposed in the spires of the Cathedral Group, but this first segment of time is so very distant that, except for the rocks themselves, little can be seen.

About six hundred million years ago, the Precambrian era fades out and the Paleozoic era fades in. The screen brightens and the picture comes into sharper focus, revealing a stark landscape in the region where the Tetons will one day rise—an endless, windswept plain extending to the horizons, covered with monolithic rocks and crossed by sluggish streams. Except for the sound of the water and the wind, all is silence, for there are no trees with leaves to rustle, no birds to sing. Life on land has not yet come into being. To the west and south, the Paleozoic Sea is advancing and has already arrived to flood the surface of what in the far-off future will be Nevada, Idaho and part of Utah.

Fifty million years pass and the sea sweeps in to cover the land with warm, shallow water, then rolls on to reach as far as the Dakotas, where it joins with other shallow seas spreading west across the continent. For millions of years, the Paleozoic Sea penetrates this section of Wyoming, recedes, then again advances. Still no animal life exists on land, but in the water extensive coral reefs are forming and primitive marine organisms are already engaged in the eternal cycle of life and death. As this long era winds down, the first venturesome amphibians crawl onto land and start on an evolutionary journey which will ultimately lead to man. But before they do, some four hundred and fifty million years ago the surface of the water in this region begins to ripple when below it the earth's crust gradually rises. Slowly, like the back of a great leviathan surfacing, land emerges and the site of the future Tetons comes into view.

One hundred and fifty million years back along the arc, Mesozoic time flashes on the screen to reveal a tropical landscape dotted with palm trees, an expanse across which huge monsters lumber, reptiles so large their footsteps make the ground beneath them tremble. Dinosaurs now dominate the earth and many of the recently

Triceratops, horned dinosaurs with bodies twenty feet long, inhabited Jackson Hole when the vegetation was tropical. *Illustration by Rod Ruth from "Album of Dinosaurs" by Tom Mc-Gowen;* © *Rand McNally & Co., 1972.*

created smaller mammals scurry to escape the shadows of these giant creatures, while in the sky strange, reptilian-like birds glide and gyrate. Again the region is invaded as down from Alaska comes the Sundance Sea, followed millions of years later by another sea, the Cretaceous, both of which leave behind deep swamps inhabited by dinosaurs, one of which is Triceratops, a horned dinosaur with a body twenty feet long. Before this era ends, all of the dinosaurs will suddenly and without our knowing why have become extinct, and with their demise other forms of life will increase in size and numbers. Also toward the end of this era, the earth's surface here begins to move and the land slowly curves upward in a long, low arch.

Cenozoic time arrives, starting as recently as sixty-five million years ago, and although the arch continues to grow, it and the land around it still lie close to sea level. Now horses the size of a dog trot across the screen, while crocodiles can be seen basking in the sun

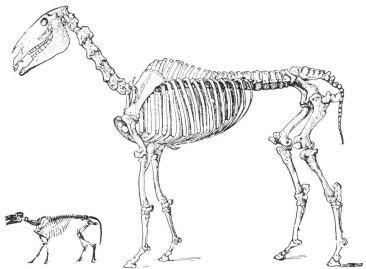

The skeleton of a modern horse towering over its Eocene ancestor dramatizes the diminutive size of the horses that once roamed through Jackson Hole. *American Museum of Natural History.*

along the banks of streams. The landscape has become one of low hills and savannah plains, and the climate has changed from tropical to subtropical. Magnolia, breadfruit and fig trees grow along with more temperate varieties such as oak, maple and redwood.

During this era, the Rocky Mountains are formed, but here in Jackson Hole the Tetons have yet to be thrust upward. To the north, in what will become Yellowstone, incredible numbers of volcanoes are created by pressures from deep within the earth and erupt for the next thirty or forty million years. Their molten output, including incomputable tons of airborne ashes, raises and levels the surface of the surrounding region by several thousand feet, and their fiery flows advance far into the territory of the future Tetons. The climate turns cooler and drier, so that plants of a subtropical nature can no longer flourish. For about a million years, an animal in size and shape somewhat like a rhinoceros, the Titanothere, roams this countryside, then disappears. Horses now grow to the size of a small colt and diminutive camels have appeared.

About twenty-five million years ago, volcanoes begin to erupt in Jackson Hole. It is a difficult time for life to survive, but two species somehow do: the camel and a pig-like animal called an oreodont. Another fifteen million years pass. The climate turns cooler and the familiar fir, pine, spruce and sagebrush are now to be seen. Meanwhile, the beaver, whose fur will one day lure the first white men to this country, is already growing fat and sleek.

The arc grows shorter, curving back to less than nine million years ago, and the stage is set for the Tetons to break upon the scene. The dramatic device making it possible is a fault, a fracture-like weakness in the earth's crust, running north and south along a line which will soon mark the base of the upcast Teton Range. For millions of years, semifluid rock has lain below the plain which will shortly become the valley of Jackson Hole, and slowly, under the weight of the earth's crust, this semifluid rock begins to move subterraneanly. As it flows under the plain, with much of it moving north toward Yellowstone, the surface of the land above is placed under great tension, until finally, unable to bear the tension any longer, the earth's crust cracks open along the fault line and the Jackson Hole plain collapses. It literally drops down, tilting toward the west and placing even more pressure on the semifluid rock below. Most of the underground rock continues to flow north, but enough is forced to the west to act like a huge hydraulic jack beneath the land just west of the fault line, where from deep within the earth rocks which have been buried since Precambrian time are heaved skyward. As Jackson Hole falls, the Teton Range rises.

This cataclysmic event does not take place in a matter of days or weeks or even months. Many years of convulsive jerks and wrenches, accompanied by earthquakes, must elapse before the Tetons will be uplifted to their eventual height. Nevertheless, the major breakthrough has occurred and there the newly-born mountains stand, although not in their familiar saw-toothed form, but rather as a blunt, massive block towering above what has become a valley. Immediately, erosion goes to work to strip the block of surface stones and sediment, and to begin the shaping of the peaks and pinnacles.

Only two hundred thousand years ago, the Ice Age comes to Jackson Hole. The first glaciation, called the Buffalo, is formed by ice flowing southwest from the Beartooth Mountains, ice flowing west from the Absaroka Range and ice flowing northwest from the Wind River Range. The Beartooth and Absaroka glaciers meet in the northern end of the valley and merge to flow south past the Tetons at a depth in places of two thousand feet, while on the eastern side of the valley all but the highest elevations are covered by the moving ice and scoured by the rocks it contains. The frozen river advances by inches, plowing the valley floor and overriding Signal Mountain and Blacktail Butte, shaping their forms. At the same time, the glacier from the Wind River Range moves through the canyon of the Gros Ventre River, streams into Jackson Hole and links up with the main flow grinding south, and together the three glaciers, now one, sculpt East Gros Ventre Butte and West Gros Ventre Butte. The glacier gradually narrows in the southern end of the valley, but before it wastes away its cold tongue twists through the Snake River Canyon and reaches into Idaho.

Just eighty thousand years ago, the second glaciation, the Bull Lake, arrives. Less than half the size of the earlier ice masses, it rises in the Absaroka Range and winds its way down the Buffalo River Valley into the northern end of Jackson Hole, where it joins forces with glaciers crawling down from the many canyons of the Tetons, broadening and carving those canyons as they advance. When the glaciers begin to melt, their powerful streams lay down outwash deposits in the southern part of the valley.

The arc shortens until it is but a mere fifteen thousand years ago, and the last glaciation, the Pinedale, moves in. As it did before, ice flows down through the canyons of the Tetons and spills out into the valley. One large glacier gouges the bed of Jackson Lake and reaches out to surround Signal Mountain, rising so high only a few hundred feet of the mountain remain visible above the ice, while other glaciers scoop out the beds of smaller lakes at the base of the range. The largest mass of ice stays mainly in the northern end of the valley, where its southernmost advance is marked by the Burned Ridge Moraine, and the outwash streams that pour from it lay down a layer of gravel for ten miles south. When the glaciers withdraw, blocks of ice a quarter of a mile and more in diameter are left behind, buried in the earth. As they melt, they leave an area dotted with circular depressions resembling craters on the moon, large pockmarks later to be called the Potholes.

The peaks and canyons of the mountains have been chiseled, the graceful lines of the valley have been contoured. Now the plowed surface of the valley begins to green with vegetation. Where the glaciers laid down fertile soil, thick stands of timber push through. Where they laid down gravel, grass and sagebrush take root. Finally, as the scene fades out some ten thousand years ago, the principal features of this masterpiece of landscape we call the Tetons and Jackson Hole have been completed—just in time to receive the first human visitors, prehistoric men.

3

The Firstcomers

While the story of the rocks in Jackson Hole is written in a legible script, the story of early man in the valley is not as easily deciphered. Because the Indians had no written language, the history of their ancient past is lost in the swirling mist of legends, and although archeologists and anthropologists have made revealing finds in recent years, the picture of Stone Age man's presence here is still somewhat blurred. But of this we can be sure: long before the glaciers on this hemisphere began their final retreat, hunting bands from Asia had crossed to Alaska over the Bering land bridge, had advanced with surprising swiftness down along high mountain valleys that served as narrow corridors through the shelf of ice then covering the upper part of the continent and, with spears in hand, were roaming the Great Plains and northern Rocky Mountains in pursuit of big game.

Pitting their not meager skills of survival against both the animals and elements of what was then truly the New World, the Early Hunters, as they are called, made their way into the region surrounding Jackson Hole by an early date. Across the Tetons, near American Falls in Idaho, bones of a bison belonging to a long-extinct species have been discovered under conditions suggesting that it may have been hunted down by men as far back as 30,000 years ago. Even closer to Jackson Hole, a cave in the Absaroka Range near what is now Yellowstone National Park was occupied by humans off and on for 9,000 years, with its many strata yielding weapons which gradually advanced from primitive stone points for spears to skillfully chipped arrowheads. Closer still, near the headwaters of the Gros Ventre River that flows into the valley from the east, and also at Astoria Hot Springs not far south of the valley, fluted stone points of a type dating back 11,000 years have been found, attesting to the fact that humans were in the vicinity by at least that time.

Although it is not known precisely when or by what route the Early Hunters arrived in the valley, there is no question they were here—and they were here in time to see the Tetons while the canyons still contained the last withdrawing tongues of Pleistocene ice. According to the foremost anthropologist who has studied the prehistoric peoples of Jackson Hole, they began arriving "probably in the summer, by at least 10,000 years ago," a time so remote that to put it into context we must remember this was seven thousand years before the first dynasty of the pharaohs in Egypt was founded.[1] Obviously, it is not possible to trace the movements of these firstcomers with any degree of certainty, but in all likelihood they were searching for game and entered the valley over one of the mountain passes or through one of the river canyons their descendants would one day use.

Double-shouldered obsidian Cody knife. Estimated to be 8,000 years old, this knife was found in 1972 near Emma Matilda Lake in the northern end of Jackson Hole. *Courtesy Dr. Gary Wright.*

The chronology of the presence in Jackson Hole of both early men and the later Indians is incomplete, to say the least, but clues in the form of artifacts they left behind are beginning to fill in some of the blanks. At Emma Matilda Lake in the northern end of the valley, an obsidian knife estimated to be 8,000 years old has been recovered, while at nearby Two Ocean Lake a quartzite projectile point of about the same age has been turned up. Also in the north, on the shore of Jackson Lake before a dam raised its water, a site was discovered where Early Hunters made camp around 8,000 years ago, probably coming down from Yellowstone in late spring or early summer to hunt mule deer and bighorn sheep and gather plants for food, then leaving before winter snows made the valley uninhabitable. Interestingly, this same campsite was used with some degree of regularity until relatively recent times, with artifacts from it revealing that over many different periods many different peoples wandered into and out of Jackson Hole, although there is no indication that any ever took up year-round residence.

Campsites in the central and southern parts of Jackson Hole apparently are not as old, but they also confirm the fact that nomadic bands visited the valley from time to time during the course of many centuries. Near Blacktail Butte, for example, an archeological excavation revealed two projectile points of a type used 4,000 years ago as well as a recognizable ring of stones used to anchor a latter-day Indian tipi.* The early occupants of this site do not appear to have been the same people who came down from Yellowstone to the northern campsites, nor does it appear that the two groups intermingled to any extent, rather preferring to keep a distance apart. However, there is good reason to believe that the bands in the south drifted into the valley from the Green River Basin to the southeast and were in some form of communication with the bands to the north, because at an archeological site in the Green River Basin obsidian originally from Yellowstone has been found. What is most remarkable is that these bands were also in communication with other aboriginal groups, as demonstrated by the discovery that obsidian from Yellowstone and from Teton Pass in Jackson Hole was traded from band to band east across the Great Plains until it finally reached southern Ohio 2,000 years ago.

While the way of life of the firstcomers to Jackson Hole can be seen only in a half-light, they were human in the fullest sense of the word. They lived and roamed in small family units, were intelligent, spoke a language, used tools and had command of fire. They also possessed the most valuable of all traits in the struggle to survive: the ability to adapt. And it was good they did, because in the period following the end of the Ice Age more than one hundred species of mammals, including the horse, mysteriously died out in North America. With meat no longer plentiful, these people who had lived almost entirely on big game were forced to change their methods of gathering food. Gradually, they learned to supplement their more limited meat supply with roots, fish, nuts, wild berries and other growing things of the areas across which they ranged.

For thousands of years, the people of the high country found an hospitable summer habitat in Jackson Hole. Entering the valley in

* On a ledge about three hundred feet below the summit of the Grand Teton, a curious circular enclosure formed by upright slabs of granite has led to the speculation that it is also an artifact from a very ancient time. What is more probable is that it was constructed for a "vision quest," a ritual in which a young Indian approaching manhood would go to a solitary place and induce a trance, usually by fasting, in order to receive a message from the particular spirit which would thereafter guide his life.

Reconstruction of a prehistoric bison hunt in northern New Mexico. In Jackson Hole, the quarry of the Early Hunters was mainly bighorn sheep and mule deer. *American Museum of Natural History*.

the spring and departing in the fall for more favorable winter hunting grounds, they adapted brilliantly to the local ecology, gathering blue camas from the meadows for food, fishing the streams for cutthroat trout, hunting in the higher elevations for bighorn sheep and obtaining obsidian from local deposits for chipping into weapons and tools—all the while observing ancient symbolic rituals that had been passed down to them over many generations. Then these people, who were probably speakers of the Athapaskan language, suddenly vanished, leaving behind no further traces of their presence in this land. What had happened is that a new and stronger people had arrived in the outlying regions.

In the sixteenth and seventeenth centuries, a great migration of Shoshonean-speaking people moved northeast from the Great

Basin and eventually drove the Athapaskan-speaking people from their traditional winter hunting grounds. Overwhelmed by superior numbers and arms, the longtime residents of the high country moved well to the north into Canada, ostensibly leaving Jackson Hole for the summer use of the new arrivals. They also ostensibly left it for the summer use of the other now-familiar Indian nations of the northern Rockies who not long thereafter appeared and claimed tribal territories along a far-reaching perimeter mostly to the north and east of Jackson Hole. Surprisingly, however, instead of being visited and utilized by these various tribes, even in summer, Jackson Hole was virtually abandoned by the Indians for more than one hundred and fifty years before white men first came into the mountains. This avoidance of the valley by native Americans of any kind for such a long period of time is a relatively recent finding, and it shatters a long-standing myth which has prevailed to this day about Jackson Hole.

When the first few white men ventured into the northern Rockies early in the nineteenth century, they encountered a number of major tribes encircling Jackson Hole. To the north in what is now Montana were the Blackfeet and the Gros Ventres, allies whose ferocity in battle made them the most hated and feared of all the tribes. To the northeast and east, from the Yellowstone River to the Wind River Basin, were the Crows, outstanding both as horsemen and horse thieves. Beginning in the Green River Basin to the southeast, the homeland of the Shoshonis (or Snakes) curved west below Jackson Hole through upper Utah, then ran north through eastern Idaho to a point roughly opposite the western boundary of Yellowstone Park. The Shoshonis shared the western section of this territory with the Bannocks, who were related to them and with whom they intermarried. Farther away in the northwest were the Flatheads, who did not flatten their heads, and the Nez Percés, who almost never pierced their noses.

All of these tribes had horses descended from those originally stolen from the Spanish by the Indians of the Southwest in earlier times, so they were able to range far outside their loosely defined territories in order to hunt and make war. Because of this mobility, it has long been assumed that the Indians of the northern Rockies were frequent visitors to Jackson Hole. In fact, over the years this assumption has persisted to the point where many now accept it as gospel that every summer and fall for centuries the tribes of the region, especially the Shoshonis, descended on the valley to enjoy

festive reunions of the usually scattered hunting bands and to engage in great buffalo hunts. It is a pleasing picture which has grown
to become part of the local lore regularly repeated to tourists, but
unfortunately there is no evidence whatever to bear it out. Quite to
the contrary, well-documented evidence compiled by Dr. Gary
Wright, an anthropologist who has conducted extensive studies in
the valley, shows that although more than three hundred archeological sites have been uncovered in Jackson Hole, not one can
be dated as having been occupied between the years 1640 and
1811—that is, between the time the Athapaskan-speaking people
were driven north and a party sent out by John Jacob Astor to
found a fur trading post on the Pacific Coast passed through.[2]

The reason why the latter-day Indians who ringed Jackson Hole
seldom went into it is that their culture was entirely different than
that of the Athapaskan-speaking people who preceded them. Because they were essentially nomadic, horse-riding hunters, especially of buffalo, they never developed the adaptive skills needed to
exploit the plant and fish resources of the valley. Further—and in
the face of still another myth about Jackson Hole—this valley seems
never to have abounded with game, at least not to the extent frequently stated. The great elk herd of later times may not yet have
been forced up into the mountains from the Great Plains, and even
if it had its migratory pattern of entering the valley when heavy
snows begin to fall would not have coincided with the time of year
when the Indians would have found Jackson Hole to be accessible.
Moreover, although there were some buffalo in the valley, they
were not present in numbers large enough either to sustain the
needs of many people or to warrant communal hunts of the size
approaching those conducted on the Great Plains to the east, in the
Green River Basin to the southeast and on the Snake River Plains to
the west of the Tetons. As a result, for a long time prior to the
coming of the white men Jackson Hole remained to all intents and
purposes forgotten and unvisited—so much so that none of the
mountain nations even seems to have claimed it as part of their
domain, although the Shoshonis may have thought of it as being on
the vague outer limits of their land. Rather, the valley seems to
have been viewed as a neutral zone between irreconcilably opposed
nations such as the Shoshonis to the south and the Blackfeet to the
north.

This is not to say that Jackson Hole was a no-man's-land avoided
entirely by Indians, for there were trails leading into it and out of it

"Indian Camp on Jackson Lake," by Herbert Collins. Contrary to popular belief, Jackson Hole was not a favorite hunting ground for the tribes of the northern Rockies. *National Park Service, Grand Teton National Park.*

when the first white men arrived. But even in historic times, which began in the early nineteenth century when trappers who moved through the area kept journals, these trails were used by the Indians less as a means to go into Jackson Hole than as a means to go through it. Although some Indians undoubtedly entered the valley now and then specifically to hunt, it served mainly as a corridor for parties traveling to other destinations for other purposes. The Gros Ventres, for instance, are reported to have passed through when they journeyed to visit their kinsmen to the south, the Arapahoes. In order to avoid the Crows, their enemies who lived to the east, the Gros Ventres are said to have entered the valley from the north and proceeded down along the foothills of the range which now bears their name. Journals of early trappers also refer to the transient presence of Flatheads in Jackson Hole, but in every instance they were either on their way to or from one of the annual fur trade rendezvous. In addition, journals mention raiding parties of

Blackfeet and Gros Ventres crossing Jackson Hole on several occasions, most notably in 1832 when a small party of trappers was ambushed in the valley by members of this confederacy and three of the trappers were killed. But nowhere is there any reference to either Nez Percés or Crows having been in the valley at any time, and as for the Shoshonis, the historical records strongly indicate that Jackson Hole was by no means their "happy hunting ground," as has been so often depicted. After 1811, when two curious Shoshonis followed the Astorians into Jackson Hole, there is no further mention of them entering the valley again until 1860. Thus, although it is true that the written records are sparse at best and parties of Indians probably traveled across the valley from time to time, it is also true that the major mountain tribes never visited Jackson Hole in anywhere near the numbers or with the frequency that has been assumed.

Still another assumption which has come to be accepted by many as fact is that a subgroup of Indians called the Sheepeaters, or Tukudikas, often camped on the shores of Jackson Lake. Speakers of the Shoshonean language who were pathetically poor compared with their linguistic cousins, the Sheepeaters had neither horses nor guns and were easy prey for other tribes. Consequently, they developed shy, withdrawn ways, living in the more impenetrable parts of the mountains rimming the Yellowstone Plateau and along the Continental Divide in Montana and Idaho. Although they left behind a few artifacts testifying to their having been in the valley, they probably did not visit it often. As for written references to them, the closest any places them to Jackson Hole is when Osborne Russell, a trapper in the 1830s, came upon several Sheepeaters high in the Washakie Range to the northeast. In their travels, the Sheepeaters gained an extensive knowledge of what is now Yellowstone National Park, which has led a number of writers to describe them as huddled around the mysterious thermal phenomena to be found there in order to frighten off their enemies. Supposedly, the geysers and boiling springs were so surrounded by superstition in the eyes of the other tribes that they would not venture near. This, too, is a colorful picture, but again no evidence bears it out.

These various tribes of the northern Rockies were dispersed widely around Jackson Hole in the spring of 1804, when far to the east a series of events was set into motion which would forever alter the lives of all the western Indians. On May 14 of that year, near

William Henry Jackson photograph of Sheepeater Indian family, taken in 1871. *Smithsonian Institution National Anthropological Archives.*

the frontier village of St. Louis, a small group of men started up the Missouri River to explore what was to them the unknown West. Although they thought of themselves only as soldiers carrying out a mission for their president, as things turned out they were much more than that. They were the advance guard of a people who had come late to North America, had built an energetic young nation out of its eastern wilderness and soon would burst across the Mississippi River all the way to the Pacific Ocean, claiming every last bit of this long-occupied land as their own. In the course of their westering, they would sweep the Indians aside like leaves in a storm.

4

Enter John Colter

Lewis and Clark did not discover Jackson Hole when their bold and brilliantly executed expedition went up the Missouri River, crossed over the Rocky Mountains and wound its way down to the mouth of the Columbia River. In fact, they did not even come close, passing far to the north through Montana on both their outward and homeward journeys. Nevertheless, because one of their men is acclaimed as the discoverer of Jackson Hole as well as the area now enclosed in Yellowstone National Park, it is appropriate to touch briefly on their travels in order to understand how he came to be in a position to do some exploring on his own.

In 1803, as a result of the most adroit diplomatic negotiation ever conducted by any American president, Thomas Jefferson purchased the vast Louisiana Territory from Napoleon, thereby instantly doubling the size of the United States and assuring that it would become a continental power of the first rank. For only fifteen million dollars, he obtained 828,000 square miles of some of the world's richest land, from which all or part of thirteen future states would be carved, including most of Wyoming. Jackson Hole, however, was not part of the purchase, because it lies west of the Continental Divide. Although the boundaries of this enormous acquisition extending west from the Mississippi River were far from precise, they were generally thought to run north of the Spanish settlements in New Mexico, south of the few British fur outposts in western Canada and as far west as to the crest of what were then called the Stony Mountains, which no one then knew for certain were a continuous, massive chain stretching from Canada to Mexico. Indeed, no one knew much of anything about what lay in this great beyond. There were rumors, to be sure—of an entire mountain composed of salt, of a race of dwarfs who terrorized the Indian tribes, of a mighty river that flowed directly to the western sea—but in reality almost the whole of the West was a blank on the map, a void into which no white man had ventured very far and about which Jefferson was determined to learn more. The instrument he forged to do this was the Lewis and Clark Expedition.

On a journey which took two years and five months and covered almost eight thousand miles, the small party commanded by the two young army officers reached the Pacific Ocean and returned, bringing back to Jefferson and the world a harvest of priceless information about the geography, climate, natural resources, flora, fauna and Indian tribes of the Northwest. The expedition also established a territorial claim to the basin of the Columbia River, a claim that would hold up against British counterclaims and would lead to the future states of Oregon, Washington and Idaho, and the western sections of Montana and Wyoming as well. Lewis and Clark's achievement was to have such far-reaching consequences that, as Henry Adams said of the Louisiana Purchase, its importance in American history is beyond measurement. Their achievement was also of importance to the history of northwestern Wyoming, because events stemming directly from the expedition soon led to the first reported sighting by a white man of the Tetons and the strange land of Yellowstone. The story, which is wrapped in legend and surrounded with controversy, began in August of 1806 when the Corps of Volunteers for Northwestern Discovery, as the expedition was called, was returning home.

One of the volunteers was a young man who had been born in Virginia and recruited in Kentucky, Private John Colter. He comes through the pages of the journals kept by Lewis and Clark as a good soldier who could be counted on to carry out his duties, and we catch glimpses of him returning to camp with the game he had shot, carrying dispatches between the two captains and serving as a scout. Once he ran into a river to avoid being attacked by a grizzly bear; on another occasion, he seized a tomahawk the Indians had stolen from Clark and stubbornly refused to let them wrest it from him; and, still later, he narrowly missed being seriously injured when the horse he was riding fell off the bank of a creek and the two, horse and rider, "were driven down the Creek a considerable distance roleing over each other among the rocks."[1] Otherwise, only a few everyday details are known about Colter's service with Lewis and Clark, but in the eyes of the captains he must have stood well, for in his case they made an unprecedented dispensation which permitted him to leave their party and set off on a remarkable journey of his own.

When the expedition arrived back at the Mandan Indian villages in what is now North Dakota, it met two men, Joseph Dickson and

Manuel Lisa, who sent John Colter out to tell the Crows about the new trading post at the mouth of the Bighorn River. *Missouri Historical Society*.

Forest Handcock, who had ventured up the Missouri far beyond the frontier in order to trap beaver. Eager to know more about the prospect for pelts farther upstream, they made Colter an offer: if he would join them and share with them his knowledge of the region he had just come from, they would share with him their traps and whatever pelts they took. At first glance, it seems highly improbable that Colter would even have considered such an offer. He had been west of civilization for more than two years, and now, almost within sight of it, two complete strangers were asking him to turn around and go back into the loneliness and danger of the wilderness. And yet, Colter went to Meriwether Lewis and William Clark and asked for his discharge, which was granted on the basis that "as we were disposed to be of service to any one of our party who had performed their duty as well as Colter had done, we agreed to allow him the privilage provided no one of the party would ask or expect a Similar permission."[2]

One explanation given for Colter's surprising decision is that he felt the "call of the wild" and, like so many mountain men who were to follow him, had come to prefer the solitude and free way of life in the wilderness to the bustle and restrictions of society. But this is more romantic than realistic. What is more likely is that Colter, a poor man whose wages as a private came to only five dollars a month, had caught a bad case of beaver fever, a disease every bit as virulent as the gold fever of the later forty-niners. The prospect of becoming rich on beaver fur would soon entice many young men to endure incredible hardships and risk their lives for years on end in an untamed mountain country a thousand miles and more from the closest frontier settlement. Colter was probably no exception.

In August of 1806, when Colter said farewell to his fellow members of the expedition and went back upriver, the wilderness closed in behind him and he was not seen or heard from for almost a year. During that year, a clever and sharp-dealing St. Louis entrepreneur named Manuel Lisa organized a company for the purpose of exploiting the beaver-rich streams Lewis and Clark reported having seen on the upper Missouri, where it flows from west to east across Montana and North Dakota. Lisa's plan was to build a series of trading posts from which his men could go out to trap and to which Indians could bring furs for manufactured goods, and in April of 1807 he started up the Missouri with a party of fifty or sixty men in two keelboats. Three of these men had served with Lewis and Clark and knew Colter, so they must have been astonished when near where the Platte River joins the Missouri their former comrade came into sight, alone and paddling a dugout canoe downstream.

In those days, when a man appeared from out of the wilds by himself, leaving his partners behind, it was bound to raise eyebrows it not suspicions, because usually violence of some kind had taken place, either from the Indians or from a falling out between the men themselves. But Colter was able to explain that Dickson and Handcock were alive and well; all that had happened was that the partnership had been peacefully dissolved and he was heading home on his own. Once again, however, he would not get there. Either Manuel Lisa was a persuasive talker or Colter still believed that beaver pelts offered a golden opportunity, or probably both, for on the spot he signed up with this first organized venture to open the Rocky Mountain fur trade. With no apparent second thoughts, this man, who had now lived beyond the frontier for more than three straight years, turned around and went back up what some have called the wide Missouri and others simply the Big

It was on a keelboat like this that John Colter returned up the Missouri with Manuel Lisa's fur-seeking expedition of 1807. *Rare Book Division, New York Public Library, Astor, Lenox and Tilden Foundations.*

Muddy, with its water "too thin to plow but too thick to drink."[3]

Today, when a jet plane can travel many more miles in an hour than a keelboat could travel in a month, it is difficult to imagine just how slow and agonizingly strenuous a trip upriver was. This less than graceful craft, from sixty to eighty feet long and designed not unlike artists' conceptions of Noah's Ark, literally had to be pushed and pulled in order to make headway against the Missouri's power-ful current. Although there were oars, they were often little more than useless, so teams of boatmen would line catwalks on the deck and push with all their might against long poles placed into the river's bed. Slowly, as the boat inched forward, the straining men would walk to the stern, then lift their poles and return to the prow to repeat the drudgery. Not infrequently, other teams would have to jump overboard and wade ahead through the river's cold water or thrash their way through underbrush along the river's banks, pulling on long tow ropes called cordelles. Now and then a sail would be raised to ease their physical labor, but the flukiness of the winds and the twisting course the Missouri weaves seldom com-bined to let it be used for long stretches. Moving upriver a distance which could vary from twenty or so miles a day to only a mile or two, Manuel Lisa's party took seven months to reach the Yel-lowstone River and go up it to where the Bighorn River feeds in. By then it was late fall, and there, in the heart of Crow country, Lisa began construction of a stockade trading post he named Fort Raymond after his son, but which most of the men called Manuel's Fort.

As the post neared completion, Lisa decided that the first order of business was to spread the word to the scattered Crow tribal bands that they should bring their furs to trade for articles such as blankets, beads, tobacco and small mirrors (the last item to become a favorite not only with the squaws, but also with the self-admiring braves). John Colter, who had at least a rudimentary knowledge of the country from the previous year, knew sign language and also seems to have been somewhat familiar with the Crow tongue, was the logical choice to carry out the mission. Late in November of 1807, he strapped a thirty-pound pack on his back, shouldered his flintlock rifle and set out on the most celebrated and debated hike ever taken by any American.

5

The Colter Case, A Mountain Mystery

Legend has it that John Colter's long walk took him as the first white man into Jackson Hole, across the Tetons, then north into what is now Yellowstone National Park. It is a treasured epic of the West: a man alone, plunging farther and farther into the wilderness, until he came upon a towering, unheard-of mountain range and the pyrotechnic marvels of a large thermal region. Unfortunately, Colter had no way to prove where he had been, so when he told others of the wonders he had seen most of them laughed it off as a farfetched tale and dubbed his imaginary fireworks "Colter's Hell." They also dubbed him a liar, for it was, after all, a preposterous story. Who could penetrate to the heart of the Rocky Mountains in the season when heavy snows begin to fall? Who could survive without shelter in often sub-zero temperatures? And who, except a wide-eyed greenhorn, would believe such a place existed where the air reeked of sulphur, steam vents hissed, mud pools gurgled and jets of boiling water shot skyward from the bowels of the earth?

For more than sixty years after Colter's return, his story was largely dismissed as just another mountain yarn. Then, when the strange works of nature in Yellowstone finally came to the attention of the American public in the early 1870s, many people put two and two together and concluded that they were in reality what Colter had described and had been scoffingly called "Colter's Hell." Overnight, Colter's story was given a credence it had not previously enjoyed and his reputation as a liar was magically transformed into that of an honored discoverer, the founding father, so to speak, of the northwestern corner of Wyoming. However, it was not to be this easy. Some years after the Colter legend had been propped up by the opening of Yellowstone, the legs were kicked from under it when scholars rediscovered what a number of excellent sources had stated all along: that although Colter had most definitely come upon a geyser basin, what he found was located more than eighty miles east of where tourists now stand and look at Old Faithful.

With "Colter's Hell" clearly established as well outside of Yellowstone, the Jackson Hole part of the legend again became suspect, and to this day a controversy continues, based on clues and theories about Colter's journey as engrossing as those of any mystery story.

After leaving Manuel's Fort, Colter headed south, probably going up the Bighorn River to where the Shoshone River joins it, then southwest up the Shoshone to the vicinity of present-day Cody, Wyoming. There, along the Shoshone River Canyon, he walked into a world no white American had ever seen, an active thermal area huffing and puffing with eerie sights and sounds. This was the true "Colter's Hell," known as such to a few of Colter's contemporaries and a number of the later trappers. George Drouillard, a fellow member of both the Lewis and Clark Expedition and Manuel Lisa's group, followed Colter into the region and told William Clark about it back in St. Louis. Washington Irving, with Captain Bonneville as his source, correctly located it on the Stinking Water River, the less than elegant name by which the Shoshone River was known to the Indians and trappers. Irving described it as the place "first discovered by Colter . . . who came upon it in the course of his lonely wanderings, and gave such an account of its gloomy terrors, its hidden fires, smoking pits, noxious streams, and the all-pervading 'smell of brimstone,' that it received, and has ever since retained among the trappers, the name of 'Colter's Hell!' "[1] The Jesuit missionary-explorer, Father De Smet, also knew about "Colter's Hell" from Jim Bridger, and mountain man Joe Meek claimed to have visited the spot, describing it with his characteristic humor as the "back door to that country which divines preach about."[2] So Colter was surely there, but he probably did not linger long to watch the geysers perform or listen to the hollow echoes of his footsteps on the earth's thin crust. Although geysers were known to exist in Iceland, few Americans had heard of them, and even for a rugged frontiersman this weird and awesome canyon was not a place to be alone.

When Colter left the "hell" he had discovered, history stopped and legend began. Some staunchly believe he walked on to reach the Tetons and even crossed them before going up to Yellowstone, while others are just as positive the story should be banished to the realm of the ridiculous. At this late date, it is impossible for anyone to prove or disprove beyond any shadow of a doubt just where this man did go. The most that can be done is to lay out the many clues

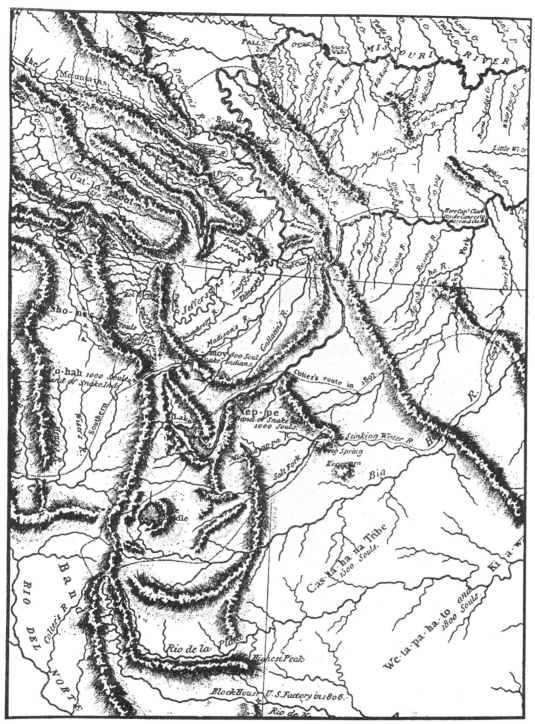

Section from William Clark's map of 1814, with dotted line tracing "Colter's route in 1807."
From "History of the Expedition Under the Command of Captains Lewis and Clark," Philadelphia, 1814.

and let those who would like to do so deduce for themselves what seems most likely to have happened.

The key document in the Colter case is a map of the West prepared by William Clark and published in 1814. On it a dotted line marked "Colter's route in 1807" runs in a long, generally westward loop from the Shoshone River into and through what those who support the Colter legend identify as Jackson Hole and Yellowstone. This section of the map was based on a visit Colter later had with Clark in St. Louis, and while one might think his personal testimony about his journey should all but clinch the matter, it must be remembered that Colter himself never claimed to have discovered the Tetons and Yellowstone. All he did was tell Clark about some nameless country he had traveled through, which Clark then put down as best he could from the description. Unfortunately, although the map is a remarkable document for its time, it leaves out or misplaces so many now-familiar topographical features of the region west of the Shoshone River it cannot be accepted as airtight evidence that Colter ever discovered anything.

On Clark's map there are two large lakes and a mountain range lying roughly in the same relationship to one another as do Jackson Lake, Yellowstone Lake and the Tetons. Those who believe the Colter legend to be true point to the map and say that the lakes Clark named Biddle and Eustis are respectively and unmistakably Jackson Lake and Yellowstone Lake, and they see the mountain range clearly as being the Tetons. The dotted line marking Colter's route shows him walking west from the Shoshone River into this region, crossing the mountains only to come back over them again, then skirting the edges of both lakes before returning to Lisa's outpost. If the lakes are Jackson and Yellowstone, as many believe they are, then by all means Colter reached Jackson Hole.

Those who belittle the legend also point to the map to support their view. They ask why the section assumed to be Jackson Hole does not depict the Snake River flowing from north to south, as it does, but instead shows a river flowing from west to east before emptying into the Bighorn River, which the Snake most certainly does not do. They argue quite persuasively that in order to cross the Tetons Colter would first have had to ford the Snake and would surely have remembered in which direction it flows, if for no other reason than that fording the river's frigid waters in winter is not an experience one is likely to forget. And yet, it may be that Clark, who made a number of errors, simply put the direction of the river down wrong. On the other hand, it may even be, as one school of thought holds, that the lake Colter described and Clark named Biddle, from which the river seems to flow, is not Jackson Lake at all, but actually Brooks Lake to the east of Jackson Hole near Togwotee Pass. It also lies at the foot of a pinnacled range and it does drain into the Bighorn system.

Clark's map, as the King of Siam says of women in *The King and I*, "is a puzzlement." The dotted line marked "Colter's route in 1807" marches across so many blank spaces that even those who agree with the legend cannot agree with each other on the exact route he may have followed. However, a composite version of their various theories about his journey runs something like this: southwest from "Colter's Hell" to the Absaroka Mountains, south along them to Togwotee Pass (or even farther south to Union Pass), west into Jackson Hole, west over the Tetons via Teton Pass, north along the Idaho side of the Tetons, back across the Tetons through Conant Pass, north from Jackson Lake to the west shore of Yellowstone Lake, across the Yellowstone River near Tower Falls, over or around the Absaroka Mountains, south to "Colter's Hell," then back to Manuel's Fort along the route he had earlier traveled. All in all, this is an impressive itinerary, having a ring of authenticity because it lists specific places with specific names. But it should not be forgotten that these are nothing more than assumptions based on Clark's dotted line, and while proponents of the legend can argue among themselves as to which particular pass or trail Colter may have taken, they cannot even tell us which way he went along the loop, clockwise or counterclockwise.

Putting Clark's map to the side for the moment, the Colter skeptics go on to ask three tough-minded questions about the journey having to do with terrain, weather and, at least as far as one of Colter's movements is concerned, his motivation. The questions are especially difficult because they place the burden of proof on the Colter loyalists, and there is simply no way anyone now can prove much of anything. Still, there are answers, partly documented and partly guesswork, that are well within the margin of the possible.

How, they ask, did Colter traveling alone make his way through a maze of wilderness, finding trails, mountain passes and fords across rivers? Possible answer: Colter may not have been alone. While it has never been suggested that he was accompanied by another white man, the original account of his journey, written by Henry Brackenridge, says that he "went upwards of five hundred miles to the Crow nation; gave them information, and proceeded from them to several other tribes."[3] Thus, Colter evidently came to Indian villages along the way, and it is not unreasonable to assume that they could have provided him with guides, or at least directions, to the next village. This would support the theories about his use of Togwotee Pass (or Union Pass), Teton Pass, Conant Pass and the path he is thought to have taken from Jackson Lake to Yellowstone, all of which lay along trails Indians are known to have followed.

How did Colter stay alive and on the move during the months of winter in deep-snow country that would tax the strongest man's stamina? Possible answer: Colter may have been not only a highly skilled frontiersman, but he also may have been endowed with more than ordinary physical powers. Thomas James, who knew Colter and trapped with him, wrote that "Nature had formed him, like [Daniel] Boone, for hardy indurance of fatigue, privation and perils."[4] To this it can be added that during Colter's more than two years with Lewis and Clark his name never appeared on their sick list, and that John Bradbury, who met Colter, described him as "a remarkably strong man."[5] Colter's later cross-country run from the Blackfeet also gives us reason to believe he had abnormal staying powers.* And while we have no way of knowing whether the winter of 1807–1808 was one of heavy snows or was relatively mild in the Rockies, there is reason to assume that even if the snows had been deep Colter would have been able to move about. An experienced woodsman, he either would have carried snowshoes or would have made a pair along the way. As a former chief park naturalist of the National Park Service has said, this would have made foot travel "easier, with underbrush buried beneath the snow, than hiking in summer over the same route."[6]

---

* Some have mistakenly associated Colter's famous escape from the Blackfeet with his return journey to Manuel's Fort after having supposedly discovered Jackson Hole and Yellowstone. Actually, the incident did not occur until much later, then far to the north on the Jefferson River in Montana. There his trapping partner was killed and he was taken prisoner, stripped naked and told to run for his life—not a generous gesture by the Blackfeet, as might be thought, but a diabolical form of torture, because he would have to run barefoot across a plain covered with prickly pears, a variety of cactus, with a pack of murder-bent braves giving him only a short head start. By an almost superhuman effort that brought blood gushing from his nostrils, Colter outran his pursuers over a distance of five miles, coming at last to what was either a large beaver lodge or pile of driftwood and hiding in it. When the Blackfeet finally gave up searching for him, he walked three hundred miles back to Lisa's trading post, subsisting by "eating roots and the bark of trees, for eleven days." (Burton Harris, *John Colter*, p. 131).

Colter arriving at an Indian village in the course of his long journey. *From "John Colter Visits the Crows," a painting by John Clymer.*

The most vexing of the questions asked, the one which all but stumps even the most ardent defenders of the legend, is why would this man who was sent out to drum up Indian customers for Manuel Lisa go into Jackson Hole in winter when any Indians he met in his travels would have told him that no tribes wintered there? One possible answer, largely overlooked by those who have written about Colter, is that at this juncture in his journey Colter may not have been searching for Indians at all. Instead, he may have been searching for another people both he and Manuel Lisa had reason to believe lived beyond the Tetons—the Spaniards, who were said by the Crows to be within a twenty-two-day walking distance from the forks of the Shoshone River.

This is not as absurd as it may first appear, for the true dimensions of the West were still undreamed of at the time, and the concept of the Spanish settlements being not very far away runs like a refrain through many of the early chronicles. Just two years before Colter set out from Manuel's Fort, the northern Shoshonis in Montana told Meriwether Lewis something he then had no way of knowing was blatantly untrue—that "they could pass to the Spaniards by way of the yellowstone river in 10 days."[7] Lewis's partner, William Clark, continued to be fascinated by the prospect, and when he sketched a map several years later from information one of Lisa's employees gave him, he entered a number of references to the Spanish settlements on it. He also marked on the map a salt cave the Crows said was a fourteen-day march from the Shoshone River, where, he noted, "the Spaniards obtain it [the salt] from this place by passing over the river Collarado."[8] Although the salt cave has never been found and the implied proximity of the Shoshone River and the Colorado River reveals the extent of confusion about western geography at the time, Clark's conviction that the Spaniards were close by is evident.

Manuel Lisa, who undoubtedly heard the same story from the Crows directly, would have had more than a passing interest in the Spaniards being within walking distance. Of Spanish blood himself, he had earlier engaged in an abortive attempt to open trade with Santa Fe, and later, in 1812, he did send a trading party to that city. Could it be that Colter was under instructions from Lisa to try to reach the Spanish settlements, that Indians along the way fed the fable and that when the Tetons loomed before him he had been walking approximately the amount of time the Crows said the trip would take? If so, then it would have been only natural for him to have wanted to look beyond the range, and instead of wandering aimlessly into Jackson Hole and over Teton Pass, as critics have questioned with ridicule, he may have acted with a definite purpose in mind.

Until 1931, all theories about Colter's movements were based entirely on Clark's map. Then another clue came to light in the form of a controversial stone a father and son unearthed while plowing a field in Teton Basin, a sparsely inhabited area just across the Tetons to the west. If the stone is what it purports to be—a memento left behind by John Colter himself—then beyond any question he was the first white man to see the Tetons piercing the sky. If it is a hoax, then the Colter legend must remain just that, a story from the past, unverifiable. The Colter Stone, as it is called, is now displayed behind glass in the Fur Trade Museum at Grand Teton National Park headquarters. A thin block of rhyolite lava about thirteen inches high, it was formed partly by nature and partly by someone's hands into a shape resembling the profile of a man's face. But the human likeness is not what makes this stone so special; it is that one side is carved with the letters J O H N C O L T E R and the other with the date 1 8 0 8.*

* Still another so-called Colter clue is a tree blazed with the initials "JC," found in Yellowstone in 1889. Although some still cite it as evidence of Colter having been there,

Is the Colter Stone authentic, or is it the work of a clever prankster? As usual, two different points of view collide. One holds that Colter carved it while holed up in Teton Basin waiting for a snowstorm to pass or for hostile Indians to leave the area, while the other rejects it as nothing more than hokum. On one issue, however, both views agree: if the Colter Stone is a hoax, it was not perpetrated by the father and son who found it in their field. The family had never heard of Colter, quietly kept the strange "stone head" in their home for two years merely as a curiosity, sought no publicity for it, made no money from it and finally traded it to a neighbor for a pair of riding boots. Only then did the stone come to the attention of Grand Teton National Park officials.

The case for the authenticity of the Colter Stone leans heavily on the testimony of a geologist and historian, Fritiof Fryxell, who examined it shortly after it became public knowledge. His judgment was that the stone had been weathered by the elements for many years before becoming covered with earth, and from this he went on to make a telling point. Because the weathering of the carved name, date and facial features appeared to be every bit as old as the weathering of the stone's other surfaces, Fryxell was convinced that no one had recently taken an already weathered stone and carved it, for if he had the knife would have peeled the weathering off the carved surfaces. Fryxell then went across the mountains into Teton Basin and found a ledge of rhyolite similar to that of the Colter Stone's composition not far from where the stone itself had been found. From this he reasoned that the stone had not been carved outside of Teton Basin, then taken to the field and buried, as some have charged, but that it was of local origin, had been carved near where it was turned up and had been left on the ground, where it weathered before sinking into the earth or becoming overblown with soil. Fryxell concluded that the stone was indeed the handiwork of none other than John Colter.

Most people find these observations impressive and convincing, but some who think the Colter Stone reeks of a hoax say there is no way to tell exactly how long a stone has weathered, and they remind

---

the claim would be thrown out of court by any objective judge. The blaze's age was never determined by a ring count (the tree was felled and sectioned, but the key section was somehow lost), and for the initials to have remained clearly legible for over eighty years is not typical of other blazes in the region, many of which have faded in half that time. What is more, it is now known that seventeen years before the blaze was discovered a botanist with the Hayden Survey of 1872 had collected specimens in the very same part of Yellowstone, and his name, by wild coincidence, was John Coulter.

The controversial Colter Stone, discovered by a father and son while plowing a field in 1931. *National Park Service, Grand Teton National Park.*

us that other hoaxers have been known to take infinite pains in order to give their forged relics the appearance of antiquity. In 1869, for instance, the figure of an oversized man, presumably fossilized, was "discovered" near Syracuse, New York, causing a nationwide sensation. Called the Cardiff Giant, it fooled many people, including the respected director of the New York State Museum and the eminent

Dr. Oliver Wendell Holmes, who drilled a hole in the monster's skull and marveled at the complexity of its cranial anatomy. When finally unmasked as a fraud, the monster was revealed to be nothing more than a large, carved block of gypsum (what an aptly named material to use for a hoax), which had been perforated with a spiked hammer, then treated with acids to create the illusion of a fossil's surface. But the Colter Stone shows no signs of anything more than many years of natural weathering, and the theory that it was carved and planted in the field shortly before it was found does not seem to hold up.

There is, however, another theory offering a reasonable explanation of the uniform weathering of the stone and its carved surfaces. It is that the Colter Stone is neither Colter's work nor a deliberate hoax, but the product of idle campfire doodling done by a member of the Hayden Survey when that government party went into Teton Basin in 1872. The supposition is that simply in order to kill time someone made the stone's already head-shaped features more pronounced and embellished the sides with Colter's name and the date 1808, then left the stone behind when the Survey moved on. The theory is tempting to accept, because it challenges the conclusions of Fritiof Fryxell without challenging his expert observations. The stone could have lain exposed to the elements for many years; the stone could have come from the rhyolite ledge close by; and yet, the stone could have been carved by someone other than John Colter. What makes the theory of a doodler even more tempting is that in the general area covered by the Hayden Survey a number of similarly carved stones have also come to light—for example, C L A R K 1 8 0 5, which is flatly impossible as William Clark was never anywhere near here. In all, this is a convincing argument, but as with so many aspects of the Colter controversy, pro or con, it too can be countered.

No one knows for certain that doodling on stones was a campfire pastime, and it does seem to have required far more work than would have been worth the effort, especially since wood would have been much easier on both the doodler and his knife's blade. Then there is the possibility that the other obviously bogus stones are latter-day hoaxes inspired by the discovery of the Colter Stone itself. But the most significant point advanced in favor of the authenticity of the Colter Stone is based on the date, 1808, which someone carved into it, and here, to understand why the point is significant, we have to turn back to Clark's map.

At the time of the Hayden Survey in 1872, the sources of information about John Colter were few and not easy to come by, with the single most important document being Clark's map of 1814. Because of the notation on the map reading "Colter's route in 1807," that year was long universally accepted as the time of Colter's journey. In fact, even into recent times many people have assumed that the date on the map was ironclad and therefore charged that the date of 1808 on the stone smacked of fraud. What they did not realize, and what would have been almost impossible for any member of the Hayden Survey to have known, is that not until well after the Colter Stone was discovered did research reveal the date 1808 to be more likely than 1807. True, Colter set out from the trading post in late November of 1807, but by the time he stopped to visit Indian villages and then walked on to Jackson Hole and crossed the Tetons (if he did), the year in all probability would have turned. If there was a Hayden doodler, he either made a lucky error or was in possession of knowledge about Colter's movements far ahead of his time. Colter, it can be said with almost absolute certainty, would have known the year.

There is one last piece of testimony to be submitted, bearing in mind that Colter did without question reach the vicinity of present-day Cody and did continue in a generally western direction from there. A few years after his long walk to somewhere, he told Henry Brackenridge of a pass along his route which was "less difficult to cross than the Allegheny mountains," and Brackenridge went on to add, "Colter, a celebrated hunter and woodsman, informed me that a loaded wagon would find no obstruction in passing."[9] There are not many passes in the entire chain of the Rocky Mountains fitting this description, but there is one not far from Jackson Hole that comes close. It is Togwotee Pass, just east of the northern end of the valley, over which first ran an Indian trail, then a wagon road and now a highway. If Colter came over Togwotee Pass and started down the mountain's western slope, the full range of the Tetons would have been revealed to him, and the inscription on the monument in the town of Jackson proclaiming him to have been the first white man to set foot in Jackson Hole is right. On the other hand, it could be his words mislead us and he crossed a lesser mountain elsewhere and looked down into a lesser valley.

There it is, the body of evidence for and against John Colter having discovered Jackson Hole. Did he or didn't he? Although the scales seem to weigh in his favor, anyone's guess is as good as anyone else's, and probably will continue to be as long as the issue is argued. Meanwhile, like the Sphinx, the Colter Stone keeps its secret. Resting on a block of wood in a glass case, it stares out at the tourists who file by and pause only briefly before moving on to other exhibits in the museum. Most of them never heard of John Colter and do not know that this strangely shaped slab of rhyolite is the subject of debate. Even if they did, they probably would not care—after all, is it important to know who discovered Jackson Hole? They may have a point, for the Tetons which rise just outside the museum door are so huge they dwarf the controversy. They were here long before man came into being, and if a solitary figure did pass this way in the early 1800s, it was not a matter of any moment to them.

"Setting Traps for Beaver," by Alfred Jacob Miller. At dawn and dusk, the mountain men waded into the ice-cold streams of the Rockies to set and clear their traps. *Northern Natural Gas Company Collection, Joslyn Art Museum, Omaha, Nebraska.*

6

Trapper Trails in Jackson Hole 1807-1822

It is ironic that a development of such far-ranging consequences as the exploration of the American West was brought about by a fad in men's haberdashery. Moreover, the fad was based on something as seemingly trivial as the soft underfur of an industrious, monogamous, bucktoothed aquatic mammal, the beaver. During the early decades of the 1800s, in London, New York and other fashion capitals, men's stovepipe-like felt hats were the height of fashion, and no fur was as soft or as easy to work into felt as that of the beaver. Thus, although they did not realize it, what the dandies who strolled along the Thames Embankment or through the narrow streets of lower Manhattan wore upon their heads was the initial economic incentive of the westward movement across the Mississippi River. Nor did they realize that this movement was being spearheaded by a small group of trappers who had gone into the Rocky Mountains for the beaver's pelt, were leading lives more savage than civilized, were opening the trails which would carry the nation to Oregon and California, and with it all were laying the groundwork for what would become a uniquely American epic, the saga of the mountain men.

The theater in which the mountain men acted out the drama of the western fur trade was nothing less than a subcontinent. Consisting of more than a million square miles, the big unknown ran from St. Louis west to California and from Taos north to Canada, an area larger than all the countries of western Europe combined. Until the mountain men came, this land mass had been probed by only a few tentative fingers of exploration, with even the Lewis and Clark Expedition leaving merely a thin pencil line across an otherwise blank map. But by the time the mountain men were gone, the map was filled in, if not on paper certainly in their minds, down to just about every mountain, river, lake, desert and valley. In fact, so thoroughly did they explore the West that when its so-called "discoverers" later came along—the celebrated John Charles Frémont and others—they almost invariably made their fame as pathfinders with former mountain men leading them by the hand as guides.

Although the mountain men came from many different parts of the nation and walks of life, they were mainly very young, very poor and very favored with the physical capacity to endure unbelievable hardships. They were also singularly blessed with the ability to adapt to an environment Bernard DeVoto described as not so much a foreign country as a different planet. And it was fortunate they were, because it was their lot to face privations and perils on a scale totally new to the American experience. Not even their lineal forefathers, the frontiersmen of the Colonial and Revolutionary periods—the Kentuckians of the long rifles and all the others before them—had been confronted by such problems of sheer survival. Everything west of the Mississippi River, from the Great Plains up to the Rocky Mountains and then on across the Great Basin, was of a vastly larger and more violent magnitude. The distances were far greater than any Americans had known before, the terrain far more treacherous. Except for a few small and isolated trading posts on the lower Missouri, there were no bases of supply and safety to fall back on; there was literally nothing out there but thousands and thousands of miles of unexplored and inhospitable country. The climate alone was a whole new enemy, with prairie storms striking with cyclonic fury, lightning-ignited prairie fires racing across the horizon faster than any animal can run, giant mirages rising over deserts to tantalize tongues already swollen with thirst and mountain blizzards raging for days on end every bit as savagely as those in Siberia. Even the wild animals were larger and more ferocious; the buffalo and that most fearsome of all American carnivores, *Ursus horribilis*, the grizzly, were not to be met with in the East. With it all, the Indians here, unlike those who had earlier been pacified with the rifle, had an extra and equalizing weapon in their arsenal, the horse. The tribes of the Great Plains and Rocky Mountains were superb horsemen, battle-trained and battle-eager, later to be described by General Charles King as "foemen far more to be dreaded than any European cavalry."[1]

That the mountain men survived was in itself a remarkable achievement. That this handful of men, whose numbers seldom came to more than five hundred in any given year, mastered the topography of the West, fought the Indians to a standstill, balked the territorial ambitions of the British and blazed the trails for the wagon trains which followed is little less than a minor miracle. As for their courage, Francis Parkman, who as a young man took a trip

Scenes of the many dangers and hardships in the life of a Rocky Mountain trapper. *Denver Public Library, Western History Department.*

One of that special breed of men of whom Francis Parkman wrote: "I defy the annals of chivalry to furnish the record of a life more wild and perilous than that of a Rocky Mountain trapper." *"The Trapper," by Charles Deas, Yale University Art Gallery, Mabel Brady Garvan Collection.*

along the Oregon Trail and met a few of the mountain men who still lingered in the Rockies, had this to say: "I defy the annals of chivalry to furnish the record of a life more wild and perilous than that of a Rocky Mountain trapper."[2]

While much that has been written about the mountain men tends to give the impression that the fur trade was an isolated phenomenon of the trans-Mississippi West, nothing could be farther from the truth. Actually, the fur trade in North America had been a basic form of commerce since the time when the first Europeans had set foot on the Atlantic seaboard. From the very outset, it played a crucial role in shaping the political and economic destiny of the continent north of Mexico, with the greater part of the history of the American colonies and the entire history of New France intertwined with the search for and trade in furs. It is no exaggeration to say that more than any other driving force the pelts of fur-bearing animals, especially the beaver, moved men to explore the unknown parts of North America, caused empires to wage bloody colonial wars and, along with the never-to-be-satisfied hunger for land, lured the frontier inexorably toward the Pacific Ocean. What transpired in the Rocky Mountains was in fact but one short chapter in a long history, although it did turn out to be the most colorful and exciting of all.

Because of its location, Jackson Hole was an important crossroad of the western fur trade from its earliest days until the changing tide of fashion turned away from hats made of beaver and the time of the mountain men came to an end. Not only did the valley lie in the heart of prime beaver country, but the passes and canyons which lead into it and out of it also provided the most accessible route over the Rocky Mountains for several hundred miles north and south. Consequently, Jackson Hole was visited at one time or another by virtually all of the men whose names resound through mountain history: Wilson Price Hunt, Robert Stuart, Bill Sublette, Jedediah Smith, Tom Fitzpatrick, Jim Bridger, Captain Bonneville, Kit Carson—the list goes on and on. At times, these men merely passed through the valley. At other times, they stayed to trap and hunt. Once, just over the Tetons in Teton Basin, then called Pierre's Hole, they assembled and put on a wild, drunken rendezvous, complete with the biggest trapper-Indian battle ever fought. There were few, if any, places in the entire West more central to the fur trade than was Jackson Hole, and by following the trails of just a few of the trappers who came and went through this great amphitheater, a most unusual phase of American history can be seen being acted out.

If John Colter did reach Jackson Hole on his long hike in the winter of 1807–1808, he was the first white man to do so. If he did not, then the first whites arrived three years later, and when they entered the valley they came in from a completely unexpected direction, the west. The Blackfeet eventually forced Manuel Lisa to abandon his trading post in what is now Montana, but before he left the mountains they drove one of his trapping parties over the Continental Divide north of Jackson Hole. Fleeing for their lives from the most feared of all the Indian tribes, these men under the command of Andrew Henry circled down to what has since been called Henry's Fork of the Snake River in Idaho, where they threw together several log cabins and christened this first American outpost on the Pacific slope of the Rocky Mountains Henry's Fort. In the fall of 1810, a few of these men went east into Jackson Hole, did some trapping, then returned to Henry's Fort, and whether or not they or Colter were the first white men to go into the valley, they were surely the first to trap its waters.

Stone carved with the name Henry and the date 1810, found near Drummond, Idaho, in 1917. Presumably left behind by members of Andrew Henry's trapping party which fled from the Blackfeet in Montana and wintered west of the Tetons. In the fall of 1810, a few of these men went east into Jackson Hole. *Jackson Hole Museum.*

In the spring of 1811, after an especially cruel and hungry winter, Henry's starving and demoralized group disbanded in what amounted to little more than an every-man-for-himself dash back to the safety of the frontier. Three of them—John Hoback, Jacob Reznor and Edward Robinson, who is said to have worn a red bandanna to cover his pate which had been scalped by Indians years earlier in Kentucky—crossed into Jackson Hole presumably by way of Teton Pass and exited by way of Togwotee Pass. They then walked cross-country to the Missouri River, where they made a dugout canoe and started down toward St. Louis. But before they reached that farthermost point of civilization, they met the westbound Astorians and were talked into turning around and heading back into the Rocky Mountains once more.

The name of the Astorians was derived from the name of a man back in New York who dreamed great dreams of wealth and rode roughshod over anyone who stood in his way of achieving it, a man who would become both the most powerful and hated figure in the history of the fur trade, John Jacob Astor. His plan was to build a chain of trading posts all the way to the Pacific Ocean, and in 1811 he acted to leapfrog all competition by forging the last link in the chain first, a post at the mouth of the Columbia River. Fort Astoria, as it would be called, was to be supplied by ships from the East Coast, which would then sail on with the furs to China and trade them for silks and other goods for the home market. To found the post, Astor sent one expedition around Cape Horn aboard a schooner and another overland from the Missouri frontier. Led by Wilson Price Hunt, the overland party consisted of sixty-two men, one squaw and two half-breed children, a force so large it seems to have given Hoback, Reznor and Robinson a sufficient sense of security to join up and try their luck another time at making a fortune by trapping "soft gold," as the beaver's fur was called. They guided the Astorians west, making sure to steer them south of Blackfoot country, until in mid-September they came to Union Pass some seventy-five miles east of Jackson Hole. There, as Washington Irving wrote when he related the adventures of the Astorians, they saw the three Tetons in the distance "glistening with snow . . . They were hailed by the travellers with that joy with which a beacon on a sea-shore is hailed by mariners after a long and dangerous voyage."[3]

Instead of going into Jackson Hole by way of the canyon of the Gros Ventre River, the hungry group swung south to hunt buffalo for several days, then followed the river they named after John Hoback through its precipitous canyon into the valley. After scouting the lower part of Jackson Hole and seeing ample signs of beaver, Hunt decided to detach four men to stay behind and trap while the main party went on to found Fort Astoria. In Irving's words, "They [the trappers who stayed behind] took leave of their comrades . . . with stout hearts and cheerful countenances."[4] While Irving made the men's assignment sound simple enough—to remain in Jackson Hole until they had taken all the pelts their horses could carry, then go on to the mouth of the Columbia River—he

John Jacob Astor, from a drawing made in 1842. *From "Century Magazine," April, 1904.*

(Opposite page) "Four of a Kind," by Edgar S. Paxton, depicts mountain men fighting for their lives during an Indian attack. *Thomas Gilcrease Institute of History and Art, Tulsa, Oklahoma.*

failed to say that close to seven hundred straight-line miles of nothing but a howling wilderness lay between the two points, a reminder of the epic scale of distance and danger the men of the mountains accepted as commonplace.

The four trappers evidently wintered in Jackson Hole and explored its upper reaches before leaving in the spring of 1812. After going out of the valley over Teton Pass and traveling north, they were attacked by a war party of Crows, who stole all their possessions, killed one man and left the other three to wander helplessly until they were taken in by friendly Indians and later rescued by fellow Astorians. In the fall of that same year, a group of returning Astorians under the command of Robert Stuart, who was carrying dispatches to Astor, went east through Jackson Hole by way of Teton Pass and Hoback Canyon and made their way homeward. In the course of their journey, they appear to have discovered historic South Pass, that key gap in the Rocky Mountain barrier which later made it possible for wagon trains to cross the

Continental Divide, and they certainly followed a route much the same as that which thirty years later would become the Oregon Trail. Beset by terrible hardships (they came so close to starving that one member suggested they draw lots to see who should be killed and eaten), the small band arrived back on the frontier in the spring of 1813 to learn that the War of 1812 had been going on for almost a year.

During that war, Fort Astoria was lost to the British and the initial phase of the American fur trade in the far West came to an end. Jackson Hole—indeed, the entire Northwest—reverted to the Indians as far as any American presence was concerned. The British, on the other hand, continued to be active in western Canada, and in 1819 a party from the North West Company came south and seems to have explored Yellowstone and Jackson Hole, at which time the French Canadian *engagés*, or hired hands, probably gave the three Tetons their name. Although the records are far from explicit, a few other British parties may have entered the valley during the next few years. However, except for the 1819 British party and any others that may have visited briefly, the primeval silence of the Teton country was not disturbed by the sound of trappers' voices throughout the long period from 1812 until the Americans finally returned in 1824.

After the War of 1812, a prolonged depression greatly reduced the demand for furs. Although some trapping continued along the lower Missouri, no penetration was made of the mountain West until 1821, when Manuel Lisa's successor, Joshua Pilcher, constructed a small trading post at the mouth of the Bighorn River. But it was not until early in the following year, after Congress did away with many of the restrictions attached to trading with the Indians for furs, that the heyday of the western fur trade began in earnest. Suddenly, the enormous empire west of the Mississippi River was thrown wide open to private enterprise and the race for the beaver-rich streams of the northern Rocky Mountains promptly got under way.

7

Trapper Trails in Jackson Hole 1822-1840

First to jump off from St. Louis for the distant mountains was the trapping expedition of General William Ashley and Andrew Henry in April of 1822. Under the command of Henry, an advance party consisting of about one hundred "enterprising young men," one of whom would lead the first Americans back into Jackson Hole, went up the Missouri River and built an outpost at the mouth of the Yellowstone River, where the men began to master the intricate mechanics of trapping and wilderness life.[1] The following year, General Ashley took two keelboats and a large force to join and resupply the first group, only to be driven back at the Arikara villages in what is now North Dakota when that tribe fell upon them in a surprise attack. Although the army sent troops to punish the Arikaras, the campaign was a fiasco and the river route to the Rocky Mountains remained closed. The only alternative was to travel overland with pack horses and mules, so shortly the main artery for supply trains ran across the Great Plains, following the Platte River and the Sweetwater River up to South Pass—the same route over which two decades later the Mormons would trudge to Utah and the wagon trains of the "gentiles," as the Mormons called all others, would roll on to Oregon.

In the autumn of 1824, six of Henry's trappers, led by an extremely capable and highly devout young man named Jedediah Smith, went into Jackson Hole and apparently traveled its length before going out by way of Conant Pass in the northern end of the Tetons. Moving north, they continued on to make accidental contact with the competition, the Hudson's Bay Company (known facetiously to the trappers as H.B.C., or Here Before Christ), at Flathead House in Montana. There the British were less than overjoyed to see this vanguard of Americans in the still disputed Northwest. In fact, the issue was of such importance to them that just a few weeks earlier a high official of the company, knowing the American fur men were steadily advancing west, had written of the Snake River country that it "is a rich preserve of beaver . . . which

Jedediah Smith, who "rediscovered" Jackson Hole in 1824. After a horrible mauling by a grizzly bear, in which one of his ears was almost torn off, he wore his hair long to conceal the scar. *Kansas State Historical Society, Topeka*.

(Opposite page) "Rendezvous," by Alfred Jacob Miller, the painter who was taken to the Rockies by Sir William Drummond Stewart and actually attended one of the annual gatherings of the mountain men. *Walters Art Gallery, Baltimore*.

for political reasons we should endeavour to destroy as fast as possible."[2] But this was not to be. The Americans soon came into the mountains in such numbers that what trapping out of the streams was to take place would be done largely by them, not the British.

After Jedediah Smith passed through Jackson Hole, the valley was not visited again until the next year, 1825, and then by a party of trappers whose ranks included two young men whose names were destined to be written large in mountain history, Jim Bridger and Tom Fitzpatrick. They arrived from the Green River country southeast of Jackson Hole, where the most famous of all fur trade institutions, the rendezvous, had just been inaugurated. Because it took so long to get to the Rocky Mountains from the Missouri frontier, it was necessary for the men to stay in the mountains year-round, and some means had to be found to resupply them with what they considered the basics of life: ammunition; blankets; a little coffee, flour and sugar; ribbons, bells, cheap jewelry and other "foofaraw" for the Indian damsels; and, not the least of all necessities, whiskey. So rendezvous was born, an annual summer assembly of the trappers at a predetermined time and place, with a supply train from St. Louis bringing goods into the mountains and taking pelts out.

The first rendezvous in 1825 was a modest and relatively inno-
cent affair, but the mountain men and the Indians who at the time
of any given rendezvous happened to be friendly soon perfected
the event into a kaleidoscopic combination of a trading fair, brawl,
orgy, gymkhana and class reunion, the trappers' alma mater being
what they jokingly referred to as the fountainhead of all their
knowledge, the Rocky Mountain College. An observer at a later
rendezvous described it, without benefit of commas, as a "drunken
crazy hooting quarreling fighting frolic," while still another observer complained of being "compelled all day to listen to the hic-
coughing jargon of drunken traders, the *sacré* and *foutre* of French-
men run wild, and the swearing and screaming of our own men,
who are scarcely less savage than the rest, being heated by the
detestable liquor which circulates freely among them."[3] In short, a
good time was had by all, or almost all, and the rendezvous became
the most eagerly looked forward to and, because of hangovers, the
most ruefully looked back on several weeks of every year.

After the first rendezvous, Jim Bridger, Tom Fitzpatrick and
thirty or so fellow trappers worked the waters of Jackson Hole
before going north into Yellowstone, where the strange sights they
saw and later told others about back home were so ridiculed that

Bridger finally decided to stop telling the truth and wove the various wonders into outrageous lies.* By the time of the second rendezvous in 1826, General Ashley, whose partner Andrew Henry had quit the mountains earlier, had done some simple arithmetic concerning the business and had concluded that greater profits could be made with far less risk by supplying the mountain men with goods at exorbitantly marked up prices than by bankrolling their trapping efforts. So, while retaining control of the supply system, Ashley sold out to Jedediah Smith, Bill Sublette and David Jackson, after whom Jackson Hole is named, ostensibly because it was his favorite trapping ground. Although this firm did not become known as the Rocky Mountain Fur Company until it passed into the hands of new owners four years later, its ranks already contained most of the men whose deeds would cause that company to be long remembered as the elite, the legendary Round Table, of the fur trade.

Between 1826 and 1830, parties of trappers seem to have gone into Jackson Hole only twice, once in 1826 when Bill Sublette's and David Jackson's brigades crossed the valley after having fought a pitched battle with the Blackfeet elsewhere, and again in 1829 when Sublette and Jackson gathered their men on the shore of Jackson Lake at the foot of the Tetons to keep an appointment they had made with Jedediah Smith two years earlier. Prior to setting the date for this meeting, Jedediah had been very active, not so much in making a fortune in beaver as in making several historic explorations. After the rendezvous of 1826, held north of Great Salt Lake, he had started out to find new trapping grounds to the southwest and had ended up on the Pacific Ocean, he and his fourteen men being the first to reach California by land from any part of the United States. There the Mexicans, who only a short time before had won their independence from Spain, did not greet this ragtag band of mountain men with open arms, for they intuitively recognized them to be the forerunners of what Americans have called "Manifest Destiny" and what those who stood in the way of it have called "Yankee Imperialism." Urged to leave, but it being too early in the season for his entire party to travel, Jedediah left most of his men in California and with two companions set out on

* In 1856, nearly two decades before Yellowstone was "officially discovered," a newspaperman in Kansas City missed what could have been the journalistic scoop of his time. He heard from Jim Bridger of "a place where hell bubbled up," but suppressed the story when told he would be the laughing stock of the town if he printed "any of old Jim Bridger's lies." (H. M. Chittenden, *The Yellowstone National Park*, fn. pp. 48–49)

Charles M. Russell's "Free Trappers" depicts mountain men in high country such as that around Jackson Hole. *Montana Historical Society, Helena.*

one of the most arduous journeys ever taken by any Americans. Riding east, they forged the first passage ever made across the Sierra Nevada Mountains, and did so while the snow was still deep. Then they crossed the desert, almost dying of thirst, finally arriving at Bear Lake in Utah in time for the rendezvous of 1827. Typical of his Spartan-like ways, Jedediah simply reported what had happened, rested briefly, made the date to meet his partners in Jackson Hole two years later and with eighteen men returned to California to bring back his men and furs.

When Jedediah Smith appeared in Jackson Hole in 1829, he had still another amazing story to tell about his travels and misadventures. On the way to California, his group had been hit in a surprise attack by the Mohave Indians and had lost ten men and most of their possessions, so Jedediah arrived back in what was to become the Golden State just as broke as he had been when he left it. Ordered by the Mexican authorities to get out of the country, and hearing that good trapping streams lay to the north, he and his men were the first to travel up the Pacific coastline to Oregon, where most of them were butchered in a massacre by the Umpqua Indians. Out scouting when the massacre occurred, Jedediah and several others made their way to the sanctuary of a Hudson's Bay Company outpost. There they were treated more hospitably by the British than they had been by the Mexicans, but they were eyed not a whit less suspiciously.

Although one historian has counted no fewer than thirty trapping and trading parties in Jackson Hole between the years 1829 and 1840, to itemize them here would be a pointless recitation of names and dates. It is enough to say that Jackson Hole and the region around it for a radius of a hundred miles was the main arena of the fur trade in its final decade, the first year of which saw Smith, Jackson and Sublette sell out to what officially became the Rocky Mountain Fur Company. The new proprietors were Tom Fitzpatrick, Milton Sublette (Bill's brother), Henry Fraeb, Baptiste Gervais and Jim Bridger, who signed the transfer papers with an X, and while every one of these men was a first-rate trapper and mountain leader, all of them together did not have the business acumen of a General Ashley. However, someone who did have business acumen to an extraordinary degree chose the same year, 1830, to send a trapping expedition into the mountains. John Jacob Astor now began moving to compete in full force, and the demise of the Rocky Mountain Fur Company was to be only a matter of time.

"A Fur Trader in the Council Tepee," by Frederic Remington. *Remington Art Museum, Ogdensburg, N.Y.*

The German-born Astor's aversion to competition of any kind is crystallized in this one sentence by Kenneth Porter: "It was his purpose to concentrate the Western fur trade in the hands of only such American citizens as had been born in Waldorf, Germany, in 1763 and had arrived in the United States from London in the spring of 1784."[4] Until 1830, Astor's activity in the West had been limited to trading posts along the upper Missouri, and his men were therefore mainly river traders who knew little of the mountain crafts. Now that he had decided to invade the heartland of beaver country, which the Rocky Mountain Fur Company men looked upon as their own, the brass knuckles came out. Never one to employ subtle techniques or soft field commanders, Astor put the nail-tough Kenneth McKenzie in charge of the Upper Missouri Outfit of his American Fur Company with orders to crush the opposition and hang the expense. With the great financial resources of Astor's fur trust behind them, McKenzie and his captains would soon be able to outbid all others for furs, bribe Indians to rob those who did not cooperate and engage in other ruthless practices, including several instances of suspected murder, designed to snap the spine of all competition.

In late June of 1832, the mountain men and friendly Indians from different parts of the Rockies began to assemble in Jackson

In "Caravan," by Alfred Jacob Miller, mountain men and friendly Indians meet a supply train on its way to rendezvous. *Northern Natural Gas Company Collection, Joslyn Art Museum, Omaha, Nebraska.*

Hole's neighbor valley just across the Tetons, Pierre's Hole. They came in company brigades, files of bearded mounted men leading pack horses piled high with beaver pelts. They came in smaller, scattered groups of free trappers, men not beholden to any company, many with their Indian wives astride beautifully caparisoned steeds and their black-eyed half-breed children perched atop bulky packs strapped on mules. They came in tribal bands of Nez Percés and Flatheads, resplendent in their finest beaded and porcupine-quilled attire. Perhaps as many as a thousand in all, red and white alike, they came to rendezvous, for summer was back in the mountains and it was time to gather once more.

The host of the party was the Rocky Mountain Fur Company, still the king of the mountains when it came to trapping know-how. It had contracted for a supply train from St. Louis that was due to arrive any day, led by Bill Sublette, who like General Ashley before him had given up trapping and become a supplier. Also in Pierre's Hole there were some ninety uninvited guests, men who owed their allegiance to Astor's American Fur Company, and they were awaiting his supply train, which was racing Sublette to get to rendezvous first and skim the cream off the business. The field leaders of both companies were on edge because the trappers, regardless of which firm they were attached to, had a year-long thirst to quench and no loyalty was so strong it could withstand the temptation to sell pelts to the supplier who won the race to fill the camp kettles with whiskey. The leaders of the rival supply trains were also tense, urging their men to push themselves and their animals to the utmost. Tom Fitzpatrick, a Rocky Mountain Fur Company partner who was traveling with Sublette, finally became so eager to carry the word to the rendezvous that Sublette was in the lead and the whiskey would soon be there that he rode ahead by himself. In so doing, he wrote one of the more terror-filled episodes into mountain lore.

Fitzpatrick left Sublette's supply train while it was still well to the east of Jackson Hole, and not long thereafter ran headlong into a band of Gros Ventre warriors. Fleeing from them, his horse broke down, but before the Indians could get to him he found a hole in an outcropping of rocks and concealed himself in it behind sticks and leaves. The Gros Ventres scoured the area for hours, coming so close to where he was hidden they almost stepped on him, at last breaking off the search at nightfall, only to resume it in the morning. For two days and nights, Fitzpatrick was the mouse in a cat-and-mouse chase, and when he finally did escape he lost his rifle trying to cross a stream on an improvised raft, was attacked by wolves, almost starved to death and weakly staggered west with failing hope that he could make it to Pierre's Hole. Fortunately, several trappers came upon this wild-eyed skeleton of a man as he was struggling with the last of his strength to ford the Snake River in Jackson Hole. Until this incident occurred, Fitzpatrick had carried the Indian name "Broken Hand," descriptive of the damage inflicted on his fingers when a gun had burst while he was firing it. From then on, his Indian name would also be "White Hair," descriptive of the change of color said to have taken place as a result of this nightmare.

Bill Sublette's supply train crossed Jackson Hole, forded the Snake River, went over Teton Pass and arrived at rendezvous on July 8, having left the American Fur Company's supply train so far behind that it failed to appear before the rendezvous broke up. By July 17, a year's trading, drinking, boasting, fighting, gambling and squaw-wenching had been done—or, put another way, a year's pent-up fears and tensions had been released in what Joe Meek described as one "crazy drunk."[5] On that day, Milton Sublette led his men out on a trapping expedition and camped for the night not far from the western foot of Teton Pass. The next morning, they saw a long column of horsemen in the distance, which they first thought to be the American Fur Company's supply train, but instead turned out to be a large party of Gros Ventres. When the two groups came closer to each other and the chief of the Gros Ventres rode forward to parley, two trappers rode out to meet him, one of whom hated all Gros Ventres because their close allies, the Blackfeet, had slain his father some years earlier. Violating every code connected with such preliminary councils, one of the trappers seized the chief's hand while the other shot him at point-blank range, killing him. The battle of Pierre's Hole was on.

The Indians immediately withdrew to a thicket where their women began constructing a timber barricade, while the trappers sent a messenger speeding back to their main force still at the site of the disbanding rendezvous. Bill Sublette and his good friend Robert Campbell brought up reinforcements, including the friendly Nez Percés and Flatheads, and as their horses raced at a full run the two men shouted their last wills and testaments to each other. Arriving on the scene, Sublette took charge and directed efforts to penetrate the Gros Ventre defenses, all of which failed and during which heavy fire was exchanged by both sides, with one of the Indian bullets hitting Sublette in the shoulder. Then the proposal was made to burn the Gros Ventres out, but this was vetoed by the friendly Indians who could not bear to see the Gros Ventre booty they counted as already in their hands go up in flames. All the while, the Indians on both sides were haranguing each other in typical battle style, loudly defaming the rival tribe's ancestry and describing in gory detail the tortures to be endured when they triumphed. Resorting to a ruse, a Gros Ventre called out that his band was merely the advance party of a large army of warriors who were sure to appear at any moment, and this was somehow garbled in the translation, leading the trappers to believe that their pelts, supplies and remaining comrades back at the main camp were being overrun. So back they raced, leaving only enough men to keep the Gros Ventres contained. By the time they learned they had been tricked, it was too late in the day to carry the battle forward, and by morning there was no more battle to be fought— the Gros Ventres had stolen away during the night and had fled

"Trappers Going to Pierre's Hole Fight," by Frederic Remington. *From "Century Magazine," April, 1904.*

over Teton Pass into Jackson Hole. Although there may have been as many as thirty-eight killed on both sides in this largest of all engagements between mountain men and Indians, it settled nothing, only serving to keep old hatreds burning brightly.

Another bloody event connected with the rendezvous of 1832 took place in Jackson Hole itself. While Bill Sublette's shoulder wound healed, seven men who had planned to accompany his fur-carrying caravan back to the frontier became tired of waiting and set off by themselves. This small, foolhardy group, which is said to have included two of Daniel Boone's grandsons, no sooner crossed Teton Pass and went down into Jackson Hole than it was attacked by either Gros Ventres or Blackfeet, who killed two of the travelers on the spot and left one to die shortly thereafter. Of more long-range importance in the history of the fur trade, however, in this same year the man who craftily manipulated the mountain men from afar read the economic signs every bit as clearly as they could read the signs of Indians. In a letter from London, John Jacob Astor noted, forebodingly, "It appears that they make hats of silk in place of beaver."[6]

A month after the rendezvous of 1832 ended, a whole new company of trappers passed through Jackson Hole, led by a man who had no knowledge of either the mountains or the fur trade, but was deeply into both. Captain Benjamin de Bonneville of the United States Army, who had been a refugee from the French Revolution, had graduated from West Point and whose friends included Thomas Paine and the Marquis de Lafayette, arrived from the Green River region of the Rockies, where he had erected a fort and named it after himself, Fort Bonneville. Although the mountain men thought the fort's location was completely impractical and derisively called it "Fort Nonsense" and "Bonneville's Folly," in retrospect its positioning may not have been the folly it appeared to be, and the leave the War Department granted Bonneville to participate in the fur trade may not have been all it appeared to be either. Whether by coincidence or not, Fort Bonneville was strategically placed to block forces which might move from Oregon, to cover forces which might move toward Oregon, to control the western approach to South Pass and to command routes leading west to the Great Salt Lake and on to California. Bonneville also both commissioned and led a number of expeditions which whether or not so intended did gather valuable topographical intelligence, much of which he incorporated into one of the first maps of the interior West that accurately depicted its principal features, including the Tetons and Jackson Hole. Although Bonneville proved to be pitifully inept as a fur man and his backers lost much money, it very well may be that his primary mission was not to supply the raw material for men's hats. What makes the supposition highly probable is that when he overstayed his leave by two years and was automatically dismissed from the army, he was returned to duty by a man who could never be accused of being lax in matters of military discipline, President Andrew Jackson.

The year 1834 was eventful and decisive. By then John Jacob Astor could see that he had the Rocky Mountain Fur Company on the ropes, but because he could see a little farther down the road than most men, he could also see that beaver were becoming less plentiful and the fashion in men's hats was changing rapidly. Deciding to concentrate his fortune in a more promising investment, New York City real estate, he sold his interest to his partners, leaving it to them to preside over the final monopolization of the fur trade in the West. At the rendezvous that summer, the Rocky Mountain Fur Company finally caved in. Fraeb and Gervais sold out, the firm was dissolved and Bridger, Fitzpatrick and Milton Sublette entered into an agreement with the American Fur Company which was tantamount to placing the mountain fur trade into that company's outstretched hands.

At the same rendezvous of 1834, two newcomers appeared who symbolized the enormous changes headed toward the West. The first missionaries, Jason and Daniel Lee, came in with the supply train, not to save the souls of the mountain men, as might be supposed, but in response to an appeal from the Nez Percés and Flatheads to learn more about the white man's "medicine." The Lees, however, did not follow through on their mission; instead, they rather callously abandoned the people they had been sent to catechize in favor of going on to both better ministerial and real estate opportunities in the huge territory called Oregon. Soon the richness of the land in Oregon would attract other Americans in such numbers that, by dint of occupancy, the great Northwest would be preempted from the British and become part of the United States.

In 1835, Osborne Russell, a Maine farm boy turned trapper, celebrated the Fourth of July with several companions on the banks of the Snake River in Jackson Hole. But they did not observe the occasion in the way the mountain men usually did, by firing their

B.L.E. Bonneville, later as an army general. Was he an authentic fur trader or on an intelligence mission for the War Department? *Denver Public Library, Western History Department.*

rifles and beating on camp kettles. Rather, Russell and his comrades spent the afternoon and night stark naked, cold and drenched by a driving rain, having had to abandon the raft that was carrying their clothing and equipment across the river when it got out of control and plunged toward dangerous rapids. Comparing his lot with "those who were perhaps at this moment Celebrating the anniversary of our Independence in my Native Land or seated around tables loaded with the richest dainties that a rich independent and enlightened country could afford," Russell bemoaned his plight. "I now began to reflect on the miserable condition of myself and those around me, without clothing provisions or fire arms . . . not knowing at what moment we might be aroused by the shrill war cry of the hostile Savages with which the country was infested whilst not an article for defense excepting our butcher Knives remained in our possession."[7] By great good luck, the next morning they found the raft lodged safely on a sand bar and recovered both their gear and their good spirits, going on to trap beaver as though nothing had happened.

In early August of 1835, two more Oregon-bound missionaries came to rendezvous, both of whom were more dedicated than the

Kit Carson in his later years, long after he had trapped in Jackson Hole. *Museum of New Mexico.*

Lees and not half as sanctimonious. Marcus Whitman, a medical missionary, hit it off with the mountain men and removed a Blackfoot arrow Jim Bridger had been carrying in his back for three years.* Whitman's older companion, Samuel Parker, was also liked by the trappers, although to the mischievous delight of Joe Meek the sermon Parker preached in Jackson's Little Hole at the source of the Hoback River was rudely interrupted by a herd of buffalo. When the buffalo were spotted, the mountain men ran for their horses and, according to Meek, "the congregation incontinently broke up, without staying for a benediction."[8]

With missionaries in the mountains, all that remained to complete the onrush of civilization was the appearance of white women, and this came to pass the following year at the rendezvous of 1836, when Marcus Whitman brought his beautiful, vivacious wife Narcissa through with another church couple on their way to Oregon. About this time, silk hats began to become more popular and twilight fell fast on the Rocky Mountain fur trade. The last ren-

* Bridger was later asked why the wound around the arrow point he had carried in his back for so long had not suppurated or become gangrenous. Straight-faced, he replied, "In the mountains the meat never spoils!" (J. Cecil Alter, *Jim Bridger*, p. 191)

dezvous was held in 1840, after which all but a few diehards among the mountain men scattered to the winds. Some went back to the old frontier and donned the garb of respectability. Some went on to the new frontier, Oregon, and became men of substance. Some enthusiastically engaged in what might be called the mountain men's second profession, stealing horses from the Mexicans in California. Several, such as Jim Bridger and Kit Carson, had their wilderness skills called upon by the army and became famous guides, scouts and Indian fighters.

As for Jackson Hole, it had two notable visitors the summer of the last rendezvous. Father De Smet, the beloved Jesuit missionary, crossed the valley in company with Flatheads to found his mission among them, and a penniless Joe Meek took a final fling at trapping the streams which feed into the Snake River. When Joe left Jackson Hole, he heard that his longtime mountain friend and brother-in-law by Indian marriage, "Doc" Newell, was looking for him. "Doc" had a crazy idea that wagons could be taken from Fort Hall, not very far southwest of the Tetons, all the way through to Oregon, something none of those who had gone before had even attempted to do. With nothing to lose, Joe packed his Indian wife and child on a wagon and helped "Doc" do just that.

After 1840, Jackson Hole was abandoned by the whites. A few of the straggling trappers who remained in the mountains may have entered the valley from time to time, but no longer did the brigades of fur men come and go. The trade which had lured them up from the frontier into the high country had vanished, and all that was left were memories—memories of hardship and danger and courage and laughter the mountain men would yearn to go back and relive as the years went by and rheumatism crept into their bones. It was a dream they cherished to the end, although in their hearts they knew it was impossible, for their day was over and silence had once again fallen upon the land of the Tetons they knew so well.

8

Mountain Mavericks

Except for a few rust-covered old traps and rifle barrels which have since been found by the sides of the streams they trapped and the trails they followed, the mountain men left behind no lasting visible traces that they were ever in Jackson Hole. Nor did they leave behind any local descendants to carry on their names, for they departed from the scene many decades before the valley was settled and families were established. As a result, unlike most other communities where there are long and continuous links with the past, here there are no family trees with roots reaching back to the first adventurous progenitors. However, this accident of history has been rectified by a simple expedient: the people of "trapping country" have adopted the mountain men as their forefathers. And few, if any, forefathers, albeit adopted, are more admired than are the mountain men by the people of Jackson Hole.

Most of this admiration stems, of course, from the fact that in terms of sheer adventure their story is without parallel. Neither before nor since, on this continent or elsewhere, has any other company of men gone into an unexplored wilderness a thousand miles from civilization and subsisted off the land year after year among tribes of savage aborigines barely removed from the Stone Age. Simply in order to survive, they had to perform feats calling for courage and stamina far beyond normal human limits, and for the most part they pushed back those limits to a degree almost impossible to believe. But their often heralded death-defying deeds, now a part of our folklore, are only one legacy they handed down. There is another, although less familiar, which is especially cherished by the people of Jackson Hole. It is the legacy of respect for individualism, even eccentricity, a long and treasured tradition of the valley dating back to these honored "forefathers."

In an age when many fear that individualism is being eclipsed and conformity is becoming the order of the day, the mountain men have a special appeal. Crude, boisterous, lawless and sometimes even brutal they may have been, but they stand as a towering

Frederic Remington's "I Took Ye for an Injin," the most flattering words a mountain man could hear about his bizarre attire. *Remington Art Museum, Ogdensburg, N.Y.*

symbol of independence, self-sufficiency and tolerance for the idiosyncrasies of others. Free spirits unfettered by the restraints of society, they dressed as they pleased (often in attire making them look more Indian than white), ate and slept when their bodies told them to, got uproariously drunk when the mood was on them and whiskey available, were suspicious of and resistant to arbitrary authority, despised sham of any kind and in a very real sense were determined to live outside "the establishment" of their time, which even in frontier towns and villages had some class distinctions. In their eyes, a man was measured solely by his courage and his mountain skills, not by who he was or where he came from. Nothing else counted, and therefore the mountain men accepted the frequently bizarre behavior of their associates as a matter of course. Long before the expression came into vogue, they believed that a man should "do his own thing."

This aspect of the mountain men is usually forgotten in the rush to extol their heroic deeds, but it is an important legacy worth recounting, if only briefly, by bringing to mind a few of these men who dared to be different. Although two of them—"Old Bill" Williams and "Pegleg" Smith—probably never made it into Jackson Hole, they, too, are legitimate "forefathers," members of that special breed who had the courage to live their lives as they wished and the forbearance to let others do the same.

As a brash young man in Missouri, Bill Williams ordained himself a circuit rider and traveled about preaching hellfire and brimstone to all who would listen. When that palled, he decided to carry the good word to the Osage Indians, making a bargain with them that led to a remarkable religious conversion in reverse. He told them that if they would accept his teachings he would adopt their Indian customs, and the Osages readily agreed. But then they blithely went right on worshiping the sun, the moon and the other powerful forces of nature, while Bill plunged wholeheartedly into the life of the tribe. Soon he became more Indian than white, marrying an Indian girl, dressing as an Indian, participating in tribal rites, coming to believe in dreams and omens, and developing a streak of wildness which in later years set him apart among men whose wildness was notorious. In the course of his long career as a trapper, he was even accused of cannibalism. Although there was no truth to it, Kit Carson, who knew "Old Bill" well, jokingly remarked that in starving times it was not a good idea for anyone to walk alone ahead of him on a trail.

If cleanliness is truly next to godliness, "Old Bill" Williams did not stand much of a chance in the hereafter, because even among the mountain men, who were not noted for their personal fastidiousness, his incredibly dirty and disheveled appearance was viewed with a fascination bordering on awe. As for life in the hereafter, he had a most unusual notion about that. Somewhere along the line he became convinced that when he died he would be transformed into a bull elk, and so real was his fear that someone would shoot him that he went to great lengths to warn all of his incredulous fellow trappers of this coming reincarnation. He even described his future markings so no one would draw a bead on what appeared to be an elk, but actually was "Old Bill." Nevertheless, for all of this man's eccentricities, which were recounted with glee around many a campfire, no one ever suggested that it was not his right to believe and act as he did.

Jedediah Smith also dared to be different. In a community of men composed of what a contemporary called "a great majority of Scoundrels," he did not drink, swear, use tobacco or sleep with squaws.[1] Moreover, he was deeply religious, carried a Bible in his saddlebag and was not ashamed to be seen in prayer. For the mountain men, who loved to poke fun at their comrades and give them nicknames for their obvious traits, young Jedediah presented a perfect target. And yet, not even the rowdiest of trappers ever jested about his piety, and by them all he was called Jed or Jedediah, nothing else, except by those who even more respectfully called him Captain or Mister Smith.

Perhaps the paramount field captain of the fur trade, and ranked by many only next to Lewis and Clark as the greatest of American explorers, Jedediah time and again saved the lives of those around him. When they were dying of thirst, he would push on by himself and find water, then bring it back to give them the strength to reach the water hole. When they were lost in unfamiliar country and apprehensive that they would not survive, he would rally their spirits, then ride ahead and find a trail. Among men where the attributes of bravery and endurance were commonplace, Jedediah more than held his own. And he also more than held his own in terms of another attribute not universally commonplace. Just as they were tolerant of what they considered his strangeness, he was tolerant of theirs, never sanctimoniously criticizing them or trying to convert them to his beliefs. He simply went his way and they theirs—men worlds apart, but with a bond of mutual esteem between them.

Then there was another Smith, "Pegleg," a completely different cut of man who presided at the amputation of his leg when it was shattered by an Indian's bullet and lived to enjoy a mountain-wide reputation for his outlandish behavior. A man with a bull voice and an unquenchable thirst for "Taos Lightning," he boasted that he had learned the alphabet only as far as the letter "k," stopping there because he never found any use for it whatever and presum-

"Pegleg" Smith as he appeared in 1860. He often un-strapped his wooden leg and used it as a weapon in brawls. *From "Hutchings' California Magazine."*

ably the balance of the alphabet would have proved to be equally worthless. Although "k" never came in handy, his wooden leg did, because he soon learned to unstrap it and wield it as a fearsome weapon in the brawls which had an uncanny way of starting whenever he was around.

Unlike most mountain men, who when they took Indian women as wives usually took one at a time, "Pegleg" seems to have had a sultan's eye for numbers. At one point, he is reported to have had five children born to him in the space of a single month, while over the years his progeny were legion. In most other times and places, this man's lifetime of fighting, drinking and wenching would have led to rebukes, perhaps even ostracism, but among his associates his antics scarcely raised an eyebrow. It was part of the code that he had a right to live as he wished.

Jim Beckwourth not only stepped beyond the conventions of his time, but he broke them as he went along. Born a slave, the son of an aristocratic Virginian and a black woman, he ran away to the freedom of the mountains, where among the trappers the color of

Mountain man Jim Beckwourth, who was born a slave and ran away to write his name large in the history of the fur trade. From a daguerreotype made about 1855. *Nevada Historical Society.*

a man's skin was far less important than his ability to carry his own weight. It is a noteworthy commentary on the mountain men that, in an era when the institution of slavery was rarely questioned and blacks were thought of as a subspecies of the human race, they accepted a number of blacks into their ranks and treated them as equals. To most of the men of the mountains, many of whom were from the South, the color line ended at the frontier.

Jim's swarthy complexion brought about one of the most extraordinary of all his adventures, leading him to become not only a full-fledged member of the Crow tribe, but a war chief as well. The way it happened was that at the rendezvous of 1828 a trapper named Caleb Greenwood told some Crows that Jim was in reality a blood relation, having been born a Crow, abducted by the Cheyennes and sold to the whites, who raised him. Caleb and Jim had a good laugh over the story, but the Indians took it seriously. The following winter, when Jim was captured by a party of Crows and did not know what sort of treatment lay in store, he quickly declared his identity and, in his words, soon "was being hugged and kissed to death by a whole lodge full of near and dear Crow relatives."[2]

Adopted into the family of "Big Bowl"—and, as he called her, "Mrs. Big Bowl"—so comfortable did Jim find life with squaws to wait on him that he stayed with the tribe for more than seven years, growing his hair down to his waist in Crow fashion and having his ears pierced for earrings.[3] He soon gained prestige for both his prowess in war and among women. He said that while with the Crows he had eight wives at one time, and the number he had in his lifetime is beyond counting. In 1860, a Kansas newspaper reported that "Jim Beckwourth, ex-chief of the Crow Indians, has once more committed matrimony."[4]

Although Jim was notorious for greatly exaggerating his adventures and achievements, he did live an amazingly diverse and active life. His mountain years aside, he was a dispatch rider for Major General Stephen Watts Kearny in the Mexican War, ran a wide-open saloon in Santa Fe, stole horses from the Spanish ranches in California, prospected for gold with the forty-niners, discovered a pass in the Sierra Nevada which bears his name and once, with gambling winnings, got the town of Sacramento drunk, or at least "all the inhabitants . . . who were disposed that way."[5] While he was disliked by some, it was mainly because of his boastfulness, not because he was black. When with the mountain men, who were remarkably color-blind, he was regarded as a peer.

Of all the unlikely members of the trapping fraternity, none was more so than Captain William Drummond Stewart, a decorated veteran of the battle of Waterloo, scion of an enormously wealthy Scottish family and shortly to inherit the title Sir William, 19th Lord of Grandtully and 7th Baronet of Murthly, owner of two ancient castles and vast estates whose lands included Macbeth's Birnam Wood. Stewart went to the Rocky Mountains in search of adventure, finding there a group of men and way of life so appealing that he returned time and again. His eccentric behavior and steadfastness in the face of danger soon made him a favorite of the crusty mountain men, who were amused by his strange accent and elegant attire, which at times included a Panama hat and tight-fitting trousers made of the Stewart plaid.

Stewart was a man full of delightful surprises, bringing with him into the wilderness such unheard-of items as vintage wines, canned delicacies, Persian rugs on which to hold councils with the Indians and, of course, the wherewithal to make and properly serve tea. Once, when the party of trappers he was with found mint growing along an ice-cold stream, he made the most of the moment by

Alfred Jacob Miller's "Attack by Crow Indians" shows Sir William Drummond Stewart keeping his British composure in the face of threats. *Thomas Gilcrease Institute of History and Art, Tulsa, Oklahoma.*

mixing and passing around mint juleps. But the biggest surprise of all was the one he kept sealed in a box on the long journey from the frontier and presented to his friend Jim Bridger at the rendezvous of 1837—a burnished steel breastplate and a gleaming, long-plumed helmet, part of the uniform of the royal Life Guards. Jim loved the gift and promptly donned the armor and paraded about, to the laughter of the trappers and the astonishment of the Indians.

A maverick among mavericks, Stewart was accepted by the mountain men for the man he was. Such was their tolerance for the right of others to be different that they even forgave him for being British, rich and titled.

Capt Bridger, a celebrated Leader or Bourgeois in the Rocky mountains, was a great favorite of Sir Wm Stewart who imported a full suit of English Armor & presented it to Bridger, who donned it on all special occasions, & rode. so accoutered at the head of his men.

"Jim Bridger in a Suit of Armour," by Alfred Jacob Miller. The inscription beneath the painting is in Miller's hand, saying that Bridger donned his gift from Sir William Drummond Stewart "on all special occasions & rode so accoutered at the head of his men." *Northern Natural Gas Company Collection, Joslyn Art Museum, Omaha, Nebraska*.

Joe Meek can hardly be called a genuine eccentric, but he was not afraid to appear to be so when it suited his purpose. On a visit back to civilization, he did and said things deliberately designed to shock those who looked askance at his tattered mountain clothing and rough-hewn mountain manners. One night in a fancy hotel dining room, Joe became tired of being stared at with disdain, so he loudly congratulated the waiter on his plate of beef by declaring it to be "better meat than the old mule I eat in the mountains."[6] Then, although he knew better, he ordered a bottle of wine he called "pain," which turned out to be champagne. After finishing his meal, he arose and regally announced to his startled audience, "I am Envoy Extraordinary and Minister Plenipotentiary from the

Jovial Joe Meek, a comedian among the mountain men and related by marriage to President Polk. *Oregon Historical Society.*

Republic of Oregon to the Court of the United States!"[7] Whereupon, he strode from the room, leaving jaws hanging open and knowing that his mountain friends would have heartily approved of what he had just done.

Like Joe Meek, Jim Bridger was not an eccentric by mountain standards, although to the military mind he must have seemed passing strange. Later in life, when serving as a scout for the army, he ignored the usual by-the-clock regimen and "ate when he was hungry and drank when he was dry and went to bed when he felt sleepy—sometimes in the middle of the afternoon. This would get him up shortly after midnight, when he would make a fire, roast some meat for his breakfast, and eat it; afterwards, like as not, singing Injun songs, using a tin pan for his tom-tom."[8] What the others thought of him did not matter. He was merely observing the mountain man's right to "do his own thing."

These are only a handful of the uninhibited, larger-than-life men who cut the first trails through the West, then vanished, leaving behind practically no signs of their having been here. But they did leave behind a legacy more valuable than precious heirlooms passed down from generation to generation. It is that a man should be free to believe as he wishes to believe and free to behave as he wishes to behave, as long as he does no harm to others, and over the years this legacy would become an important part of the heritage of Jackson Hole.

9
Interlude

During the three decades following the final fur-trade rendezvous in 1840, the American people were busy populating Oregon, founding Deseret in Utah, laying railroad tracks, inventing baseball, seizing land from Mexico, singing *Oh! Susannah*, rushing for gold in California, reading *Moby Dick* and settling the long-festering issues of slavery and the Union. While all this was going on, Jackson Hole was virtually forgotten. Located far from the trails over which the first settlers streamed into the West, the valley remained part of a remote wilderness that was bypassed for many years. Except for a few holdover trappers who remained in the mountains and may have wandered in from time to time, on only six occasions during the long interval between 1840 and 1872 was Jackson Hole visited by white men in any numbers, then only briefly.

The first of these visits is one of the most perplexing and elusive pieces of all of Jackson Hole's history. It is based entirely upon hearsay evidence, yet it has the ring of truth, if for no other reason than that the story seems to be too improbable to have been made up. Writing in *Scribner's Monthly* in 1873, Nathaniel Langford, who was the first to claim the ascent of the Grand Teton, mentioned in passing that as early as 1843 a group led by a French trapper named Michaud, equipped "with ropes, rope-ladders, and other aids," tried and failed to reach the top of the tallest of all the Tetons.[1] Langford cited as his source Beaver Dick Leigh, the first settler of Teton Basin, but Beaver Dick did not come into this country until long after the attempted climb, and from whom he obtained his information is unknown. At the close of the century, C. G. Coutant wrote in his *History of Wyoming* that Michaud "with a well-organized party and with a complete climbing outfit ascended to a point directly beneath the summit, but here he encountered perpendicular rocks and was unable to proceed further. This was a great disappointment to the explorer and he never ceased to regret his failure."[2] Where Coutant came by his information he did not say.

The story is fascinating and frustrating, with the sum of what is known about this obscure group as bare of details as those recounted here. Who was Michaud? Langford calls him a French trapper while Coutant calls him a French explorer, but the truth of the matter seems to be that neither knew enough about him to be able to tell us his first name. Who were the members of his party? Where did they come from? And what in the world were they doing hundreds and hundreds of miles ahead of the advancing frontier trying to climb a Matterhorn-shaped mountain 13,770 feet high with rope ladders? Unfortunately, none of these questions is ever likely to be answered, unless somewhere in an old trunk someday to be opened there is a faded journal written by one of these mystery-enshrouded men who, like so many others who came after them, were drawn to the challenge of the Grand Teton way back in 1843.

In that same year, Jim Bridger hung up his traps and built Fort Bridger, which was more of a store and blacksmith's shop than a fort, and went into the business of selling supplies to the first few wagon trains just beginning to appear on the Oregon Trail where it crossed southern Wyoming about one hundred and fifty miles south of Jackson Hole. But Bridger, who was not cut out to be a shopkeeper, soon found ways to leave the establishment in the charge of others while he went hunting or hired himself out as a guide. On one of these occasions, he is reported to have led a trading expedition north through Jackson Hole and Yellowstone on the way to do business with the Crows and Sioux. This was in 1846, and it is the only record other than that of the Michaud venture when a group of white men came into Jackson Hole during all of the 1840s.

If the 1840s were lean in terms of visitors to the valley, the 1850s were even more so. There is no record indicating that a party of any size entered Jackson Hole during the entire decade, although Beaver Dick Leigh and a companion were evidently on the western slopes of the Tetons as early as 1858. Not until the spring of 1860 did white men in numbers return to Jackson Hole, and when they did arrive it was quite by accident, their intention having been to go elsewhere.

Before the Civil War consumed the nation's energies, the army sent an expedition into the West which had among its numerous missions the exploration of "the headwaters of the Yellowstone and Missouri rivers, and of the mountains in which they rise."[3] If these men had reached the place they were supposed to go, they would have come across the geysers and other freaks of nature the mountain men had earlier told others about only to be ridiculed, and which when "officially discovered" a decade later so captivated the American public that the world's first national park was created almost instantly. But this expedition of 1860 never made it to Yellowstone, although it did go into Jackson Hole, where a man's life seems to have been lost needlessly.

Under the command of Captain William F. Raynolds, the expedition consisted of one lieutenant, thirty infantrymen, seven scientists and a guide Raynolds called "The Old Man Of The Mountains," Jim Bridger, now fifty-six years old.[4] To the southeast of Jackson Hole, near where the town of Riverton, Wyoming, is now located, the expedition was broken into two divisions. One, under the lieutenant, had instructions to go due north, then west to the Three Forks of the Missouri River, while the other, under the captain, had as its assignment the discovery of the source of the Yellowstone River. Traveling northwest through the Wind River Valley, Captain Raynolds told Bridger he wanted to stay on the Atlantic slope of the Continental Divide, to which Bridger replied that Yellowstone could not be reached by such a route because a basaltic ridge five thousand feet high blocked the way. Ignoring this advice from the then outstanding authority on Western geography, the West Pointer gave orders to push on, so Bridger dutifully led them to the base of the impossibly sheer ridge, where he could not contain himself any longer, declaring gleefully, "I told you, you could not go through; a bird can't fly over that without taking a supply of grub along."[5]

Bridger seems to have enjoyed this moment of triumph, but not much later the usually faultless direction finder inside his head went out of kilter. After guiding the party over the Continental Divide through Union Pass (which Raynolds named), he became confused when he tried to forge a path north through the Mount Leidy Highlands to Two Ocean Pass. Raynolds wrote, "My Guide seems more at a loss than I have ever seen him."[6] Then, after an unnecessary and laborious crossing of a ridge, Raynolds added, "These little errors in matters of detail on his part are not remarkable, as it is fifteen years since he last visited this region, and they fade into insignificance when compared with his accurate general knowledge of the country."[7] Perhaps Bridger's memory was a little rusty, or perhaps the thick timber and deep snow in the Mount

"The Old Man Of The Mountains," Jim Bridger, in the 1860s, not long after he had guided the Raynolds Expedition into Jackson Hole. *Kansas State Historical Society, Topeka*.

Leidy Highlands briefly disoriented him, but he quickly regained his bearings and led the expedition down through the canyon of the Gros Ventre River into Jackson Hole. There they saw a hunting party of Blackfeet in the foothills along the eastern side of the valley and met a band of Shoshonis swimming horses across the swollen Snake River from the Teton side.

While Bridger's temporary confusion in the highlands is understandable, what he now told Captain Raynolds—or, more importantly, did not tell him—is inexplicable. He said there was no ford across the Snake River north of where they were camped, which is true and which Raynolds confirmed for himself by riding some miles up the river's east bank. What he left unsaid is that the best way to Yellowstone from Jackson Hole is not to cross the river, but to stay on its east side up to Pacific Creek, then on to Two Ocean Pass. Why he did not inform Raynolds of this pathway to the north is bewildering, to say the least, and it cannot be dismissed lightly as a lapse of memory about a topographical detail, for this had been a major route of the mountain men and had been traveled too many times by Bridger himself to have been forgotten. The only explanation that makes sense is the one offered by Frank Calkins in his book *Jackson Hole*. He speculates that Bridger probably remembered the Yellowstone region in early June to be a morass of melting snow and flooded streams, and, further, since he was being paid by the day he may have been in no hurry to get there. Whatever the reason, Bridger's omission had tragic consequences which all of his biographers, in their desire to make him a superhuman hero, have chosen to ignore.

In order to leave Jackson Hole, Raynolds now had no alternative but to put his men and supplies over the Snake River and go out by way of Teton Pass, and when Lance Corporal Bradley attempted a crossing where the Shoshonis had been seen swimming their horses over, he was drowned. Although Jim Bridger was indisputably one of the greatest of all the mountain men and guides of the West, he was, like everyone else, not without flaws. There are several other instances in his long and distinguished career when he did things not consistent with the image of the all-wise and ever-fearless man the myth makers have handed down. In this particular instance, there is simply no avoiding the conclusion that his failure to inform Raynolds of the route to the north to Yellowstone, no matter how wet it may have been, resulted in an unnecessary death.

After the drowning, Captain Raynolds ordered a raft to be constructed to ferry the men and supplies over the Snake River, at the time running high with the melting of snow in the mountains. When the raft proved to be inadequate, Bridger built a bull boat, that ingenious invention of the Indians which could be easily assembled on the spot with tipi hides or other skins, then dismantled when it was no longer needed. Soon everyone was across, and on June 18, 1860, they went out of the valley over Teton Pass, after which Bridger guided them north, apparently with a plan in mind to attempt an approach to Yellowstone from the west. They never reached Yellowstone, however, because one of the expedition's other missions (which it also failed to carry out) was to arrive near the Canadian border by a certain date in order to observe an eclipse, and they were running out of time. Although Captain Raynolds wrote, regretfully, that "the valley of the Upper Yellowstone . . . is as yet *terra incognita*," along the way Bridger made a believer of him with his accounts of what he had seen years before in the land of rumors north of Jackson Hole. The captain said his guide "described an immense boiling spring, that is a perfect counterpart of the geysers of Iceland. As he is uneducated, and had probably never heard of the existence of such natural wonders elsewhere, I have little doubt that he spoke of that which he had actually seen."[8]

Strangely, the first penetration of Yellowstone after the time of the mountain men (or, more precisely, after Sir William Drummond Stewart and Bill Sublette led a hunting party there from the frontier in 1843) was not made by this army expedition which had been sent to find it, but by a group of men who were not looking for Yellowstone at all, and who, when they did find it, were disappointed that it did not contain gold. In 1863, a gold strike was made at Alder Gulch, Montana, and overnight the boom town of Virginia City sprang up. Arriving too late to stake worthwhile claims, a group of prospectors elected as their leader a surveyor named Walter DeLacy and set out to try their luck along the Snake River. Following its twisting course, they traveled south, then looped north through the Snake River Canyon, entering the southern end of Jackson Hole in August of 1863. As they moved up the valley, panning its waters, they found no gold in quantities worth the effort, so near Jackson Lake they split into two groups. One group left Jackson Hole by the way the party had come, while the other, under DeLacy, continued north into Yellowstone by the route Captain Raynolds and his men should have taken. Most of the prospectors were too preoccupied looking for gold to appreciate the visual riches of the region, passing through the Lower Geyser Basin without stopping to camp, or, for that matter, even slowing down their march. But DeLacy himself was observant enough to realize that they had stumbled onto something most unusual. Back in Montana, he told others of what he had seen and published a crude map of the area, which excited curiosity and eventually led to Yellowstone's final, once-and-for-all "official discovery."

The following year, 1864, another band of prospectors came into Jackson Hole, having no more success in finding the metal that makes men go mad than their predecessors had, and leaving behind no signs of their having been here other than that Phelps Lake at the base of the Tetons was later named for one of their leaders.* Then, in 1867, A. Bart Henderson and three companions, all "two sheets in the wind and the third fluttering with 2 bottles of whiskey in our cantinas," left Montana on a prospecting venture and, following the Snake River upstream from Idaho along the route DeLacy and his men had taken, made their way into Jackson Hole before moving up to Yellowstone.[9] Not until five years later would still another party visit the valley, but to say that during the long interlude between 1840 and 1872 the only white men to see the Tetons were the members of the six groups previously noted would not be entirely accurate.

A few anonymous itinerant trappers probably wandered through the valley during this period, and in 1865 a trapper named Tim Hibbard is known to have had the temerity to hole up and winter in Jackson Hole (something the Indians would never think of doing) near the present-day village of Wilson. It appears, however, that one wind-swept, snowed-in winter was enough for him, because the few subsequent records mentioning his name indicate that he changed his abode to less rigorous Teton Basin. Even earlier than Hibbard, a Mormon boy who had run away from home in

---

* For years to come, the traces of placer gold to be found in the Snake River and its tributaries in Jackson Hole would raise high hopes in many would-be forty-niners, only to break their hearts in the end, as it was too fine to be taken in amounts large enough to make any dream of wealth come true. One anonymous prospector composed a poem and posted it near Deadman's Bar to warn others from wasting their time, and while it may not scan like a quatrain from *The Rubaiyat of Omar Khayyam*, it does make its point:

> *Payin gold will never be found here*
> *No matter how many men tries*
> *Theres some enough to begile one*
> *Like tanglefoot paper does flies.*

(Fritiof Fryxell, *The Tetons*, p. 34)

Utah and joined Chief Washakie's band of Shoshonis went into Teton Basin with them in the mid-1850s and saw the Tetons from the western side. And not long thereafter, an unusual Englishman named Beaver Dick Leigh somehow found his way into this wilderness and became so taken with it that he married an Indian woman and remained in the region for the rest of his life. The story of Nick Wilson, the runaway who was a Huck Finn kind of kid long before Huck was invented, and the story of Beaver Dick Leigh, who left some truly remarkable memorabilia in the form of letters and diaries, are both part of the richest lore of Jackson Hole. More than that, they are part of the richest lore of the frontier West.

10

Runaway Boy with the Indians

Many a frontier boy, badgered by his parents to do his chores, comb his hair and learn his "three R's," dreamed of running away from home to live with the Indians. It was an exhilarating prospect offering all the freedom of the wilderness, not to mention freedom from soap and Sunday School, but for most boys the dream faded and vanished as they were gradually broken to the harness of social conventions. Not Nick Wilson. As a lad of only eleven, about to turn twelve, Nick ran off and joined the Shoshonis, and for two years he was an Indian boy in every way except for the color of his skin.

The small village of Wilson at the foot of Teton Pass in Jackson Hole was founded by Nick, who as a grown man came to the valley and homesteaded land. While his youthful adventures that he described later in a book took place outside of Jackson Hole, there is reason to give a brief account of them here. Not only was Nick one of the valley's most prominent early settlers whose tales became local legends, but his experiences also convey to an unusual degree what it was like to be young and live on the frontier, which Jackson Hole was part of for many years.

Nick lived to be an old man—a short, rotund, merry old man—adored by the children of Jackson Hole and fondly known throughout the valley as "Uncle Nick," a teller of stories about his boyhood that glued listeners to their chairs. And little wonder, because the runaway Nick first became the adopted son of the powerful Chief Washakie's mother, then a Pony Express rider, then an army scout, then an Overland Stage driver. What makes his story even more unusual is a touch of bittersweet involving two women, one white and the other red, Nick's two mothers, both of whom loved him very much and came to know and like each other.

Born into a Mormon family in Illinois in 1842, Nick remembered traveling by ox-drawn wagon to Utah, where his family broke land for a farm south of the Great Salt Lake. He was, however, a young-ster with such a fiery spirit and restless foot that he could not long be

"Uncle Nick" Wilson in later life in Jackson Hole. He always wore his hat, indoors and out, to cover the scar from an arrow wound he received while riding for the Pony Express. *Teton County Chapter, Wyoming State Historical Society.*

content with the humdrum life of a farm boy. Sent out to herd sheep, he became so bored that to pass the time he learned the Gosiute language from an Indian boy who was working with him, little realizing that his ability to speak an Indian language would soon provide his passport to adventure. Even in his wildest imaginings he could not have foreseen that many miles away his future was being shaped by a dream in which the widowed mother of the chief of the Shoshonis saw a white child coming to live with her.

Chief Washakie was a powerfully built man of commanding presence to whom his people looked for counsel in all matters. But there was one person who refused to heed his counsel—his own grieving mother, an old woman of many "snows," whose husband had been killed by a Crow arrow, whose other two sons had been buried by an avalanche and whose only daughter had been dragged to death by a horse. In her despair, she dreamed that one of

Chief Washakie of the Shoshonis, Nick Wilson's Indian brother. *Smithsonian Institution National Anthropological Archives.*

the dead sons would return as a white child to console her, and the idea became such a fixation nothing the chief said could change her mind. When a few roving Shoshonis camped not far from Nick's home and learned that he could speak an Indian language closely related to theirs, to please the chief they volunteered to kidnap the boy for the old woman. Washakie, who always believed in staying on the right side of the white man's law, at first sternly forbade them to consider such a thing, but then he made a subtle distinction, bending enough to say that if the boy could somehow be lured away from home that would not be kidnaping and he therefore would not disapprove. And that is how Nick came to be offered a beautiful pinto pony along with the promise that as an Indian boy he could spend all his time hunting, fishing and riding horses, which, as Nick later wrote, "looked better to me than herding a bunch of sheep alone in the sagebrush."[1] So, on an August night in

1854, Nick slipped away from the family farm, met the waiting Indians in a grove of willows and galloped off to become a Shoshoni.

Nick took naturally to Indian life and quickly became fond of his Indian mother, who welcomed him with tears of joy and dressed him in the finest buckskins. He was given the name Yagaiki, easily picked up the Shoshoni language and learned to hunt with a bow and arrow, but his early days with the tribe were far from idyllic. Because he was the protégé of the chief he was resented by some of his elders, and because he was white he was resented by many of his own age-group, who spat at him, teased him and constantly re-

Nick runs away from home to join the Shoshonis. *From "The White Indian Boy," World Book Co.*

minded him that he was an outsider. Nick more than held his own, however, earning a reputation as a quick-tempered scrapper who kicked "worse than a wild horse," and those who came within range of his flailing feet soon learned not to taunt him again.[2]

Not with his feet, but in other ways, did Nick finally win the favor of the tribe. He went to the aid of a girl who had been attacked by a bear, and he saved his Indian mother's life when her horse fell while fording a river and she was swept downstream. He also built a sled and introduced the boys of the village to the thrills of downhill coasting, meanwhile showing others how to use it to haul wood. As much as anything that made him more likable in the Indians' eyes was an incident in which he came out the goat, for no one more than the red man enjoyed a good laugh. While out hunting elk with

Washakie, Nick became separated and lost. Then his horse ran off and night began to fall, so he climbed a tree to avoid the possibility of being attacked by a bear. There he sat for hours until he heard a search party calling his name, "Yagaiki, Yagaiki," whereupon he directed the party through the darkness to the foot of the tree. When one of the Indians asked him what he was doing perched on a branch high above the ground, Nick, not wanting to admit that he was afraid of bears, replied, "Looking for my horse." The Indian thought about this for a moment, then dryly suggested that Nick might as well climb down, because "you won't find him up there."[3]

During his two years among the Shoshonis, Nick saw and did

Nick and his old Indian mother in their tipi. *From "The White Indian Boy," World Book Co.*

things few white men, let alone white boys, were ever privileged to see and do. He hunted buffalo on horseback with the tribe; he saw Washakie lead his warriors to victory in a major battle with the Crows; he became friendly with an old Indian who remembered Lewis and Clark; and he attended a grand encampment of the Shoshoni nation, where Pocatello, chief of the Bannock Creek Shoshonis and opposed to Washakie's policy of peace with the whites, proudly displayed the spoils of a wagon train he had just massacred—not only "new quilts, women's clothes, and new guns, watches, saddles, and hats," but scalps as well.[4] One of the more pleasant sights Nick saw in his travels was the land of the Tetons when Washakie's band camped and hunted in Teton Basin in the mid-1850s. While they did not go into Jackson Hole, it may have been his memory of the beauty of the region, among other things, which brought him back years later to settle in the valley.

All the while, the attachment between the white boy and the old Indian woman deepened. She pampered him, worried about him in all the ways that mothers do and praised him for his willingness to help her with the heavy work, which was the lot of every squaw and with which no right-thinking Indian male would condescend to lift a hand. When writing of her later, Nick called her "my dear old Indian mother" and remembered the long talks they had together, during which she expressed much curiosity about his real mother, wanting to know what his life at home was like.[5] She feared that Nick would want to go back to his own people, and nothing delighted her more than to hear him say he would like to stay with her. "This," he wrote, "always seemed to please her, for her face would light up and sometimes a tear would steal down the brown cheeks and then she would grab me and hug me until you could hear my ribs crack."[6]

Chief Washakie was also fond of Nick, treating him as a brother and grateful for the happiness he had brought back into his mother's life. At one point, Nick overheard the chief say, "I do believe it was the Great Spirit that sent the little white boy to her," seeming for the moment to have forgotten it was he, Washakie, not the Great Spirit, who had allowed Nick to be lured from home.[7] What Washakie did not forget was that Nick was white and this could lead to trouble for the tribe, and on a number of occasions he offered Nick the opportunity to return to his family.

As it turned out, the decision that Nick should go home was made for him. A delegation from Pocatello's band came to the village with the report that Nick's father was raising a large force to rescue Nick and would "kill every Indian he could find."[8] Nick told Washakie he did not believe a word Pocatello's men said, and the chief shared his opinion, but after a lengthy debate in the tribal council Washakie was outvoted and agreed to have two of his braves escort Nick to the vicinity of the nearest white settlement. Nick's Indian mother was heartbroken, and even his promise to return soon gave her little solace. Hanabi, Washakie's wife, was also sorry to see him go, and with other squaws set to work to make sure the prodigal son would appear on his family's doorstep wearing the very best Indian clothing. A few days later, when Nick rode out of the village and looked back at his sobbing Indian mother, he did not know that this was the last time he would ever see her.

Nick's real mother greets him upon his return home from living with the Indians. *From "The White Indian Boy," World Book Co.*

Arriving in the yard of the family farm dressed in buckskins decorated with beads of many colors and leggings trimmed with red flannel, Nick frightened his little sisters, who ran to tell their mother an Indian was outside. But, as Nick wrote, "She came to the door and knew me as soon as she saw me."[9] Never one to dwell on emotional scenes, Nick described the reunion with his family after an absence of two years in a single, matter-of-fact sentence: "I cannot tell you just what passed the next hour, but they were all glad to have me back safe at home again."[10]

Not long after Nick's return, President Buchanan sent an army to force the Mormons to discontinue the practice of polygamy, and the Wilson family was one of many who fled from the path of the advancing troops. When a peaceful settlement was negotiated, the Wilsons had no sooner returned home than Nick's father died, so Nick had to put aside his plans to rejoin the Shoshonis and help his brother with the farm. Finding farming no more to his liking than herding sheep, he took a job breaking horses for a man named Faust, whose humorous nickname, "Doc," suggests that some fellow pioneer was familiar with the writings of either Marlowe or Goethe. Then, by the time he thought the family's affairs were well enough in hand that he could rejoin Washakie's band, a whole new opportunity for excitement had come along, one which to the still young and adventure-prone Nick was too good to pass up.

Early in 1860, a San Francisco newspaper published one of the most bluntly honest advertisements ever written:

Wanted — young, skinny, wiry fellows, not over
18. Must be expert riders, willing to risk death
daily. Orphans preferred. Wages $25.00 a week.[11]

The Pony Express lasted for only nineteen months before the transcontinental telegraph made it obsolete, but in that short time it wove one of the most colorful of all threads into our history. On April 3, 1860, a rider left St. Joseph, Missouri, racing west, while at exactly the same moment another rider left Sacramento, California, racing east. All along the trail, which crossed plains, mountains and deserts, there were way stations seven to fifteen miles apart where each young rider quickly remounted, then spurred his fresh horse into a full run. Every seventy-five to one hundred miles, there were home stations where the rider turned his leather pouch over to another rider and rested briefly before heading back over his section of the route. Wearing gaudy red shirts and blue trousers, armed with Colt revolvers and with the brims of their hats rakishly turned back, these boys relayed the mail two thousand miles in ten days, cutting the best previous delivery time by more than half. Overnight, the Pony Express fired the nation's imagination and the riders were applauded as the brave heralds of a marvelous new era of communications.*

A roll of honor has been compiled listing the names of one hundred and twenty-nine Pony Express drivers. Except for Buffalo Bill Cody, the names are now forgotten, and to the casual peruser of the list the name Wilson, Elijah Nicholas means nothing. But this was Nick, the future founder of the village of Wilson in Jackson Hole, whose adventures while carrying the mail read like a dime novel. When Nick heard that the service was to be started, he joined up and was assigned to a home station in Utah, where he appears to have ridden in the inaugural run. He certainly was riding for the Pony Express when a month later the Paiutes went on the warpath. Then Nick quickly learned just how precarious the calling he had chosen was. When a raiding band killed a rider Nick was scheduled to meet at one of the stations, he rode on to the next station, which

---

* Among its accomplishments, the Pony Express is credited with having inspired the invention of the doughnut, or at least there is a legend to that effect. Where the route lay near settlements, the girls came out to watch the riders pass, and one of the riders, a youth named Johnny Frey, soon became a favorite. The girls would hold out cakes and cookies for him to grab on the run, but this proved awkward, so they came up with the idea of baking circles of dough with holes in the center. Thereafter, Johnny merely had to spear the doughnuts with a finger as he flew by.

Copyrighted, 1891, by BEADLE AND ADAMS.   Entered as Second Class Matter at the New York, N. Y., Post Office.   June 17, 1891.

No. 388. $2.50 a Year.   Published Weekly by Beadle and Adams, No. 98 WILLIAM ST. NEW YORK.   Price, Five Cents.   Vol. XXX.

THE PONY-EXPRESS RIDER.

The exploits of young Pony Express riders such as Nick Wilson inspired many pulp "thrillers."
Rare Book Division, New York Public Library, Astor, Lenox and Tilden Foundations.

came under siege by nightfall, and for a time it was nip and tuck until the Indians were driven off. Soon after this, he again almost had his scalp lifted. While racing through a canyon, he saw the trail blocked by four Indians with bows and arrows drawn, and wheeling his horse around to escape, there, having appeared from nowhere, stood the rest of the war party. Taken prisoner, Nick was so sure he was done for that when the Indians built a fire he could see himself being burned alive. However, by a stroke of almost miraculous good luck, one of the Indians had known the Wilson family and persuaded the others to let the boy go.

A wound Nick received while with the Pony Express left him with a deep scar in his forehead that, in turn, left him with a lifelong habit those who visited Jackson Hole and did not know him thought peculiar: he never took off his hat in public, even indoors. When chasing several Indians who had stolen horses from a station, he was struck by the arrow above his left eye and given up for dead. But the next morning a burial party found him to be still alive and sensibly decided, in Nick's words, "they would not bury me just then."[12] A doctor was finally found to remove the arrowhead and soon Nick was riding again.

Before the Pony Express was discontinued, Nick served as a scout for the army, infiltrating an Indian camp and learning of a planned attack, which led to the army surprising and routing the Indians. Then, when the need for the Pony Express ended, Nick became a driver for the Overland Stage and was posted to Virginia City, Nevada, where the sound of gunfire on the streets was not unusual and spur-of-the-moment hangings were not infrequent. After a few months, this young man who had not been afraid to run away with the Indians, to ride for the Pony Express and to be an army scout found himself too frightened to go out at night, so he quit his job and went home.

Nick arrived home to hear a story from his mother every bit as extraordinary as the stories he had to tell her. While he had been away, his old Indian mother had appeared at Mrs. Wilson's door, asking for her missing Yagaiki and expressing great disappointment when told he was not there. Nick later learned that after he left the tribe the old woman became despondent and began to act in strange ways, wandering off by herself for days and returning to the village only when she was half-starved. At last, she set out in search of Nick and somehow managed to find her way to Mrs. Wilson's house in Utah, where she was welcomed and given a room.

Nick's real mother and Indian mother in Mrs. Wilson's home. *From "The White Indian Boy," World Book Co.*

For more than two months, Nick's red mother stayed with Nick's white mother, during which time the two women grew attached to each other. Finally, when Nick did not return and "no words could comfort her," the old woman went off with some passing Indians.[13]

Nick's mother urged him to go and find the woman who had been a mother to him in the wilderness, telling him it was his duty to take care of her. Nick agreed, and now a young man he set off to keep the promise he had made as a boy to return to the tribe. Hearing that a small party of Shoshonis was in Bear Lake Valley, he went there hoping to learn where Washakie could be found. What he learned was that his Indian mother was dead.

Nick traveled with the Shoshonis he had met to South Pass, where Washakie was camped. There the chief greeted him as a brother, but could not tell him where their mother was buried as he had been away when she died and the village had been on the move. All he knew was that her body had been hidden somewhere on Ham's Fork of the Green River, where Nick then went to try to find the grave. That he was unsuccessful is not surprising, for the Shoshonis, unlike other mountain tribes who placed their corpses on scaffolds or in trees, concealed their dead beneath rocks in deep crevices with no markings above ground. In common with other Indians, however, the Shoshonis did inter their dead with articles they had treasured in life, and Nick was touched to learn that wherever his old Indian mother lay, next to her were his quiver for arrows and several other of his little possessions that she had kept and prized.

Nick wrote the account of his youth much later in life when he was living in Jackson Hole and was urged by two professors who were visiting the valley to record his earlier adventures. Putting his story on paper must have taken almost as much courage as breaking horses for "Doc" Faust or riding for the Pony Express, for although his wife had taught him the alphabet he could barely read or write. But with his hat jammed down over the arrowhead scar on his forehead, and using a typewriter of such ancient vintage it had no ribbon and the keys had to be inked by hand before being struck, Nick stayed with the task until he had pecked out his story. While more than half a century had gone by since he had run away from home, his memory was still green, with his concluding words echoing the warmth he felt as he looked back to those two magical years when he was transformed from Nick Wilson, Mormon boy, into Yagaiki, Indian boy. "The old friends of my boyhood days with Washakie have almost entirely passed away," he wrote. "Only once in a great while do I find one who remembers Yagaiki, the little boy, who once lived with their old chief's mother. But when I do happen to meet one . . . then we have a good time, I tell you, recalling the days of long ago when Uncle Nick was among the Shoshones."[14]

11

A Man Called Beaver Dick

Although his spelling was phonetic and his punctuation nonexistent, in his own fashion Richard "Beaver Dick" Leigh was, as a diarist, the Samuel Pepys of the Teton country in the 1870s. Not that he had much in the way of social events to record, for Jackson Hole and most of the region around it remained uninhabited until 1884, when the first settlers came into the valley and took up land. But earlier than this a handful of men had gone into Teton Basin across the Tetons to the west, the first of whom was this transplanted Englishman whose diaries and letters give us a rare insight into what daily life was like on the raw edge of the frontier.

As might be expected, many of Beaver Dick's diary entries are a monotonous listing of the game he trapped and shot to support his Shoshoni wife, Jenny, and their children. Fortunately, however, his gift from the past is more than a catalog of game killed, because despite his shortcomings with the niceties of spelling and grammar, at times he wrote with a clarity that illuminates his world as it was. And what we see is a way of life of an almost Old Testament simplicity, with Beaver Dick and his family living close to the land and precariously from it, and where the matters of greatest moment were the providing of food and the turning of the seasons.

Theirs was a life so lacking in material possessions it is difficult for us today to imagine, so poor a cup of coffee was a luxury and a cast iron cooking stove an article to be treasured. Once, when Beaver Dick made a table for Jenny, he noted proudly, "this is the first real table we ever ad [had]."* Yet, nowhere in his words is there a hint that Beaver Dick thought of himself as poor, or of his life as one of hardship. To the contrary, he was a man content with his place and time, happy in his family until tragedy struck them down and thoroughly in tune with the deep wilderness surrounding him.

Most of what we know about Beaver Dick comes from his own

* All quotations in this chapter, unless otherwise noted, are from "Writings of Richard 'Beaver Dick' Leigh," a collection of his original diaries and letters in the Western History Research Center at the University of Wyoming.

pen, which he wielded to form a flowing, almost elegant script difficult to account for when we realize that he probably had little formal education. In four short sentences, he summarized his life as follows:

> *i am the son of Richard Leigh formely of the Britesh navey and grand son of James Leigh formly of the 16 lancers england. i was borne on Jenury 9th in 1831 in the city of Manchaster England. come with my sister to philadelphia u s a when i was 7 years old. went for the Mexcin war at close 48 atched to E co [company] 1st infentry 10 months then come to rocky mountons and here i die.*

Just when Beaver Dick arrived in the Jackson Hole area is unclear, although in a letter he said that he and another man tried unsuccessfully to cross the Tetons from the west as early as 1858. But it is unlikely he was living in Teton Basin at that time, because in the same letter he also said he did not begin his trade as a local trapper, hunter and guide until 1863. For several decades, he guided occasional parties of prominent and well-to-do sportsmen from the East on hunts in Jackson Hole, and it is evident these hunters were impressed with Beaver Dick's qualities as a man, for some of them remained his lifelong friends, encouraged him to keep his diaries and sent him magazines to read and pictures for Jenny to look at.

In 1872, when the Hayden Survey came into northwestern Wyoming, Beaver Dick first guided it into the Tetons from the west, then later through Jackson Hole. Although he received little for his efforts in the way of money, he and his wife were given a touch of immortality when members of the Survey named Leigh Lake and Jenny Lake at the base of the Tetons for them. William Henry Jackson, one of the first great photographers of the West, was with the expedition and took a picture of Beaver Dick and his family posed outside their tipi. In it the bearded Dick leans on his rifle and stares off at the horizon; Jenny, her raven-black hair parted in the center, sits on the ground with their small children, holding a surprisingly towheaded little boy in front of her; and off to one side their oldest child, Dick, Jr., sits on a jackass that looks as though it is about to fall asleep on its feet. For those who know Beaver Dick's story, a shadow of sadness falls across the old photograph, but in the early 1870s their life was good, and we can share the flavor of their days through the faded script written so long ago.

William Henry Jackson photograph of Beaver Dick Leigh and his family in 1872. *Western History Research Center, University of Wyoming.*

William Henry Jackson photograph of members of the Hayden Survey of 1872, one division of which was guided by Beaver Dick. *U.S. Forest Service.*

It does not seem right to meddle too much with the way Beaver Dick put words on paper. Actually, except for breaking his nonstop writing into sentences, the reader needs little help if it is understood that he spelled words the way he spoke them and that he dropped his "h's." Therefore, huckleberries are "uckleberrys," have is "ave" and a man whose name sources elsewhere suggest was Hain is rendered as "Anes." Otherwise, only now and then does a word need to be puzzled out in the few diary entries which quickly establish the simple rhythm of the family's wilderness life and serve as a prologue to the drama that follows.

> *rane with heavy thunder and lightning every 2 hours thrue the night. betwixt storms the moone wold shine out clere. the heavy clouds comenced to rase to the top of mount moran and the Big teton.*

> *i aroused my family at the brake of day. Dick Juner went for the horses wile i fineshed fixeng the packs. we took a hasty Brexfast then sadled and packed the horses and ad my trane on the way for Moody Creek in duble Quick time but not before the misqutos gave us a little of thare musick.*

> *2 comarade trappers came along from Jacksons Lake . . . thay report nothing to trap or hunt in that vercinaty but Bair this seson and thay ware so plenty that it was unsafe going the rounds to thare traps.*

> *Jinny made some good Butter. the first time she ever tryed she beat me all hallow.*

> *some indans came hear. they ad shot a Boflo [buffalo] Bull Braking his hind leg . . . he came downe hear and crosed to the west side of the river. the indan hunters crosed this eavening to hunt him up. this is the first Boflo that as beene seene since the spring of 1871.*

> *when i got to camp Jinny and the childron ad taken horses and crosed the river . . . to dig yamp. it is very plenty thare and is a good substatute for potatos. i cooked and eate my dinner then took 3 traps to set at the Juncon [junction] of sarvesberry creek. i pased Jinny and childrn. thay ware diggeng away like good fellows.*

> *i comenced cuting house logs for winter quarters . . . lade the foundaton 3 logs high of my cabben to day.*

And so it went, a busy life, a hard life, but not once does Beaver Dick complain, although it becomes obvious as the days of the diary pass that he had his hands full just keeping his family in food. Still and all, this man, who had every excuse in the world not to become involved in the problems of others, did not hesitate to go to the aid of an old couple who were in terror and despair. In fact, he even risked his life to help them.

On May 16, 1875, an old man named E. W. Lyons came to Beaver Dick and appealed to him for protection from his own two sons. The sons, who had been in Teton Basin for about two years and had unsavory local reputations, had induced Mr. Lyons and his wife to sell their property in New York City and move west. Then, shockingly, the sons tried to take everything their old father and mother owned, and even "beet and abused the old man shamfully." Beaver Dick responded to Mr. Lyons' plea and went to his home, where an ugly confrontation took place, described by Beaver Dick in these words:

> *alven [Alvin Lyons] struck his father 8 times in the face and John [the other son] snatched a duble barl rifall. when i turned my gun on him and made him lay it downe he sead he was going to shoot me [and] that he was going to shoot the dambd old broot mening his father . . . Mistrs [Mrs.] Lyons and hur daughter Mrs Berry begd of me to stay with them and proct [protect] them. i told them i ad a big famly to mantane and if i should stay i wold ave to kill All and John or they wold Kill me. so i [told] the young men that thare father and mother and sister ad cald on me to proct them and i should cirtnly do so and i wold hold them responsable for thare father and mothers lives untill i could get some asistance for them. they called thar old father a lyer a brute and son of a bitch. alven took a club in his hand abot 4 feet long and 3 inches thrue wile he was cursing and abusing his father and made towards him saying he wold mash him to the ground. i told him if he struck the old man i wold shoot him. that ended the fuss.*

It seems that Beaver Dick's willingness to stand up to the two bullying sons did indeed end the fuss, at least for the time being, because more than a month passed before the Lyons family was mentioned again in the diaries. Then Alvin Lyons was quoted as having said that he would kill Beaver Dick if he attempted to protect the old people, a threat Beaver Dick shrugged off with the comment, "i think he as got his match for onst." But a little later things must have taken a bad turn, for Beaver Dick and two friends "went to Mr Lyons at his call and prayers" and made what appears to have been a citizen's arrest of the sons. They took them to Malad City, Idaho, where court was in session and where Beaver Dick, to

Beaver Dick's handwriting, as illustrated in these pages from his diary, was curiously elegant for a man who had little, if any, formal education. *Western History Research Center, University of Wyoming.*

his outrage, came up against the sometimes strange workings of the law. Alvin and John Lyons were put under bail—we never hear of them again, so it can be hoped the old folks were left in peace—but for his efforts as a good Samaritan Beaver Dick was placed under a three hundred dollar bond for six months, the technicality seeming to be that during the confrontation back in May he had leveled his rifle at the sons. Knowing he had done it only in self-defense, Beaver Dick's pen exploded in anger:

> the law in this secton is only a Bilk and god keep me a long ways from it for i shall try and never Bother with such law a gane. the lyons [the sons] was wel Knowne along the road and the people came out Boldly and sade we ad ought to ave tryed them by Mountin Law.

In October of 1876, Beaver Dick's diary breaks off abruptly and does not begin again for more than a year. Then, in one of his very first entries, we are jolted upright as we read that he camped "about a quarter of a mile from the grave yard of my Wife and children." Jenny dead? All the children dead? It cannot be possible, for it seems that just a moment ago we were watching them churn butter, dig yamps "like good fellows" and come running to meet Beaver Dick as he returned from his traps. But dead they are, and the story of what happened in the fading firelight of a winter-bound cabin just west of the Tetons is one of the most moving narratives to come down from the days of the early West.

Beaver Dick was a man of physical courage, as we already know. Now, however, he was called on for a completely different kind of courage, the fortitude to stand up to a Job-like adversity against which there was little he could do to fight back. How he struggled gallantly to save his family is told in the following passages from a long letter he later wrote to a friend, Dr. Josiah Curtis, one of the hunters he had guided.

> *My Dear Frend*
>   *i set downe to give you an accont of my self and my lost famley. i moved up to the elbo of the teton river on the 25th of Aprl 1876. thare i bult a log cabin and fenced me a farme and rased some little fegetobls. i allso bult a horse corall and a hay corall and put up 6 ton of hay in it . . . on the 11th of november we past humpys camp [an Indian family] . . . humpys wife came out and asked me for some bread. i told hur i ad none backed [baked] and went 6 miles to the foot of the Crator butts and camped. wile we were eating supper by the light of the camp fire humpys Wife and Daughter 3 years old came and sade humpy ad comited sueside and hur and hir child were starving. we gave hur something to eate and blankets to sleep in. the next morning she came to were we were crosing our suplys with the boat and sade she wanted to go over the river to see my Wife. i put hur acrost. when we ad got every thing acrost we went home. my wife told me humpys father ad died and his mother ad broke out in the face with little lumps. tom [Tom Lavering, a trapper friend] sade it might be the small Pox or mesals so i told my wif to give this woman som provishons and tel hur to go to the boat . . . and i wold put hur acros the river in the morning so that she could go and tel the doctor on the resirvation. but when i went to the boat i could not find hur. [The woman later reappeared, and when Beaver Dick told her to go away, she said that she was about to have a*

child and could not walk.] so i told my wife to give hur our lodge [tipi] and some provishons and let her camp in the bushis [with] my Wife and children keeping away from [her] untill she took in labor. then my wife packed hur eatibls and wood to the lodge door but did not go in. now none of [us] knew eny thing of the small pox and we suposed she was going to give birth to a child and if there was small pox at the camp she was clere of it as she ad beene 10 or 12 days from it. so me and tom and Dick Juner went to the island to Kill a large Buck for mocksons and camped out one night. the next day when to withen 2 mils of home on our retrune we met my wife and the rest of my famley coming to meat us. i knew what was the mater as soone as i saw them. the indan womon was dead. when we got home we went and examined the womon and could see nothing suspisus about hur and come to the concluson that she died in child bed. i asked my wife to take the little indan girle to the house and wash and clene it. she sade not to do it. something told hur that the child wold die but at my request she took it to the house and clened it up. it played with my childron for 4 days as lively as could be and that night it broke out all over with little red spots. we thought it was a rash from being wased [washed] and cept [kept] in a warme house as the child ad a cold at the time . . . my famley all feling and looking wel only my wife she complaned of drowesenes but i thaught nothing of it in hur state. [Jenny was in the last days of pregnancy.] . . . we [Beaver Dick and Tom Lavering] went hunting the next morning tom on one side of the river and me on the other. the dogs run some deer out and i Kiled one of them. wile i was dresing it i looked a cros the creek and saw some one with tom. thay was a long ways from me but somthing told me it was my son Richard and that thare was somthing rong at home. i started for the cabin and thay did the same. when thay saw me Dick sade his mother ad a bad head ake and wanted me at home . . . he ad road from thair to hear in 2 hours. 20 mils. and i got on the same mair and went home in les time then that. when i got thare it was an aufall sight to see. My Wife was seting on the flore by the stove and my youngest daughter with hur boath thair heads tyed up and sufring very mutch. my oldest daughter was in bed complaning with a pane in her back and bely. hur looks when she answard my qustons struck my hart cold. Williams legs ad wekned 2 hours before i got home and he was in bed. just as i rode up to the dore of the house Johns legs gave way and i put him to Bed. Tom and me was taken the same day . . . well my wife was in labor and i ad a hard time all a lone with my famley all night and nex day about 4 oclock my Wife gave birth to a child. [Beaver Dick never mentions what happened to the newborn child, but surely it could not have survived.] she ad broken out all over with small red spots but after the birth of the child thay all went back on hur. i knew what the desise was as soone as i came in the house allthoe i ad never seene it before . . . in the morning my Wife sade she wanted to get up and set by the stove. i got hur up and as i layed her on a palit i ad fixed for hur she fanted. she shook all over and made a rumbling noyse. when she came to she sade to me what is the mater dady. i told hur she ad fanted from weknis that was all. i was satisfide that hur hours was numbard and i spoke incougenly [encouragingly] to hur but my hart was ded within me. about noone she asked me to give hur some harpers magaryens [magazines] and those pictors that you sent to us. she wanted to look at pictors. she looked at them and talked and asked me qustons about them quite lively. it was hard work for me to answar hur without betraying my felings but i did so. the children ad got quite [quiet] and some of them aslpe [asleep] and i told my wife i wold go out and set fire to a bush pile to signol for tom and dick to come home. wile doing so my legs got weake and it was all i could do to get back to the cabbin. i ad beene back about 10 minuts when tom drove up with dick taken with the small pox . . . i got Dick in the house and to bed and tom went over to get Mr Anes. wile tom and Anes was sounding the ice to see if a horse could cros my wife was struck with Death. she rased up and looked me streaght in the face and then she got excited . . . and she sade she was going to die and all our childron wold die and maby i wold die. Dor [Doctor] this was the hardist blow i ad got as yet. she then layed downe and smiled to me. all at wanst she turned over to the fire place and comenced stireng the fire. she was cold. she was layeng betwixt the stove and the fire place but thare was no fire in the stove. i layed hur downe agane and at hur request i put 2 pare of my socks and hur shoose on hur feet and coverd hur well with blankits and a roab. she smiled and sade she felt a little warmer. i then took my gun and shot a signol for tom and Anes . . . she was alayeng very quite now for about 2 hours when she asked for a drink of water. i was layeng downe with one of my daughters on eatch arme Keeping them downe with the fevor. i told Anes what she wanted and he gave hur a drink and 10 minuts more she was ded. Dick turned over in bed when he hurd the words and he sade to me father maby we will all die. i was talking as incorigenly as i posably could to him when he sade well if we ave to die it is all right. we might as well die now as some other time. that remark was a nother hard blow on me . . . i cannot discribe my felings or situaton at this time. i knew i must ave sleep but could not get it . . . i could not sleep so i got up and adminestrad to my famley a gane with *the ditermaton [determination] to doing all i could until i died witch i was shure i could not [last] more than 24 hours longer for my eyes would get full of black spots and near blind me and death would ave beene welcome only for my children . . . this night i felt some sines of sleep but with the sine came a heavy sweting and burning and tremors. my close [clothes] and the beding was ringeng wet in half an hour. when it left me i told tom and Anes were everything was that thay might want and asked them to save some of my famely if it was posable and turned over to die. i can not wright one hundreth part that pased thrue my mind at this time as i thaught deth was on me. i sade Jinny i will sone be with you and fell a sleep. tom sade i ad beene a sleep a half hour when i woke up. every thing was wet with presperaton. i was very weak. i lade for 10 or 15 minuts and saw William and ann Jane ad to be taken up to ease them selves every 5 minuts and Dick Juner very unrestlas [restless]. i could not bare to see it. i got up and went to elp tom and Anes. i saw that the spots ad gone back on Dick. my Detirmaton was to stand by them and die with them. this was cristmos eve. Ann Jane died about 8 Oclock about the time every year i used to give them a candy puling and thay menchond about the candy puling meny times wile sick espeshely my son John. William died on the 25 about 9 or 10 Oclock in the evening . . . on the 26th Dick Juner died betwixt 5 and 6 oclock in the evening . . . my son John had comenced to swell agane about day light and about 8 oclock on the 27 in the eveng he died . . . [Elizabeth, the last child alive] caught cold and sweled up a gane and died on the 28 of Dec abot 2 Oclock in the morning. this was the hardist blow of all . . . i shall improve the place and live and die near my famley but i shall not be able to do eny thing for a few months for my mind is disturbed at the sight that i see around me and [the] work that my famley as done wile thay were liveng. the meny little presants you ave sent to me and famley i shall keep in memory of you and them.*

A refrain of loneliness understandably runs through the diary entries Beaver Dick began to make again in 1878. "i am all alone," he wrote, "and i keep doing at some thing from day light to dark every day. i am very lonsome." Even the hunt for game no longer interested him. "the antlope comes and looks in to my little vally nearly every day," he noted, adding, "i dont kill eny. dont want to. no one to eate the meat and i cannot waste with a good conshus [conscience]." When he traveled to a trading post to which he had taken his family two years earlier, the sight of a little boy Jenny had taken care of while they were there brought back a rush of memories:

that night after going to bed my mind run a grate deele about my wife and that child so i could not sleep and i must tell the truth i ad wet eyes that night. when i go over all a gane i intend to take a little . . . filley 3 years old with me for the child. i intended braking it for my youngest daughter before she died.

But Beaver Dick did not remain a widower. He later married a Bannock girl and raised another family. Theodore Roosevelt met them while he was on a hunting trip and wrote that his party "came on the camp of a squaw-man, one Beaver Dick, an old mountain hunter, living in a skin tepee, where dwell his comely Indian wife and half-breed children."[1] When Beaver Dick died in 1899, he was buried at his request on a bluff overlooking Teton Basin. In one of the last entries he made in his diaries, he wrote, "i ave the pleshur of knowing that i ave led the setlements on snake river and showed them ware they could keep stock and farme."

It is clear throughout his writings that Beaver Dick was a humble man who did not think of himself as in any way unusual. He was grateful for the smallest gift, apologized for his lack of education and looked up with respect, even a touch of awe, to the prominent men he served as a guide. But those who know his story know better. Here was a man of both courage and compassion, battered by life but never allowing it to brutalize him, and never more valiant than when he fought and failed to save his family in their wilderness cabin that dark December of 1876.

The first photographs of the Tetons were taken by William Henry Jackson in 1872, from the western side. This is one of a number he took at that time. *National Park Service, Grand Teton National Park*.

12

Storm Over the Grand Teton

Orestes St. John, W. R. Taggart, Joseph Leidy, Frank Bradley, Thomas Moran. For those acquainted with Jackson Hole these names are faintly familiar, yet it is almost impossible to place them as people. Only when the names are repeated in a somewhat altered form do they become instantly recognizable: Mount St. John, Taggart Lake, Mount Leidy, Bradley Lake, Mount Moran. All are prominent topographical features of the valley, and all were named for members of government surveys that passed through during the closing decades of the nineteenth century. Today, with the exception of the artist Thomas Moran, these men are forgotten, but in their day they and their friends had a fine time playing God by using mountains and lakes it had taken nature millions of years to form as a means of bestowing instant immortality on one another.

In 1872, when the Hayden Survey was in Jackson Hole, some of its members even rechristened the Grand Teton in honor of their leader, an army surgeon turned geologist, who wore a frock coat in the field and collected rocks so energetically he was known to the Indians, some of whom thought him mad, as "Man-Who-Picks-Up-Stones-Running."[1] One of Hayden's men confidently proclaimed that the tallest of all the Tetons "has received the name of and will hereafter be known as Mount Hayden."[2] But he was wrong. The Grand Teton shrugged off the name and went right on being the Grand Teton, although in fairness to Dr. Ferdinand Vandiveer Hayden it must be said that he was not in favor of the name change in the first place.

By March of 1872, Walter DeLacy's account of what he and his band of prospectors had seen in Yellowstone had been confirmed and the world's first national park had been created, partly as the result of the efforts of Dr. Hayden, who went there in 1871 and used William Henry Jackson's photographs and Thomas Moran's sketches to convince Congress that the thermal wonders were real and should be preserved. On the other hand, no such preferential

William Henry Jackson and assistant working in the Tetons. Before taking pictures, he had to prepare his negatives by floating chemicals on plates of glass. *U.S. Forest Service*.

treatment was even considered for Jackson Hole and the Tetons, perhaps because the West was full of valleys and mountains but not geysers, and their fate would go right down to the wire in a race between the forces of conservation and exploitation. In the summer of 1872, however, all this lay far in the future when Hayden fielded his second Survey, one division of which he led back into Yellowstone, while the other division, under James Stevenson, went into Jackson Hole. The Snake River Division, as Stevenson's group was called, came up from Utah and before entering Jackson Hole moved north along the west side of the Tetons, meeting Beaver Dick Leigh and employing him as a guide. While Stevenson and his men were still on the western slopes of the Tetons, two "firsts" in local history took place.

Leading a mule packed high with his many pieces of equipment, William Henry Jackson made his way to the top of Table Mountain and took the first photographs of the Tetons. While that sounds easy enough in this age of compact cameras, in Jackson's time it was strenuous and time-consuming work. Not only were the cameras heavy and cumbersome, requiring tripods and with lenses at the end of long bellows, but before the photographer could even begin to take his pictures he had to set up a tent or other extemporized darkroom and prepare his own negatives by floating chemicals on plates of glass. Nevertheless, Jackson's photographs of the Tetons are so magnificent they remain among the finest of the many millions taken since. Oddly, although no mountain in the Tetons was named for Jackson, whose pictures did so much to bring them to the attention of the American public, one of the largest in the range was named for Hayden's painter, Thomas Moran, who never set foot in Jackson Hole and never saw his namesake, Mount Moran, from its most impressive side, the east, except from a very long distance away.

Shortly after Jackson was the first to photograph the Grand Teton, James Stevenson and Nathaniel Langford were the first to climb it, or at least they said they were. Fourteen members of the Survey established a high base camp on the western side of the mountains on July 28. Then, on July 29, undaunted by the words of Beaver Dick, who told them of Michaud's unsuccessful attempt in 1843 and added, "You can try, but you'll wind up in the same way," eleven members of the group set out.[3] As the ascent became steeper and more difficult, all of them discontinued the climb except for Stevenson and Langford, who went on by themselves, returning to announce that despite many obstacles and a few close calls the Grand Teton had finally been conquered. And so it appeared that it had, until at the end of the century a scathing attack was made on their claim.

In 1898, after several previously unsuccessful attempts, William O. Owen reached the summit of the Grand Teton along with three companions, one of whom was the Reverend Franklin Spalding, a clergyman from the East, and the other two Frank Petersen and

Artist's depiction of James Stevenson almost falling when climbing the Grand Teton in 1872. *From "Scribners Monthly," June, 1873.*

John Shive, Jackson Hole ranchers. From then on, Owen, who was an ambitious and politically influential Wyoming official, spent the better part of thirty years denouncing Stevenson and Langford as frauds and lobbying for his climbing party to be acclaimed the first to have scaled the mountain. He based his charges on the fact that at the summit he and his fellow climbers had found no marker or other piece of evidence indicating that anyone had been there before them, which it must be said most first-climbers usually do leave behind. Further, he controverted Langford's written description of the summit, saying it in no way resembled what his party had seen, although he twisted Langford's words when he ridiculed the presence of wild flowers and the tracks of mountain sheep at the top. Owen wrote, "There isn't a flower within a thousand feet of the summit, and a mountain sheep would no more be able to climb the last six hundred feet than he would to climb the Washington monument."[4] All well and good, except a careful reading of Langford's account reveals that he did not say he and Stevenson saw wild flowers and tracks *on* the summit, but rather *from* the summit when they were looking down.

The controversy no sooner got hot than it got nasty. At the time of Owen's climb, C. G. Coutant was preparing his *History of Wyoming* for publication and, according to Owen, had promised to credit his party with having made the first successful ascent. Instead, when the book was published Stevenson and Langford were given the credit and Owen hit the roof, lashing out with the charge that Langford had bribed Coutant with one hundred and fifty dollars to write what he had. This was quite an accusation to make against both the historian and Langford, a prominent and highly respected man who had earlier served as the first superintendent of Yellowstone National Park. It was denied, of course, and Owen offered no solid evidence to support his slanderous allegation. But the damage had been done, and to this day there are those who believe a bribe may have been paid. What the truth is there is now no way of knowing, although it can be said that Owen was less than scrupulous throughout his long crusade to attain recognition. It can also be said that throughout this whole wretched affair many men behaved like children.

There was, however, one notable exception, the Reverend Franklin Spalding, who had accompanied Owen and the two ranchers on the climb and had actually led the party to the summit. He wrote, "I believe that Mr. Langford reached the summit because he

COMMEMORATING
FIRST ASCENT OF THE GRAND TETON, AUG. 11 1898
BY THE PIONEERS
HON. WILLIAM O. OWEN, ENGINEER AND SURVEYOR
REV. FRANKLIN S. SPALDING
FRANK L. PETERSEN AND JOHN SHIVE, RANCHERS
THIS TABLET PLACED HERE DURING THE CONVENTION OF THE
NATIONAL EDITORIAL ASSOCIATION HELD IN JACKSON HOLE
IN CONNECTION WITH THE DEDICATION OF THE
GRAND TETON NATIONAL PARK
JULY 29, 1929
BY DIRECTION OF THE STATE LEGISLATURE OF WYOMING'S J R NO 3, 1929
BY F. M. FRYXELL, PHIL SMITH, WILLIAM GILMAN
THE TABLET IS THE GIFT OF EMMA MATILDA OWEN

W. O. Owen in 1929, with plaque voted by the Wyoming legislature to designate his party the first to have climbed the Grand Teton. *National Park Service, Grand Teton National Park.*

says he did, and because the difficulties of the ascent were not great enough to have prevented any good climber from having success-fully scaled the peak . . . and I cannot understand why Mr. Owen failed so many times before he succeeded."[5] Not only was the Rev-erend Spalding a gentleman, but he was also accurate about the difficulty of the ascent. Over the years, hundreds of men and women have reached the Grand Teton's peak, for despite its for-bidding appearance it does not pose as many problems as do some other peaks in the range.

Geraldine Lucas at her moment of triumph atop the Grand Teton. *National Park Service, Grand Teton National Park.*

Owen pursued his claim so tenaciously that in 1924 he persuaded the Alpine Club of London of its validity. Then, in 1929, as the result of what appears to have been some backroom politicking with his fellow state officials in Cheyenne, the Wyoming legislature by joint resolution declared the Owens party the first to have scaled the Grand Teton. But even before this, Owen had personally received the supreme accolade. In 1927, the second highest peak in the Tetons was named Mount Owen in his honor, whereupon he composed a poem to it, just one stanza of which is enough to demonstrate that he was a more gifted politician than poet.

> *Ten times ten thousand years have flown*
> *Since first thy mighty form was thrown*
> *From depths so great to heights sublime*
> *No mountaineer could hope to climb.*[6]

Mount Owen may rise to "heights sublime," but in the light of a devastating discovery made years later it cannot be said that W. O. Owen did. Even if he had been right in challenging the claim of Stevenson and Langford (and he may have been), all the while he fought for recognition he was in possession of information which, if correct, would have preempted his own claim—and he withheld it. After his death, a letter was discovered among his papers that had been written to him in 1899 by a Dr. Charles Kieffer, an army surgeon. Dr. Kieffer wrote that as early as 1893, five years before Owen's climb, he and two soldiers had taken time off from hunting in Jackson Hole and had succeeded in reaching the summit of the Grand Teton. The doctor even included a map of the route they had followed, but what is most striking about his letter is that receiving credit for the first climb was not important to him, and he did not press for it. Somehow this seems to add to his credibility, and surely is a refreshing change from Owen's style. The man for whom Mount Owen is named kept Dr. Kieffer's letter a secret.

The first ascent of the Grand Teton by men, whoever they were, is tainted by all the bickering and backbiting that followed. On a brighter note, when women got around to climbing the mountain they did it without recrimination or slander, and one of them celebrated her moment of triumph in a disarmingly enthusiastic, although most unusual, way. Mrs. Geraldine Lucas, a spirited Jackson Hole lady in her fifty-ninth year, was the second woman to reach the top. Standing there, she unfurled an American flag and jubilantly waved it in the wind.

Lieutenant Gustavus Cheney Doane, whose ill-conceived Snake River expedition turned into a nightmare. *Library of Congress*.

13

The Shipwrecked Cavalrymen

Lieutenant Gustavus Cheney Doane was a man so seduced by the dream of achieving fame through exploration that he went over the head of his commanding officer and arranged an expedition which for sheer foolhardiness was never surpassed in the history of the West. Not only did he cause his men to undergo a dreadful ordeal on the Snake River in winter, almost costing them their lives, but even if he had succeeded he would not have added any truly significant information to geographical knowledge. What is more, after the expedition had to be aborted in the Snake River Canyon just south of Jackson Hole because its boat had been destroyed and the men were starving and battered by sub-zero weather, the lieutenant blithely proposed to lead them all the way back to a point far north of Jackson Lake and start again so he could rewrite the notes he had been keeping that had been lost. Mercifully, he was prevented from doing so.

Doane's military career began during the Civil War when he was in his early twenties. Rising to the rank of sergeant, he was broken to private when he fell behind his company's line of march and was taken prisoner by two Confederate soldiers, who disarmed him without any resistance on his part, then charitably showed him the road his company had taken. Later, commissioned a lieutenant, he became confused and led his men into the center of a Confederate camp, only this time he managed to escape without Confederate assistance and was not court-martialed for the error. By 1870, Doane had received a commission in the regular army and was stationed in Montana, where he led Company F of the 2nd Cavalry (commanded by Major Eugene Baker) in the Marias River massacre of one hundred and seventy-three Piegan Indians, mostly women and children. Not long after the massacre, he commended one of his sergeants for having "displayed good judgment" in destroying the lodges of the Indians, leaving the survivors without shelter in the dead of winter in a "tremendous windstorm."[1] As for the lieutenant's own good judgment, it is exemplified in the application he later made for the position of Superintendent of Yellowstone National Park. Among the outstanding accomplishments he thought would qualify him for the post, he had the audacity to boast that he had been the "first and last man in Piegan camp January 23, 1870 . . . [the] greatest slaughter of Indians ever made by U.S. troops."[2] Mercifully, again, he did not get the job.

Doane greatly admired John Charles Frémont, whose meteoric rise from obscurity to national adulation, a seat in the United States Senate and nomination for the Presidency was achieved by his discoveries, or at least by what the American people were led to believe were his discoveries, the truth being that Kit Carson and other mountain men had guided him over what were for them old, familiar trails most of the way. That Doane dreamed he could also attain renown through exploration is evident in his own words: "A poor subaltern, yet unknown, while traversing with weary steps the barren wilderness, or scaling the mighty summits from which the waters part and flow, may stumble, under fortune's favor, upon some new discovery, the merit of which will secure to him all that history vouchsafes to greatness—a paragraph in the encyclopaedia of the human race."[3]

The closest Doane ever came to writing his name in such a paragraph was in 1870, when he played a contributing role in the opening of Yellowstone. Other than that, his life was mostly one of frustration and failure, for which he usually blamed others. At one point, he sent a preposterous letter to the Smithsonian Institution, saying that if it would sponsor him he would discover the source of the Nile River in Africa, citing his uncanny ability to find his way through unfamiliar country without ever becoming lost, but failing to mention that just a few years earlier in Yellowstone he had lost his way and traveled in a circle. He then went on to propose that a launch be built and the expedition move on water, because, among other reasons, it would be "a more healthy way of journeying, as water is a powerful absorbent of Malaria."[4] In the same letter, he also took a slap at the noted explorer Sir Henry Stanley of "Dr. Livingstone, I presume" fame, observing that he lacked caliber and adding, "He does well what he is sent to do, but does not rise to the Conception of Great Achievements."[5] That Doane used, let alone capitalized, the phrase "Conception of Great Achievements" should give us some insight into the caliber of his own mind.

By 1876, the course of the Snake River was well known except for a long section in Idaho, between roughly the present-day cities of

Pocatello and Lewiston, and even a large part of this section had been covered by the Astorians, who more than half a century earlier had reported that the wild waters of what they called the "Mad River" were not to be navigated. While there was no question that sometime it would be helpful to explore this part of the river, there was no urgency in doing so. Nor was there any valid reason for the nature and timing of the expedition Doane now conceived and proposed to lead into the field from Fort Ellis, Montana. Ignoring his commanding officer's disapproval of his plans, Doane worked behind the scenes to have orders issued from higher headquarters instructing him to explore the *entire* length of the Snake River, from where it rises near the southern boundary of Yellowstone Park to where it joins the Columbia River a thousand miles away. This was senseless. About half of the river's course was already known territory and there was no need whatever to explore it. Further, an exploration of the balance, much of which had previously been described both by the Astorians and by several later fur traders, could add little knowledge of real value. What was even more senseless is that, according to the orders Doane arranged to have written, a boat which could be disassembled and packed on mules was to be built and floated down the river in *winter*. Not only is this the worst of all seasons to travel in the West for obvious reasons, but it is also the time when the Snake is at its lowest and most of the rapids are dangerously exposed. Between the boat and the weather, the six cavalrymen Doane had detailed to him would experience a mortal hell.

On October 11, 1876, Doane's small party of a sergeant and five enlisted men, augmented by two men who were to return with a wagon when the road ended, started on horseback from Fort Ellis and went south into Yellowstone Park. From this point on, most of what is known about the expedition comes from a journal Doane wrote several years later from memory with the help of his sergeant's diary, his own notes having been lost in the Snake River Canyon. While Doane's journal is, to say the least, a greatly understated account of the difficulties encountered and the hardships endured, a few extracts from it can give some idea of how the going became progressively harder and harder, until at last it became desperate.

> Oct. 16. *During the night a cold blast blew up the valley and a sleet storm came on after dark.* (They are in Yellowstone after an un-

eventful trip, except for the wrecking of the wagon, and the storm is only a small foretaste of things to come.)*

Oct. 18. *This [a hill] was very slippery and most of the animals slid or rolled down into the creek. One of the boat bundles burst its lashings and several packs were badly wet. Busy all night gathering wood and keeping things dry.*

Oct. 19. *Snow 18 inches deep . . . washed all the available soiled clothing in the boiling springs near by.*

Oct. 21. *Abandoned a mule. This left us eight. Snow fell heavily all day . . . camped in snow two feet in depth.*

Oct. 27. (The boat, having been carried over Mount Washburn, then assembled and launched in Yellowstone Lake, is swamped by a wave.) *Worked hard all the afternoon and half the night keeping up fires in a circle to dry out the baggage.*

Oct. 30. (Having gone ahead with the pack train while three men stayed behind to recall the boat and bring it along the lake, Doane becomes anxious when a storm comes up and the boat does not arrive. At last, it appears.) *The oars were coated an inch thick and the boat was half full of solid ice. When the three men came in front of the camp fire, they were a sight to behold. Their hair and beards were frozen to their caps and overcoats and they were sheeted with glistening ice from head to foot.*

Oct. 31. *During the forenoon we brought the boat down in front of camp and dug the ice out of her with axes. Then threw in hot ashes to dry her out inside.* (The rest of this day and the next are spent getting the boat over the Continental Divide to Heart Lake, an exhausting effort for men and animals like.)

Nov. 8. (For several days they wrestle the boat down Heart River, the water of which is so low the boat has to be hauled by hand.) *Worked very hard all day dragging the boat over rocks in a channel where she would not float at any point . . . wore out the bottom of the boat as well as ourselves making three miles. Abandoned one horse and one mule.*

* All quotations in this portion of the chapter covering the expedition itself are, unless otherwise noted, from the journal Doane wrote later. The original, drafted in longhand, was subsequently lost, but fortunately not before the National Park Service had made typewritten and mimeographed copies. One of these copies is in the library at the headquarters of Grand Teton National Park.

Nov. 11. The boat runs a little faster since the junction of Barlow Creek. We can now walk alongside in the water and keep it going by lifting over the larger boulders . . . It is now so cold that we do not mind ordinary leakage. A cup full of water inside the boat mends the leak by freezing when poured in, thus keeping out the water of the stream.

Nov. 15. We are all getting worn out by the excessive labor with the boat.

Nov. 18. Reached camp in the forenoon with all the calking melted out of the seams and all the ice thawed out of the interior of the boat by the floods of boiling water passed through in the river channel just above. (They have gone over thermal springs.) *When it is remembered that the wood had to be dry before the pitch would adhere, and that we were obliged to keep a bed of coals under the boat constantly to effect this, on ground saturated with snow water and with the snow falling most of the time, it can be realized that the labor was of the most fatiguing description.*

Nov. 23. (They come down the Snake River into Jackson Hole.) *When the sky cleared we were under the shadow of a mighty curve of bare rock, the upper end of the Teton Range. An hour after, we ran out into Jackson's Lake, and passed the train just as a mule fell under a log across the trail, struggled a moment and died.* (They are now down to six horses and one mule, having started out with a total of fifteen animals.)

Nov. 24. (The pack train begins seven long, debilitating days beating its way through the labyrinth of boulders and fallen trees along the western and southern shores of Jackson Lake.) *Followed the lake shore under the shadow of the great range . . . Terrible severe travelling for the train . . . Abandoned one horse . . . Ate our last flour today.* (They kill and cook an otter, but only one of the men can keep it down.)

Nov. 25. (When they kill a deer on Moran Bay of Jackson Lake, the discharge of the rifle sets up such an echo in Moran Canyon in the Tetons that the party at first thinks an avalanche is falling.) *We spent hours testing it afterward, and surely nothing on earth can equal it . . . Time, one minute and 26 seconds.*

Nov. 26. *The animals had a frightful day among the rocks and heavy timber . . . My horse was abandoned on the trail.*

Nov. 28. (All the men are taken violently ill with diarrhea.) *As we had nothing in the form of bread, we lived on baked beans for the time.*

Nov. 30. (They reach the outlet of Jackson Lake with the sergeant, Fred Server, too weak to ride on horseback.) *Took him in the boat . . . started down the river, making good time as the channel is narrow and the current rapid . . . Warren saw a large herd of Elk but was unable to get one.* (They camp along the Snake River below the junction of Spread Creek.)

Dec. 1. (They camp in front of the Grand Teton near the site of the present Grand Teton National Park headquarters.) *Fishing good, but fresh fish is too thin a diet to subsist on alone. We now have no coffee, sugar, tea, bacon, and worst of all, no tobacco. Nothing but a few beans left.*

Dec. 2. *Our hunting was without avail. The animals were too weak to carry us far uphill, and the game was far up on the eastern foothills . . . Shot Warren's horse for food . . . He had not a particle of fat on his carcass, and we had no salt or other seasoning. Drew the powder from a package of cartridges and used it [for salt] . . . We ate it ravenously, stopping to rest occasionally our weary jaws . . . River running ice in cakes which screamed and crashed continually through the night.*

Dec. 4. *The boat ran with tremendous speed on a sunken rock, and knocked a hole in her bottom also pitched Starr, who was sitting astride the bow, into the roaring torrent . . . Everything in the boat very wet. Spent the night in drying out and boiling more horse meat.* (They camp near where the Gros Ventre River joins the Snake River.)

Dec. 5. *White very ill from constant working in the water.*

Dec. 7. (They are in the southern part of Jackson Hole, not far from the site of the future village of Wilson.) *As the country was open the Sergeant and Davis went hunting, and Warren fishing. Sergeant found at the base of the range the cabin of an old trapper, John Pierce, who was greatly surprised to see anyone with animals this time of year in the Snake River Basin. He was evidently incredulous as to the boat, but gave them a substantial meal and some salt which improved our regal fare by somewhat smothering the sour perspiration taste of the old horse.*

Dec. 8. *The old trapper came to our camp before we started bringing on his shoulder a quarter of fat elk, also a little flour. He was a gigantic rawboned and grisled old volunteer soldier. We gave him in return some clothing of which he was in need and a belt full of cartridges . . . He told me that he had not believed the Sergeant's story about the boat at first, and throughout his visit was evidently completely puzzled as to what motives could have induced us to attempt such a trip in such a way and at such a season.* (It is not surprising that John Pierce is puzzled. He has probably never seen anything like this in all of his days—half-starved cavalrymen trying to navigate a boat through Jackson Hole in winter, led by a lieutenant who, despite all he and his men have gone through to date, has no questions of his own about attempting "such a trip in such a way and at such a season." Before they part, Pierce tells Doane the location of a small mining settlement lying up a tributary of the Snake River beyond the dangerous Snake River Canyon Doane and his men are about to enter, information which will have much to do with the fact they survive.)

Dec. 9. Entered the cañon which cuts through the Snake River Mountains in a constantly deepening gorge . . . The channel is narrow and the water deep, boiling over boulders and swirling in numerous eddies. (Walking on an ice shelf along the side of the canyon, Doane and three of the men let the boat down through the whirlpools with a line, while Sergeant Server and two men lead the four remaining animals along the top of the canyon's walls.) *Kept awake most of the night by the screaming of an ice gorge which passed down.*

Dec. 10. Found the river in bad order. The gorge had torn away the icefoot and the ice was massed in the eddies grinding and crunching in a very ominous way . . . Sergeant and party did not get in till next morning, having been obliged to sleep by a campfire and go without food 24 hours.

Dec. 11. Cañon deeper and wilder . . . No food left but a handful of flour. Shot White's horse, and feasted. It was now evident that we were not going to run the cañon with the boat, but must tug away slowly . . . I desired to get the boat through if we had to risk everything in order to do so. This Cañon was the terrible obstacle and we were more than half way through it. Apparently the worst had been gone through with. (Not so, although Doane at the time had no way of knowing this. As full of churning white water as the Snake River Canyon is, it is gentle by comparison with Hell's Canyon of the Snake River farther on. There is little likelihood the expedition could have avoided disaster if it had reached that far.)

Dec. 12. The River was becoming better, the ice foot more uniform and the channel free from frozen pools when all of a sudden the boat touched the margin, turned under it, and the next instant was dancing end over end in the swift bold current. All of the horse meat, all the property, arms, instruments and note books were in the roaring stream. A few hundred yards below there was a narrow place where the ice foot almost touched the middle of the river. We ran thither and caught whatever floated. The clothing bags, valise, bedding, bundles, and the lodge [tent] were saved. All else, excepting one hind quarter of the old horse meat went to the bottom and was seen no more. All the rubber boots were gone excepting mine. The warm clothing all floated and was saved. We dragged in the boat by the tow line and pulled her out of the water and far up on the ledge of rock. (With the two horses and one mule now left, Sergeant Server and a private who has become very sick are sent ahead to find and bring back food from the mining settlement the trapper John Pierce had told them about.)

Dec. 13. Last night was bitterly cold, and we slept by a roaring fire on a ledge of rock . . . Cooked our horse meat on sticks, Indian fashion. Started early and worked over frozen pools and open rapids, all day without accident . . . Pulled the boat out as usual at night.

Dec. 14. The boat is becoming ice bound and we have no axes or hatchets with which to chip out the rapidly accumulating ice . . . Camped in a pocket in the cañon and pulled the boat into what we thought a place secure from ice gorges. We had eaten our last horse meat for breakfast, and had no food left.

Dec. 15. (The situation has now become so bad that Doane, as willing as he had been to risk everything to get the boat through, suddenly decides to leave it and lead the men on foot in what is to be, in his words, "a race for life" to the safety of the mining settlement.[6] They are in such a weakened condition they cannot even carry their bedding with them, but must travel with only the clothes on their backs, and for the first time Doane's words reflect his uncertainty about the outcome.) . . . *started, unarmed, without food, and in an unknown wilderness to find settlements seven miles up on a stream which we had no positive assurance of being able to recognize when we came to its mouth.* (They climb up the canyon wall and work their way along its brink, where at one especially precipitous place Doane becomes dizzy and has to rest until his nerves steady. Then they move on, coming out of the canyon and wading two rivers before finding an aspen grove, where they build a fire and sit by it through the night, listening to one of the starving men talk about nothing but food.)

Dec. 16. *Weather bitterly cold. We were obliged to build fires whenever we stopped to rest to prevent our feet from freezing. The snow was knee deep on level ground and crusted so that the leader on the trail had to break through at every footstep. We alternated at this labor. Could not make over a mile an hour.* (They camp but cannot sleep because of their hunger.)

Dec. 17. *A couple of miles farther on we stopped to build a fire and warm ourselves. Davis showed signs of undue restlessness. We had to call him back from climbing the hill sides several times.* (Davis is not "restless"; he has become temporarily deranged and is beginning to wander aimlessly. Nor was Davis the only one who apparently acted peculiarly. Shortly after the expedition came to an end, one of the privates wrote a friend that in the final stages of the ordeal "Doane nearly went crazy."[7]) *In a couple of hours we came to an old flume. Shortly after Applegate declared he smelled the smoke of burning pine. In half an hour more we reached a miner's cabin and were safe.*

As incredible as it may seem, after sixty-eight days of brutal hardships and privations, during which nothing of consequence had been accomplished and the last eighty hours of which had been spent without food or shelter in temperatures ranging from ten to forty degrees below zero, Doane was still stubbornly determined to continue the madness. He moved his emaciated and half-frozen men to a nearby small mining town and let them recuperate for a few days, then set out with them for Fort Hall in Idaho, fully intending to acquire fresh animals and supplies, return to the boat and resume the expedition. Fortunately, he was prevented from doing so by what he thought was a stroke of bad luck, which those who over the years have written about the expedition have accepted as what happened. However, it now appears that Doane's plan to relaunch the boat was thwarted not by bad luck, but only because Sergeant Server took matters into his own hands and acted in a most unmilitary, yet eminently sensible, manner.

While Doane and his men were on their way to Fort Hall, they were intercepted by a rescue party sent out from that post to find the long overdue expedition. Doane immediately ordered Sergeant Server to take four enlisted men, at least one of whom was a

Early Jackson Hole settler Emile Wolff, his wife Marie and son Willie in 1900. Formerly a member of the army rescue party sent out to find the long overdue Doane and his men, Wolff said his ax was used to smash the expedition's boat. *W.C. "Slim" Lawrence Collection.*

member of the rescue party, back up the river to bring the boat down, but they soon returned to report that the boat "had been crushed into splinters by an ice gorge which had piled up in masses twenty feet high."[8] The lieutenant attributed the loss solely to chance, never suspecting for a moment that it could have been the men, not the ice, who destroyed the presumably safely cached boat. And that seems to have been what actually happened, as Private Emile Wolff, a member of the rescue party who accompanied Sergeant Server back upriver, told his son on a number of occasions in later years.[9] Arriving at the boat, which had not been damaged by the ice, Sergeant Server asked Private Wolff, who was carrying an ax, whether he could keep a secret. Assured that he could, the sergeant then took the ax and chopped the boat to pieces.

But Doane was not yet finished. Although his men had suffered terribly and the worst of winter still lay ahead, he now proved that he was a man obsessed. He announced to his men that they would proceed to Fort Hall, obtain lumber, rebuild the boat and continue the journey, first "going back far enough beyond Jackson's Lake to take a renewal of the system of triangulations and notes, lost in the river when the boat capsized."[10] This was absurd. Jackson Hole had been so well mapped by the Hayden Survey four years before Doane's expedition that while in the valley he had referred to its topographical features by the names Hayden's party had given them, and there was not a single item of worthwhile information to be gathered by a suicidal return to the upper reaches of the river. By now, however, higher headquarters had finally had enough. While Doane was still at Fort Hall planning to continue, a telegram ordered him to break off this badly conceived expedition that only because of providential luck, with an apparent assist from Sergeant Server, did not end in tragedy.

Over the years, the impression has been fostered that Doane was an heroic, though ill-starred, figure, a man to be ranked with the foremost explorers of the West. And the myth still marches on, with various writers hailing him in terms such as "a great and gallant soldier," "one of that special breed of American explorers" and "an explorer in every sense of the word . . . in truth, a man 'to ride the river with.' "[11] Quite to the contrary, the records reveal that except for his participation in the opening of Yellowstone Doane made no discoveries of any kind, and, in fact, the two expeditions he commanded—on the Snake River in 1876 and in the Arctic in 1880—were both dismal failures. Further, the records reveal that Doane was a petty, frequently vindictive man whose lust for fame was not counterbalanced with good judgment, and who was not above attributing his lack of success to the machinations of others. Perhaps the best measure of the man is that when he was ordered to discontinue the Snake River expedition and report back to Fort Ellis, he insinuated that his commanding officer had sabotaged the venture from the outset, and he even went so far as to suggest that the same officer had sent out word that Doane and his men were deserters. Needless to say, there was not a grain of truth to it.

Although Doane did not contribute an iota to the knowledge of Jackson Hole, or, for that matter, to the knowledge of the Snake River, in 1938 Doane Peak in the Tetons was named for him. As Frank Calkins wrote, "It rises in the northern part of the range, but, like its namesake, does not loom large on the horizon."[12]

President Arthur, seated in center, and friends in Yellowstone at the end of the pack trip that took them through Jackson Hole. Lt. Gen. Philip Sheridan is seated second from left; Secretary of War Robert Lincoln is seated second from right. *F. Jay Haynes photo, Haynes Foundation.*

14

The Bottle Trail

In May of 1883, when President Chester A. Arthur went to New York to dedicate the Brooklyn Bridge, it was noticed that his complexion was sallow and his usual vigor was missing. Evidently, the President needed a vacation, but where in 1883 could a president who liked to fish and was not averse to a drink or two go to escape both the pressures of his office and the hounding of reporters, who at the time were giving his administration a rather rough going over? The answer is that any number of private resorts in the East probably would have filled the bill nicely, which is why the vacation President Arthur chose to take was so surprising. He and a select group of nationally prominent men traveled two thousand miles to camp and fish in a remote and uninhabited wilderness, Jackson Hole and Yellowstone Park. And not only did they do so, but they "roughed it" in high style, with a long pack train of horses and mules carrying several tons of supplies, including what subsequently was alleged to be an inordinately large amount of whiskey.

In early August, when the presidential party detrained at Green River, Wyoming, among the many dignitaries who stepped off were Lieutenant General Philip Sheridan, of Civil War fame; Secretary of War Robert Lincoln, Abraham Lincoln's son; and Senator George Vest of Missouri, a good friend of Yellowstone Park who once rose on the Senate floor to rebut a fellow senator's anti-Yellowstone argument that the government had no right being in "show business."[1] At the station to meet them was Troop G of the 5th Cavalry, some seventy-five well-armed mounted men who would provide an escort thought to be desirable in light of Custer's massacre at the Little Bighorn less than a hundred and fifty miles from Yellowstone just seven years earlier. Also at Green River were two Chicago newspaper reporters to whom General Sheridan, in his typically blunt way, made known the policy decided upon regarding press coverage of the junket. He flatly told them that if they followed the President any farther he would have them arrested and thrown in jail.

In what amounted to a total blackout of the press, no correspondent of any kind was permitted to accompany the outing. Instead, official news releases were written by Lieutenant Colonel Michael Sheridan, the general's nephew, and by Lieutenant Colonel James Gregory, then sent to the outside world by a relay system of mounted couriers stationed every twenty miles along the route. Although newspapers across the country were outraged at this high-handed form of censorship, it was not relaxed, so some of the more enterprising editors decided that if their reporters could not cover the news for themselves, they could at least manufacture it. Consequently, a number of wholly fabricated stories were written which are of no help when one tries to find out what really happened when the President and his friends went packing in the Rocky Mountains. Nor do the two colonels' official releases provide much illumination. Oblivious of their rare opportunity to report what may have been the most unusual vacation ever taken by any American president while still in office, their stilted, West Point prose was devoted almost exclusively to descriptions of the scenery and the number of fish caught.

The first stop before jumping off into the wilderness was Fort Washakie, Wyoming, a reservation for the Shoshoni and Arapahoe tribes. As the wagons carrying the vacationers approached the reservation, Indians rode out in large numbers to greet the Great White Father and "dashed around the President's party most gaudily and fantastically arrayed, displaying their skill in horsemanship and gratifying their curiosity."[2] The next day, the Indians entertained their distinguished guests by having several hundred braves astride war ponies charge across a plain to where the President and his group stood, at the last moment reining up in a cloud of dust. Then the chiefs of the two tribes dismounted and stepped forward to be introduced—Coal Black of the Arapahoes and none other than Nick Wilson's brother by adoption, Washakie of the Shoshonis, the great old chief in whose honor the fort had been named. Following this, the Indians and the cavalry escort staged a spectacle which was wildly incongruous, at the very least, especially since the memory of Custer was still fresh in everyone's mind. Mounting their horses, they engaged in a spirited sham battle, complete with war whoops, bugle calls and the firing of rifles and revolvers, all of which were fortunately loaded with blanks.

On the morning of August 9, the pack train started along a route that would take it west into the Wind River Range, across the Continental Divide, down along the Gros Ventre River into Jackson

Many packers and pack animals were needed to transport supplies for President Arthur's "cavalcade" through the wilderness. *F. Jay Haynes photo, Haynes Foundation.*

Hole, then north into and through Yellowstone Park, a journey of about three hundred and fifty miles. Later described by an authority on the West as "one of the most complete pack trains ever organized in this or any other country," the column on the march was most imposing, with Indian guides riding ahead, the cavalry troop fore and aft of the presidential party and, bringing up the rear, one hundred and seventy-five pack horses and mules all piled high with provisions and equipment.[3] Once the caravan plunged into the mountains, a curtain descended through which it is now impossible to see, but, at least according to one account, President Arthur and his friends went on a spree.

Other than Lieutenant Colonel Sheridan's and Lieutenant Colonel Gregory's sterile dispatches, the only document purporting to give a glimpse of what went on is a burlesque in doggerel verse entitled *The Rajah, or the Great Sporting Excursion of 1883*, published the following year and written by someone who used the pseudonym "Unc Dunkam." Who "Unc Dunkam" was is unknown, although he seems to have been either a member of the party or a newsman who obtained his information after the trip, perhaps from some of the soldiers and packers who went along. Highly exaggerated for dramatic effect, the poem is certainly no Rock of Gibraltar as a reliable source of history, but here and there, particularly in his footnotes, "Unc Dunkam" mentions small details and characteristics of the various personages that add a touch of credibility. Whether history or not, his version has become part of the word-of-mouth lore of Jackson Hole, and it does add spice to what is otherwise only the colonels' prosaic travelogue.

The size and opulence of the President's caravan inspired "Unc Dunkam" to use a rajah as the central symbol of his parody, in one verse of which he wrote that three hundred mules were "All laden with the choicest wine."[4] Surely there were not three hundred mules, and surely they were not laden with wine, but it appears that enough bottles of what was more likely rye or bourbon were taken along to stock a special tent set aside as a bar. "Unc Dunkam" described it in a footnote as "located in the center of the camp, and . . . *generously* supplied with all kinds of '*liquid refreshments*,' except '*water*' . . . These refreshments were to be had 'without money,' and simply for the asking, at any time of the day or night."[5] Thus, according to the anonymous poet, did the illustrious campers blaze a trail with "broken bottles, Every mile, of *their* wilderness *way*."[6] But "Unc Dunkam" most certainly stretched a point. While some partying undoubtedly took place, Chester A. Arthur and his friends would never have made it to Yellowstone if that much alcohol had been imbibed. Long before then, they would have fallen off their horses and broken their necks, or would have fallen into the streams they fished and drowned.

As might be expected of an ardent fisherman who was camping along some of the finest trout waters in North America, the President enjoyed himself thoroughly, although it must be said he sometimes resorted to the less than sportsmanlike use of gang hooks to catch more than one fish at a time. According to an official release, "At one cast the President landed three trout, weighing in the aggregate four and one-quarter pounds, and at each of some six other casts took two fine specimens."[7] On another occasion, the President was reported to have reeled in "thirty-five fish, weighing forty-five pounds" in just a few hours.[8] Even for his time, long before the concept of conservation had to any extent entered the American conscience, Arthur's catches were embarrassingly large, which probably explains why he refused to let the party's official photographer, F. Jay Haynes, take any pictures of him while he was fishing.

Two of President Arthur's Indian guides (one in shadow on right) at the foot of the Tetons in Jackson Hole. *F. Jay Haynes photo, Haynes Foundation.*

The scenic highlight of the trip was Jackson Hole and the Tetons, described at length by the official chroniclers. As the pack train came out of the canyon of the Gros Ventre River into Jackson Hole, "there suddenly burst upon our view a scene as grand and majestic as we had ever witnessed . . . Along the whole westerly edge of this valley, with no intervening foothills to obstruct the view, towered the magnificent Teton Mountains, their snowy summits piercing the air 8,000 feet above the spot where we stood in reverent admiration, and 14,000 feet above the level of the sea. It was the voice of every member of the party that this sight alone would have fully repaid all the toils and perils of the march."[9] The use of the word "perils" is puzzling, because up to this point not one had been reported. On the other hand, "Unc Dunkam" wrote that later, while in Jackson Hole, the President came close to losing his scalp when Indians staged a war dance in his honor. If he is to be believed, one of the Indians became so carried away by the dance, or by the contents of one of the bottles in the bar tent, he

> *Swung high in air*
> *His warclub, dire and dread,*
> *And would have* whack'd
> *Great Chester on the head!* [10]

According to the poem, a member of the party pulled a gun and prevented the Indian from carrying out what surely would have been the most bizarre assault ever made on the person of any president of the United States. Also, according to the poem, late one night some of the thirsty packers invaded the bar tent and became so intoxicated they began shooting at imaginary hostile Indians, which by the light of morning turned out to be several dead mules. But other than these two incidents, if anything even remotely resembling them did occur, the entire journey went off without mishap.

While in Jackson Hole, three camps were made: the first in the Gros Ventre River Canyon near where the Sheep Mountain landslide would later take place, the second along the Gros Ventre River south of Blacktail Butte and the third along the Snake River just below the fork of the Buffalo River. The cavalcade then moved up to Yellowstone, where more fishing was done and where President Arther encountered the first member of the fourth estate he had seen since the two Chicago reporters at Green River. Despite General Sheridan's expressed dislike of journalists, this corre-

Indians staging a war dance for President Arthur and his companions. *F. Jay Haynes photo, Haynes Foundation.*

spondent of the *London Times* was not thrown in jail, but probably only because he was in the company of some wealthy and titled Europeans who were on a sightseeing tour of the West. The Englishman was much more awed by Arthur than the dancing Indian in Jackson Hole was reported to have been, writing that "no one would have supposed that the tall, robust man in blouse and white felt hat, with checked shirt and sunburnt face, who shook us heartily by the hand and talked freely to anyone who chose to approach him, was the head of the nation and the lineal descendant in office of the most dignified and punctilious of rulers, George Washington"—which may have been the only time the twenty-first president of the United States and the first have been compared in any way whatever.[11]

On September 1, 1883, President Arthur boarded a Northern Pacific train at Cinnabar, Montana, and started back to Washington to resume the duties of his office. As far as the records go, he showed no signs of a hangover.

John Carnes. In 1884, he, his Indian wife Millie and friend John Holland became the first permanent settlers of Jackson Hole. *Courtesy Beatrice Edwards.*

15

"Pioneers! O Pioneers!"

Jackson Hole was not settled in the way Hollywood would have us believe the West was won. No long train of covered wagons streamed into the valley delivering God-fearing, law-abiding pioneers with their sunbonneted wives and freckle-faced children into a virgin promised land. Rather, when what might by some stretch of the imagination be called a wagon train eventually did come over Teton Pass, it was to find a number of settlers already in residence, all but two of whom were bachelors, many of whom were not especially God-fearing and a few of whom had been attracted to this far-off corner of Wyoming primarily because it was a comfortable distance beyond the reach of the law.

The first permanent settlers of Jackson Hole were John Holland, a former trapper in the valley, his friend John Carnes and Carnes' wife, an Indian girl named Millie. In 1884, they packed some primitive pieces of farm equipment on horses and led them from the Green River region into the Gros Ventre Range, then down through the Gros Ventre River Canyon to that part of Flat Creek now within the National Elk Refuge. There they began to homestead land, a procedure a wag once defined as "the government betting you one hundred and sixty acres against starvation, and the government always winning."[1] Despite those ominous odds, the first settlers did not starve, and close on their heels a number of other homesteaders, mostly unmarried men, came into the valley, among them a bearded giant who became one of Jackson Hole's most eccentric and beloved characters.

Jack Davis, or "Uncle Jack" as he was called, sought refuge in isolated, unpoliced Jackson Hole in 1887 after killing a man in a barroom brawl in Montana. The experience evidently transformed him, leading him from that time on to treat all creatures with a profound reverence for life. Although he was a recluse, the few people who came to know him were impressed by his gentleness, and the birds and beasts somehow seem to have sensed that he would not harm them, for the wildlife in the canyon where he built his one-room log cabin soon became his friends. Squirrels went into and out of the cabin as they pleased, sharing it with an old horse, a burro, two cats and a doe named "Lucy," who lived with "Uncle Jack" for many years, raising her fawn "Buster" under his protection. A pair of bluebirds also made the inside of the cabin their home, returning each spring for six straight years to hatch their young and always finding the door removed from its rawhide hinges in expectation of their arrival. So fearful was "Uncle Jack" of hurting any living thing that he even planted a small vegetable garden and gave up meat entirely, thereby inscribing his name in the annals of Jackson Hole not only as its homespun version of Saint Francis, but also as its first vegetarian.

Late in the fall of 1889, a wagon train appeared at the top of Teton Pass, if six wagons and five Mormon families totaling twenty or so men, women and children can be called that. One of the leaders was the former Pony Express rider Nick Wilson, now a rancher fleeing drought in Idaho for the rich stands of wild hay in Jackson Hole. With his brother Sylvester, Nick had triple-teamed the horses and slowly worked the wagons to the crest of the 8,500-foot pass, but there, looking almost straight down into the valley, they could see that by comparison the ascent had been easy. What lay before them was a grade so steep that years later, even after the horse trail they were on had been made into a road, an army engineer described it as "incomparably the steepest road I have ever seen. It appears utterly incredible that a wagon can be hauled up and held back going down."[2] Nick and his brother now set out to perform the "incredible," the lowering of the wagons into the valley far below. First, they reversed each wagon's wheels, mounting the larger rear wheels in front to reduce the chances of the wagons tipping over forward. Then they wrapped chains around the wheels so they would not turn. Then, as a further brake, they cut down trees and lashed them to the backs of the wagons to be dragged behind. Thus, with the "wagon train" sliding and bumping down the mountainside, did the Wilson clan arrive in Jackson Hole.

Although the Wilsons survived the crossing of Teton Pass without misfortune, it is doubtful they would have survived their first winter in the valley had it not been for the charity of some of the resident bachelors, who shared their sod-roofed cabins with them. Nick Wilson's nephew, Ervin Wilson, his teen-age bride and their six-week-old son were given a room by John Cherry, with whom, after their two cows died, they lived until spring on a diet consisting almost entirely of elk meat, the baby seeming to have thrived on nothing but elk soup. However, not all of the original settlers were as openhanded with the newcomers. Robert Miller, who was destined to become a founder of the valley's first bank, loaned the hard-pressed Mormons hay on terms requiring one and a half tons to be paid back for every ton borrowed, an even higher rate of interest than the usual one he later charged that earned him the nickname "Old Twelve Percent." By the following fall, the Wilson family was cutting its own hay and living in its own cabins in the southern part of the valley, where the village named after Nick would spring up. The year after that, in 1891, Ervin Wilson's wife made local history when she gave birth to Effie Jane, the first white child to be born in Jackson Hole.

During the early years, life in Jackson Hole was hard, very hard. Cut off from the outside world for months on end, the first settlers, a number of whom "imported" wives, had to fend for themselves as best they could. Frequently improvising their own tools, the men worked long hours digging irrigation ditches to increase the yield of the wild hay, laying in cord after cord of firewood against the interminable winters and hunting for game to feed their families. For their part, the women labored every bit as much, struggling to keep dirt-floored cabins clean, making their own soap, carding wool for clothing and sewing animal hides into gloves and moccasins, often working in the early darkness of winter by the light of a burning rag inserted as a wick in a dish of elk tallow. And when it came time to have their babies, they had them at home with, if they were lucky, a neighbor woman in attendance, for the first doctor did not come to Jackson Hole until 1916. (For a long time, there was no dentist either, although at one point a blacksmith did develop a crude expertise at pulling teeth.) Even the children were not spared the hardships. In winter, they had to draw water from frozen streams that first had to be chopped open with an ax, and in haying season, to quote Frank Calkins who reports elderly people remembering the days before mowing machines were brought in, "getting down on hands and knees . . . and helping to cut wild hay with the only tools they had—butcher knives."[3]

There were, of course, moments of humor that served as a tonic when spirits flagged. One such story is told of Marie Wolff, who was brought from Luxembourg as a young bride by the former soldier Emile Wolff, whose ax had been used to destroy Lieutenant

An old sod-roofed cabin, typical of early Jackson Hole homesteads. *National Park Service, Grand Teton National Park.*

Doane's boat and who eventually settled in Jackson Hole. Trained to be a fastidious housekeeper with an abhorrence for dirt, she busied herself one day while her husband was away by prying all the mud chinking from between the logs of their cabin's walls. When winter struck and snow blew through the cracks, she soon discovered why the mud had been put there in the first place. But by then it was too late, and the cabin had to be sealed with the only unfrozen material at hand—fresh cow manure. The story brightened the valley, and even the young woman could see the humor of it, later saying that was when she made up her mind never again to be finicky about housekeeping.

While the settlers were trying to make a go of things, slowly building an economy based for the most part on small cattle ranches and guiding wealthy Eastern and European sportsmen who came to Jackson Hole to hunt, a sinister drama began to unfold in a solitary setting on the shores of Jackson Lake. There, in 1890, an outcast from the East constructed a ten-room log lodge he named Merymere, which soon became as surrounded with suspicion and dark rumor as Heathcliff's Wuthering Heights. John Sargent, a relative of the painter John Singer Sargent, was the well-educated, illegitimate offspring of a member of a distinguished

Mowing hay on a homestead in Jackson Hole. *Teton County Chapter, Wyoming State Historical Society.*

New England family and a Maine seamstress, a man described as "a tortured, hampered, damned sort of poet" with a maniacal temper.[4] For several years, Sargent, his young wife and their several children lived quietly on their remote ranch. Then an old friend from the East, Robert Hamilton, a descendant of Alexander Hamilton, arrived in Jackson Hole and moved in with them. A handsome man with polished ways, Hamilton was said to have left New York because he had become involved in a scandal and had been divorced, and soon some tongues in the valley were wagging about the possibility of a scandalous relationship between him and Mrs. Sargent. What the truth is will never be known, but when Sargent and Hamilton went looking for stray cattle along the Snake River, Hamilton disappeared. After an extensive search, his drowned body was found, and although there was no evidence that Sargent had any hand in the drowning, some residents of Jackson Hole thought he had deliberately misled Hamilton as to the depth of a ford in the river.

Some time later, a soldier on his weekly snowshoe patrol from Yellowstone Park to Jackson Hole came by the lonely lodge on a winter night to see all the windows ablaze with light, while inside someone was loudly playing the piano. Refused admittance by Sargent, the suspicious soldier forced his way through the door and found Mrs. Sargent critically injured, with both of her hips broken in what, according to Sargent's unlikely story, had been a skiing accident. The soldier rushed on and brought back men and a sled to take her to the nearest settlement, but she died before she could, or would, tell them what had taken place. Meanwhile, Sargent, against whom there was again no tangible evidence of wrongdoing, hastily left the valley and was not seen for a number of years.

John Sargent by the fireplace in front of which he later shot himself to death. *Jackson Hole Museum*.

Sargent finally returned and lived by himself before bringing another wife to Merymere. She was an apparently demented woman he had met when she was playing a violin on an excursion boat in California, and her wealthy family paid Sargent to marry her and keep her out of sight in Jackson Hole. As far as the people of the valley were concerned, however, she was highly visible, for she soon displayed a penchant for removing all her clothes and sitting in a tree beside the trail leading from the valley to Yellowstone Park. A vague, pathetic creature she must have been, at times on moonlit nights playing the violin for hours, while at other times, when her husband asked her to play for him, she would play nothing but discords. A local rancher left a haunting vignette of this tormented couple when he described the time he stopped by the then shabby Merymere and found Sargent dressed in Eastern riding breeches and puttees, reading an old copy of a New York newspaper under a lithograph of John L. Sullivan. From out of the blue, Sargent asked, "Did you by any chance hear Tetrazzini sing last winter?"[5] A few moments later, a thinly clad Mrs. Sargent floated into the room carrying a French novel and, staring vacantly, observed, "There aren't many huckleberries this year, are there?"[6] Then she floated out of the room as quietly as she had come, bringing down the curtain on a scene it is hard to believe was acted out in frontier Wyoming and not in an off-Broadway play.

When the poor woman was finally taken away for her own good, the impoverished Sargent, to whom no more remittance checks were coming in, opened a small store along the trail to Yellowstone, but it failed. This strange New Englander, who was so grotesquely out of place in Jackson Hole and contributed so little to it, except to add to the darker side of its lore, then sat down in front of the fireplace at Merymere and blew his brains out with a rifle.

Every western community would like to be able to boast of an Indian attack in its past, preferably a massacre followed by the cavalry rushing to the rescue of the besieged survivors. And that is what the *New York Times* of July 27, 1895, announced to the world had happened in Jackson Hole, featuring the story on the front page under a deck of headlines reading: "SETTLERS MASSACRED—Indians Kill Every One at Jackson's Hole — Red Men Apply the Torch to All the Houses in the Valley — U.S. Troops Are Nearing The Scene."[7] But the *New York Times* was completely in error. The Indians had neither killed anyone in Jackson Hole nor had applied any torch to any homestead. Unfortunately for the Indians, however, a massacre of sorts had taken place, with one of them slain, another wounded, a child separated from its mother and other members of the tribe roughed up and intimidated. To make matters worse, the incident seems to have been manufactured by some of the settlers as part of a deliberate scheme to drive the Indians once and for all from what they considered to be their legitimate hunting grounds in the valley.

By the terms of a treaty signed at Fort Bridger in 1868, the Bannock and Shoshoni tribes had the right to hunt game on unoccupied government land, provided "peace subsists among the

SETTLERS MASSACRED

Indians Kill Every One at Jackson's Hole.

COURIER BRINGS THE NEWS

Red Men Apply the Torch to All the Houses in the Valley.

ALARM IN THE SURROUNDING COUNTRY

Another Messenger with Details of the Successful Ambuscade Is on the Way.

U. S. TROOPS ARE NEARING THE SCENE

They Can Reach the Place Sunday Night—Gen. Coppinger in Command.

Constable William Manning, who led the posse that shot two Indians during the so-called Bannock War of 1895. *National Park Service, Grand Teton National Park.*

The less than accurate headline that alarmed the country about the fate of the settlers in Jackson Hole. *From "New York Times," July 27, 1895.*

whites and Indians on the borders of the hunting districts," and for years these tribes had received passes to leave their reservations and go to Jackson Hole to supplement their near-starvation rations with elk meat.[8] Then, in 1890, Wyoming became a state and shortly thereafter enacted game laws limiting big game hunting to a two-month season, something the Indians could not comprehend and therefore did not observe. Moreover, by the early 1890s the elk herd had become a commercially valuable asset to the people of the valley, with the heads of some twenty-five families, out of a total of only about seventy-five families, earning more money by guiding trophy hunters than they did from growing crops or raising cattle. Viewing the Indians as a threat to their livelihoods, the settlers complained to state and federal authorities, accusing the tribes of wantonly destroying great numbers of elk for their hides alone, leaving the carcasses to rot. Although a later army investigation found no evidence of any such slaughter, by the summer of 1895 the issue had become so emotionally charged that a clash of some kind was all but inevitable. Indeed, it may even have been foreordained the year before when the township officers of Jackson Hole were elected on the understanding that "they would take decided steps to . . . keep the Indians out."[9]

The series of events which culminated in what local historians have seen fit to call the "Bannock War" began on June 7, 1895, when twelve deputies under Constable William Manning, who had been brought in from Teton Basin, arrested a lone Bannock for shooting elk in violation of Wyoming law. A few weeks later, the constable and his men went to an Indian camp to make more arrests, but this time they found themselves outnumbered and had to back down, returning to report, with the use of a quaint phrase, that "the trespassers were saucy."[10] Then, on July 4, eight Indians were taken into custody and led to Marysvale, a small settlement now gone but at that time located about five miles north of the present town of Jackson. When the Indians could not pay their fines, no one seemed to know what to do with them, so they were allowed to escape. Until this point, the campaign to clear Jackson Hole of Indians had been less than a success, but upon learning that a large party of Bannocks was camped in Hoback Canyon south of the valley, Manning formed a posse of twenty-six settlers who, in his words, were determined to "bring matters to a head."[11] He later said, "We knew someone was going to be killed, perhaps some on both sides, and we decided the sooner it was done the better, so that we could get the matter before the courts."[12]

On July 13, the posse surrounded the Bannock camp and at gunpoint arrested the group, which turned out to consist of only ten braves, thirteen squaws and five children. Stripping them of their few arms and possessions, meanwhile frightening them by saying that some would be hung and the others sent to jail, Manning ordered the prisoners to mount their horses and begin the march back to Marysvale. What happened next is clouded, but along the trail the Indians bolted and shooting began. According to the white men's version of the story, at a prearranged signal the Indians spurred their horses and raced for a woods. According to the Indians' version, they made a run for their lives when members of the posse slammed cartridges into the chambers of their rifles, which the prisoners interpreted as a sign they were about to be massacred in cold blood. Whatever the case, in the melee that followed one old and nearly blind Indian man was shot four times in the back and killed, another Indian was wounded and a little Indian boy who was riding with his mother was scraped off by an overhanging branch. The child, about four years old, was the only member of the band to be recaptured. Taken to Marysvale and placed in the care of the wife of a member of the posse, he was described as "shy as a deer," rejecting any friendly advances from white children by drawing "his little blanket over his face."[13] He was later returned to the wrong reservation and more than a year passed before he was reunited with his mother.

Whether the shooting was premeditated, as one newspaper reporter who investigated the incident thought it was, or whether it was the result of reflex action on the part of the posse, it was unjustified. The Indians had violated no federal law, and even under Wyoming law had committed only the misdemeanor of hunting out of season, for which the maximum penalty was a small fine or short jail sentence. But Manning and his men had accomplished what they had set out to do—"bring matters to a head."

With several hundred armed Indians still scattered throughout the Jackson Hole area, the settlers now had good reason to be worried. An urgent telegram requesting protection was sent to the governor of Wyoming, who forwarded it to Washington, where the Secretary of War ordered four companies of cavalry to the scene. Western movies to the contrary, the cavalry was not always just over the hill waiting to rush in, so during the few weeks it took the troops to arrive the residents of Jackson Hole gathered in armed camps behind hastily thrown together fortifications at three ranches throughout the valley. There they waited for an attack that never came. Well before the cavalry appeared, the Indians had returned to their reservations and the less than glorious "Bannock War" was at an end.*

* If the Indians had chosen to fight and a battle with the cavalry had taken place, it would have been a scene which, as the saying goes, could have happened only in America—members of the white race being defended from members of the red race by members of still another race, for most of the cavalry troopers who were sent to Jackson Hole were black.

But even with the Indians gone, gunplay was not over. Among the members of a civilian relief force that had come into Jackson Hole from Lander, Wyoming, there were, in the words of William Simpson, a number of "half outlaws" and "tin horn gamblers," who on their way out of the valley robbed the John Holland ranch and stole the possessions of William Arnn.[14] Simpson, who went along with Arnn in an attempt to regain the stolen property, later wrote that Arnn was "one of the coolest and most self-possessed men I ever knew in the face of a possibility such as prevailed at that time."[15] What Simpson referred to is that having ridden into the center of the looters' camp, the chances were good that he and Arnn would be gunned down, a possibility Arnn calmly averted by drawing his pistol and declaring, "The first son of a bitch that tries to pull his gun, I am going to kill."[16] Then, having recovered his property, Arnn "went up on a little knowl in view of the camp and took out his rifle and after he had done this, he said to the outfit 'solong.'"[17] It is perhaps worth noting that during the "Bannock War" the only pillaging that had been done had been done by white men. All the while the Indians had been in the valley, not a single theft was reported. *

As the nineteenth century drew to a close, more and more wealthy Easterners came to Jackson Hole to hunt, and in 1897 what has been called "the most spectacular sporting expedition that ever crossed the nation" left Vermont to obtain trophy elk heads in Wyoming.[18] Having taken a party to Yellowstone Park and Jackson Hole the year before, W. Seward Webb, a railroad tycoon and son-in-law of William Vanderbilt, seems to have been in a hurry to return, for he arranged to have the tracks all along the way cleared so his luxurious ten-car train could set a new cross-country speed record as it barreled past other trains shunted off onto sidings and was waved on by special flagmen stationed at crossings. Once in Jackson Hole, the pace slowed down. The large and lavishly outfitted group camped near Jackson Lake, where its members enjoyed the scenery as much as the hunting and fishing, although at

---

* For a time, it appeared that the right of the Indians to hunt in Jackson Hole would be upheld. In a test case involving a Bannock named Chief Race Horse, the United States Circuit Court ruled that the Fort Bridger treaty of 1868 took precedence over the later enacted laws of Wyoming and the attempt to drive the Indians from the valley had been illegal. But in 1896 the United States Supreme Court overruled the lower court, declaring that the state had complete power to enact and enforce game laws. The decision was based on an Alice-in-Wonderland kind of logic which held that the treaty, solemnly signed and sworn to by the federal government, had been annulled by the same federal government when it granted statehood to Wyoming.

Wealthy hunters from the East and Europe were important to Jackson Hole's early, struggling economy. *S.N. Leek Collection, Western History Research Center, University of Wyoming.*

first it was discovered that no one had remembered to obtain hunting licenses and a rider had to be sent galloping to Jackson to get them before the shooting could begin. One of the guests, Sir Rose Lambart Price, astonished the local guides by wearing a monocle at all times, even when aiming his rifle, wryly observing, "One sees almost as well with it as without it."[19] Sir Rose turned out to be as good a sport as he was a sportsman, with an admiring guide paying the knight the ultimate compliment by saying that if he would only learn how to speak English he could pass for a native of Wyoming.

While guiding provided an important source of income for many of Jackson Hole's residents, the backbone of the economy was the cattle business. It was not, however, the cattle business on the heroic scale usually associated with Wyoming, because no herds were ever driven here from Texas to graze, nor were there any vast spreads running many thousands of cattle on the open range. Instead, the ranches were small, family-sized units, growing their own hay to carry the animals through the winter months, and the total

One of the earliest known photographs of the town of Jackson, taken on June 1, 1907, by M. W. Trester. *Jackson Hole Museum*.

number of cattle in the valley in 1900 may not have exceeded one thousand. Although there was very little money to be made in Jackson Hole by ranching, the ranchers fared better than did those who tried to farm this uncongenial land, where the growing season was woefully short and just as a crop was about to be harvested a hail storm could sweep in over the Tetons to level fields and break hearts in a matter of minutes.* Even the storekeepers in the town of Jackson, founded in the southern end of the valley in the late 1890s, felt the pinch, for money was in such short supply the community was likened to "localities where there is only fifty dollars in cash and this is passed around from hand to hand at harvest time."[20] And so, with an economy precariously balanced on the shaky legs of ranching and guiding hunters from the East, the

---

* As early as the 1830s, Osborne Russell, a Maine farm boy who had become a mountain man, predicted the future of farming in the valley. He noted in his journal that "The great altitude of this place however connected with the cold descending from the mountains at night I think would be a serious obstruction to growth of most Kinds of cultivated grains." (Osborne Russell, *Journal of a Trapper*, p. 18)

several hundred residents of Jackson Hole prepared to move into the twentieth century, unaware that an entirely different kind of ranch had come into being elsewhere. When adopted here, it would not only bring a steady flow of cash into the valley, but would also once and for all bring Jackson Hole's frontier way of life to an end.

Just as Archimedes discovered the principle of volumetric displacement by observing what happened to the level of the water when he stepped into his bath, Howard Eaton discovered the principle of dude ranching by observing his guests eat. Hosting his

T. Lloyd's saloon in Jackson in the early 1900s. *Jackson Hole Museum.*

many friends from the East at first his ranch in South Dakota, then at a later ranch near Sheridan, Wyoming, he saw clearly that they consumed far more than he could possibly make raising cattle, so he reversed matters, charging them for both the food they ate and the horses they rode. In doing so, this unsung genius laid the groundwork for a whole new industry.

On the surface, the business should never have succeeded. In return for chuck wagon fare, lumpy beds in drafty cabins and saddle sores, Easterners were expected to travel great distances and pay fancy prices. But travel they did and pay they did, and gladly, because dude ranches filled a previously unseen need by giving city

Louis Joy, who changed the history of Jackson Hole when he started the first dude ranch in the valley. *Jackson Hole Museum*.

Cowboys next to an early gasoline pump symbolize the pioneer era drawing to a close in Jackson Hole. *Jackson Hole Museum*.

dwellers a chance to shed their city ways and get out into some of the world's wildest and most beautiful country. Many Easterners became so taken with both the West and Westerners they returned year after year, usually to the same ranch, where they were treated as members of the family and expected to accept the vicissitudes of ranch life without complaint or have a timetable of east-bound trains thrust into their hands. Howard Eaton's simple formula worked so well that dude ranching quickly spread throughout the West, particularly to Jackson Hole, which soon became one of its most flourishing centers.

In 1908, Louis Joy forever altered the future of Jackson Hole by starting its first dude ranch, the JY Ranch on Phelps Lake at the foot of the Tetons. In the years that followed, many ranchers who had earlier only run cattle opened their doors to guests, and the advance guard of generations of Eastern families began to descend on the valley. In time, many of them built summer homes and some even bought ranches, becoming either seasonal or year-round residents. For better or for worse—and almost every Jackson Holer even today has a strong opinion on the subject—the character of Jackson Hole would be greatly shaped by the presence of these people from the outside world. But in the dawning years of the twentieth century, all this was masked in the future when the passing of the pioneer era was graphically symbolized by a quiet little incident that took place on the streets of the town of Jackson. As the first automobile ever to be seen in the valley drove through, a small colt decided to throw in his lot with the new century by following it and not his mother.

16

"Mountin Law"

Early-day Jackson Hole was so widely reputed to be a haven for outlaws that a traveler on a train, astonished to learn the destination of a perfectly respectable valley resident, automatically asked whether he was going there to arrest someone or was making a getaway. In a curious Western way, the question was flattering. Just as Atlantic seaboard communities pride themselves on the notables who slept there, Western communities pride themselves on the bad men who shot someone or were themselves shot there. This inverted form of civic pride, which rejoices in perpetuating the bloodier side of the past, is nowhere celebrated with more fanfare than in the town of Jackson. There, every summer evening promptly at seven o'clock, the main street of the shopping district is cleared of traffic so a mock shoot-out between bandits and a posse can be performed for the benefit of the tourists who line the wooden sidewalks. Guns blaze, horses neigh, dancehall girls cringe and cowboys buckle and fall, until the last blank is fired and justice prevails.

The melodrama is both a good show and good for business, but it is not history, because there is no record of any shoot-out ever having taken place in the town of Jackson. For that matter, Jackson Hole, the valley itself, was never the stronghold of desperadoes it was thought to be, an impression heightened by the similarity of its name to the notorious "Hole-in-the-Wall" hideout of outlaws elsewhere in Wyoming. By no means is this to say that Jackson Hole did not earn its spurs at least as far as part of its fearsome reputation went, for over the years it did play host to as authentic an assortment of bad men as any community might wish to entertain, and it did witness as many killings as any community might covet. Where it differed from most other Western communities was in the tolerance with which the first settlers viewed the presence of outlaws in their midst. Because the valley was so isolated, settlers so few and law enforcement officers so far away, the principle of live and let live was generally observed, at least as long as the lawbreakers

Teton Jackson with his wife and child. Jackson Hole's most famous horse thief, he is said to have mended his ways and become a man of respectability. *W.C. "Slim" Lawrence Collection*.

had familiar faces and did not practice their trade at the expense of the valley's residents. On the other hand, when they were outsiders, or when they posed a threat to the valley's well-being, that was different. Then the people of Jackson Hole banded together and dispensed a swift form of justice which, while effective, was not exactly a model of due process of law.

Two of the outlaws whose faces were familiar to the early residents of Jackson Hole were Ed Harrington, alias Ed Trafton, and Harvey Gleason, whose assumed name, Teton Jackson, showed no reticence on his part to let the world know the location of his favorite sanctuary. Teton Jackson may have run stolen horses through the valley well before it was settled, and he was surely doing so after Jackson Hole's founding fathers, John Holland and John Carnes, began their homesteads. At one point, he and his cronies had a log cabin hideout in the area of the present National Elk Refuge that seems to have served as a halfway station for an ingenious shuttle operation based on stealing horses in Idaho and driving them east to be sold in central Wyoming, then stealing horses in central Wyoming and driving them west to be sold in Idaho. First arrested in 1885 and sentenced to fourteen years, Teton Jackson escaped by burrowing a tunnel under the prison walls and making a beeline back to the Teton country, where he was looked upon as "an accommodating fellow, a good singer and [one who] had many friends."[1] He eventually left the valley and somewhere along the line mended his ways, because although the stories about his later life differ, they do agree that he ended up a man of respectability. One story says that he became a rancher, another that he became a successful bank director.

While Teton Jackson specialized in stealing horses, Ed Trafton chose to spread his talents more widely across the spectrum of crime. Not only did he serve two sentences for horse theft, another for holding up stagecoaches in Yellowstone National Park and still another for robbing his mother of ten thousand dollars, but late in his long career he is said to have been apprehended before he could carry out a cherished plan to build an armored car and use it to kidnap the head of the Mormon Church. He, too, was viewed with a tolerant eye, for despite his prison record no objection was raised when he was appointed the first carrier of the United States mail in Teton Basin, a job he soon tired of. Trafton came and went to a cabin he had on Jackson Lake, and at one time he appears to have made the acquaintance of Owen Wister, who had a summer home in Jackson Hole and used the Tetons as a backdrop for his novel *The Virginian.* Although Trafton frequently boasted that the hero of the book was modeled after himself, there is little doubt that if Wister used him at all it was as the model for the villain, Trampus, whose name is somewhat similar to Trafton and who, as delineated by Wister, would also not have been above robbing his own mother.

While serving time in 1887, Trafton and a partner broke out of prison with a revolver that had been smuggled to them, but they were quickly recaptured and given extended sentences. Only after his mother had worked long and hard to have his sentence reduced was she successful, and in time her son found a way to express his gratitude. Many years and several prison terms later, Trafton, upon learning of his father's death, returned home to find his mother with ten thousand dollars of insurance money in the house, which she asked him to deposit in a bank. Not surprisingly, the money never got there. Trafton claimed he was robbed on the way to the bank, a story so improbable that even his mother could not believe it, so she had him arrested and sent back to prison. When he was finally released, he returned to the Jackson Hole region and carried out his boldest crime. With a rifle in hand, he stood by the side of the road through Yellowstone and held up sixteen sightseeing stagecoaches one by one as they came by, making the tourists file past a blanket spread on the ground at his feet and drop their valuables onto it, all the while warning them not to try to cheat "a poor Westerner" or "ye'll get a bullet in you."[2] Although he made a getaway, it was not long before he was tracked down, and once more Ed Trafton was looking at the world from behind bars.

The end of this Jackson Hole version of Jesse James (his boyhood idol) did not come at the hands of a posse or in a saloon gun fight, as might be expected, but in, of all places, Hollywood. Trafton went there in the early 1920s to try to sell the story of his life to the movies and, according to one account, had a heart attack and fell forward dead on a bar. Only it was not the kind of bar customarily associated with rip-roaring Western bad men. It was a soda fountain.

Teton Jackson and Ed Trafton were just two of the outlaws who frequented Jackson Hole during the early years of settlement. There were others, who as long as they behaved themselves while in the valley were also tolerated. On the other hand, lawmen from the outside world were not always greeted with open arms, and understandably so. At least two of the initial homesteaders were wanted men themselves—Dick Turpin, reputedly for murder, and

Ed Trafton, who held up sixteen stagecoaches in one day, at the wheel of a mock automobile in a photographer's studio. *Jackson Hole Museum.*

Iron kettle and skull, macabre mementos of
the triple murder at Deadman's Bar in 1886.
Jackson Hole Museum.

"Uncle Jack" Davis, for manslaughter—both of whom were so well
liked that no one would have wanted them to go to jail. Also, the
Mormon members of the community, an upright, law-abiding
people except when it came to the law forbidding polygamy, had
long been conditioned to cast a wary eye on men who wore stars.
But there was still another reason why Jackson Holers preferred to
administer law and order for themselves rather than have it administered for them from the then county seat of Evanston almost
two hundred miles away. During the very first years of settlement,
when the grisliest killings in all of Jackson Hole's history came to
light, a jury in Evanston so miscarried justice, in the opinion of
Jackson Holers, they decided from then on to take matters of crime
and punishment into their own hands.

On a summer day in 1886, a fishing party floating down the
Snake River rounded a bend where the river cuts by a steep gravel
bank and made a discovery that gave this spot the macabre name it
has been known by ever since, Deadman's Bar. There they saw
three bodies half-submerged in the water, each partly covered with
stones and each bearing the marks of having met a violent end.
One man had been shot twice in the back, another had been struck

in the head with an ax and the third had also died of head wounds evidently inflicted by the same ax. Hurrying on, the fishermen reported the triple murder to residents of the valley, who went to the scene and identified the three men as T. H. Tiggerman, Henry Welter and August Kellenberger, all natives of Germany who had recently come to Jackson Hole from Montana to prospect for gold. To add to the mystery, the fourth partner was missing, a man named John Tonnar, also a German, who had joined the group at the last moment on the promise of sharing whatever gold might be found. Had he also been killed and his body not yet discovered, or was it he who had committed the crime?

A posse was formed and a search began which eventually led over Teton Pass into Teton Basin, where Emile Wolff, the former member of the rescue party sent out to find Lieutenant Doane's expedition, then had a small hay farm. When the posse arrived at Wolff's cabin and asked him whether he knew anything of Tonnar's whereabouts, he was shocked, because he had employed Tonnar a month earlier to cut hay and at that very moment the wanted man was working in one of the fields. Wolff said, "My God! Grab him while you can!" explaining that while Tonnar had lived with him he had always worn his gun or kept it close at hand, a trait Wolff had thought suspicious but had dismissed because he had no reason to think the man dangerous.[3] The posse went to the field and surprised Tonnar while he was on a haystack, capturing him before he could draw his gun and discovering among his possessions a silver watch and a wallet containing twenty-eight dollars, which were thought to have belonged to the murdered partners, although this could not be proved. Tonnar was then taken to the distant county seat of Evanston, where it was assumed that justice would be meted out swiftly. Meanwhile, acting on the belief that they were preserving important evidence for the court, Wolff and another man contributed a further gruesome touch to the episode by going to Deadman's Bar and severing the heads of the victims, then boiling the flesh from the skulls in an iron kettle. Later recovered, the kettle and one of the skulls are now displayed in the Jackson Hole Museum as part of the valley's treasured memorabilia.

As it turned out, justice in Evanston was not only far from swift, but when it did come Jackson Holers felt that it had been badly served. Tonnar was not brought to trial until the following spring, and although he admitted killing the three men he claimed he had done it in self-defense, his story being that they had beaten him in an attempt to make him abandon his stake in the prospecting partnership. He testified that one day, while two of the partners were away from camp, the third quarreled so violently with him that he had to kill him or be killed himself. This may or may not have been true—no one had any way of knowing—but it did not explain how his plea of self-defense applied to his admitted killing of the two other partners, or how he managed to accomplish it with no apparent resistance from them. Dismissing Tonnar's story as a flagrant lie, those who had visited the scene at Deadman's Bar had no question that he had killed all three men while they were asleep, then had rolled the bodies down the gravel bank into the river, hoping they would not be found.

To a man, Jackson Holers were convinced that Tonnar was guilty of murder, and it appears that the judge shared their opinion, but the jury did not see it their way. With no eyewitnesses to the killing and with nothing but circumstantial evidence to go on, the jurors rendered a technically proper but highly unpopular verdict of not guilty. The upshot of the trial was that Tonnar left Evanston on the first freight train and the Jackson Holers returned to their valley embittered against the law in much the same way Beaver Dick Leigh had been years earlier when, for having leveled his rifle at the Lyons sons in self-defense, he had been required to post a three hundred dollar bond. At the time, he had written, "the law in this secton is only a Bilk and god keep me a long ways from it," adding, "we ad ought to ave tryed them by Mountin Law."[4] Angered at Tonnar's acquittal, the people of Jackson Hole would for years to come subscribe wholeheartedly to this view and, rather than turning to far-off Evanston for justice, would resort to "Mountin Law," their euphemism for vigilance committees.*

The incident known as the affair at the Cunningham cabin, which was less than Jackson Hole's shining hour in terms of administering its own brand of law and order, began in the fall of 1892 when Pierce Cunningham was cutting hay at his ranch on Flat Creek. A neighbor introduced him to two "well-spoken, pleasant-appearing" strangers, George Spenser and a younger man named Mike Burnett, who had come into the valley with a herd of horses

---

* During the more than two decades following Tonnar's acquittal, there seems to have been only one occasion when a lawman was called in from the outside world. This was at the time of the "Bannock War" in 1895, and then the call went out only as far as neighboring Teton Basin for the services of Constable William Manning, who had experience as an Indian fighter.

Pierce Cunningham in later years. His ranch near Spread Creek was where the shoot-out with the suspected horse thieves took place. *National Park Service, Grand Teton National Park.*

and now wanted to buy hay for them.[5] While making the arrangements to sell them hay, Cunningham also arranged to let them have the use of a second place he owned, a ranch near Spread Creek toward the northern end of Jackson Hole, where it was agreed they would spend the winter with Cunningham's partner, "Swede" Jackson.

During the winter, rumors that the strangers were horse thieves began to circulate through the valley, with one local rancher saying that he recognized some of the brands on their horses as belonging to a man in Montana. To see for himself, Cunningham snowshoed to the ranch and spent several days with Spenser and Burnett, coming to suspect that the rumors might be true because it looked to him as though a few of the brands had been altered. But he could not be certain, so when he returned home he did not sound any alarm or make any effort to have the men apprehended. Instead, after thinking it over, he merely went back to the ranch to tell Spenser and Burnett to leave.

Not long after Cunningham visited the ranch, a small group snowshoed into the valley over Teton Pass, led by two men named

Williams and Anderson, who presented themselves as lawmen from Montana on the trail of Spenser and Burnett for having stolen horses there. (Some later said Williams and Anderson claimed to be United States marshals.) They and several companions, also ostensibly from Montana, had recruited two volunteers in Teton Basin, and when they asked others to join their posse and go after the alleged horse thieves, eight Jackson Holers signed on. Reaching the ranch before dawn, the heavily-armed men took up positions giving them a clear field of fire on the sod-roofed cabin and a nearby corral, then settled down to wait for the men inside to awaken and come out. By all rights, Spenser and Burnett should not have been in the cabin. They had taken Pierce Cunningham at his word and left the ranch, but the day before the posse arrived they had returned to track down some horses which had either strayed or had been left behind. Now they were asleep along with Cunningham's partner, "Swede" Jackson, unaware they were surrounded.

It all happened very quickly. At dawn, a dog in the cabin began to bark, evidently sensing the presence of the men outside. Spenser got up, strapped on his revolver and went to the corral to see what was wrong. No sooner was he inside than a member of the posse shouted to him to "throw 'em up," and when he instead fired two shots in the direction of the voice, the posse opened fire.[6] As Spenser fell to his knees, emptying his gun, his body was riddled with buckshot and bullets. Burnett then came out of the cabin and was almost hit by a bullet that threw splinters from one of the cabin's logs into his face. Quickly drawing and firing his revolver, he knocked off the hat and creased the scalp of the partially hidden man who had shot at him, then called for those who were out there to show themselves. Meanwhile, from inside the cabin "Swede" Jackson was pleading with Burnett to come back in, and when Burnett turned to enter the door he was struck by a bullet and killed instantly. The shooting was over. All that remained to be done was to bury the bodies in unmarked graves, from which, as Raold Fryxell wrote in his account of the shoot-out, "Years later badgers threw out some of their bones into the sunlight."[7]

Doubts soon set in about what had happened at Pierce Cunningham's cabin. Not only did those who had joined the posse refuse to talk about it except to relatives and close friends, but their neighbors were equally tight-lipped, seldom discussing the matter among themselves and never with outsiders. Over half a century later, when Raold Fryxell wrote about the incident from notes previously made by his father of conversations with early settlers, the subject was still so sensitive he deliberately avoided giving the names of the members of the posse, many of whose sons and daughters still lived in the valley. The reason for this secretiveness was that shortly after the self-proclaimed lawmen rode away with the dead men's horses, Jackson Holers began to wonder whether Spenser and Burnett had been horse thieves after all. Further, they began to wonder whether the men from Montana were authentic lawmen or were themselves horse thieves who had duped those they had recruited for the posse into believing they were acting in the name of the law. To add to the gathering cloud of suspicion, no one could remember having seen any warrants for arrest, and although there were varying recollections as to whether Williams and Anderson had carried credentials, even those who said they had could not say exactly what kind of credentials they were.

The residents of Jackson Hole now found themselves with a delicate problem on their hands. If the lawmen had been imposters, then the local members of the posse had abetted horse thieves, or, worse yet, had helped to commit murder. This could lead to friends and neighbors having to stand trial in distant Evanston, where it was not believed that justice was to be found, so the already close society of Jackson Hole drew even more closely together and tacitly agreed to keep the matter quiet. No inquest was held, nor were the shootings even reported at the county seat. Instead, a curtain of silence descended on the Cunningham cabin affair.

To this day, no one knows whether or not the two lawmen were legitimate. But one fact is known: although it is possible they were local sheriffs from Montana, they were not United States marshals, for research done by a recent writer reveals that there were no federal marshals named Williams and Anderson in Montana at that time. The same writer, Elizabeth Wied Hayden, also found an old newspaper story dating back to 1909 in which Pierce Cunningham, who had refused to join the posse, stated his belief that what had occurred at his cabin was an offshoot of the Johnson County War of 1892, when the Wyoming Stock Growers Association imported gunmen from Texas to rid the central and northern part of the state of rustlers, as well as to harass smaller ranchers who were a thorn in the sides of the cattle barons. According to Cunningham, the men who tracked Spenser and Burnett to Jackson Hole, pretending to be lawmen, were nothing more nor less than hired killers who for one reason or another had been paid to do a job. While Cunningham may or may not have been right, he was not

Mose Giltner, a member of the posse at the Cunningham cabin, who later had second thoughts about the legitimacy of the shootings. *Courtesy John Ryan.*

alone in suspecting that all had not been what it appeared to be. A member of the posse named Mose Giltner later had second thoughts, which unlike the others he did not keep to himself. Fully accepting responsibility for his role in the shoot-out, he had the courage and honesty to say, "It was just plain murder."[8]

Still another puzzling aspect of this possibly dark chapter in Jackson Hole's history is that whereas known horse thieves such as Teton Jackson and Ed Trafton enjoyed a free run of the valley, two men who were only suspected horse thieves were not even given the opportunity to tell their side of the story. It was later recalled that from the start the posse's plan had been to shoot to kill, not to take the two suspects alive, an action which can be only partially explained on the basis that Spenser and Burnett, unlike Jackson and Trafton, were strangers. Moreover, even though Jackson Holers continued to have nagging doubts as to whether justice had been done or had been abused, they still did not question the practice of "Mountin Law." As other problems having to do with local law and order arose, Jackson Holers stubbornly persisted in the belief that they, not the authorities in Evanston, were best equipped to deal with them. Tonnar's acquittal in the slayings at Deadman's Bar had indeed left its mark.

While horse thieves and cattle rustlers ranked high on the list of undesirables in the West of the late 1800s, ranchers reserved the number one position for a group of men who broke no laws of any kind but all the same were detested with a passion it is hard to imagine in our time, the sheepmen. Because of the way sheep eat grass, nibbling it down almost to the roots so cattle cannot reach it, and also because their sharp hooves damage the root system, these otherwise harmless animals were viewed as the destroyers of the open range, the source of most ranchers' livelihoods. In Jackson Hole, where the economy was based on elk as well as cattle, both of which require extensive grazing lands, so strong was the loathing for sheep that it is said some residents refused to wear woolen socks and that children, seeing a lamb for the first time, were dumbfounded, not knowing what kind of an animal it was. Despite this animosity, when sheepmen attempted to bring their flocks into the valley and vigilance committees were formed to keep them out, no one was killed in the tense confrontations that took place, which is more than can be said for other sections of Wyoming, where sheepherders were often "bushwhacked." To this extent, the deaths of Spenser and Burnett may still have been on the community's conscience, causing Jackson Holers to think twice before pulling triggers.

There were at least three instances when the people of Jackson Hole practiced "Mountin Law" against the sheepmen. The first was in 1896, when sheepherders from Idaho drove four thousand sheep over Teton Pass, ignoring posted notices reading:

Sheep Men Warning
We will not permit sheep to graze upon the elk range
in Jackson's Hole. Govern yourselves accordingly.
Signed: the Settlers of Jackson's Hole [9]

This is one of the earliest recorded expressions of concern about the well-being of the elk herd, a concern partly based on mercenary reasons, to be sure, but also reflecting a growing awareness that the destiny of the elk herd and the destiny of the valley were somehow intertwined. While it is doubtful the sheepmen understood the significance of this reference to the elk, it is almost certain they had planned their invasion of Jackson Hole well in advance, because upon reaching the Snake River they quickly assembled a bridge of wagon bodies piled high with brush, across which they began to pass the sheep into the main part of the valley. What they had not planned on was the swift and formidable greeting they received from a vigilance committee. With guns in hand, which they gave every sign of being willing to use, grim-faced Jackson Holers suddenly appeared and demolished the bridge, then ordered those sheep which had not yet crossed the river to be herded back to Idaho and those which had already crossed to be herded to the east. Prohibiting any grazing along the way, they escorted the sheepmen with the flocks that had already passed over the bridge out of the valley through the canyon of the Gros Ventre River, a route leading to high and inhospitable country for men and sheep alike.

Two years later, in 1898, forty armed sheepmen came up from Utah with flocks numbering in the tens of thousands, intending to graze them in Jackson Hole. Met by a hastily assembled group of defenders, some sixty-five in all, the Utahans backed off and herded their sheep to the Green River country. There irate cattlemen were not nearly as restrained in their treatment of the trespassers, serving their warning in blood, not with posted notices, by killing eight hundred sheep and beating up a herder.

When violence against the sheepmen finally did break out in Jackson Hole, it was at the hands of a small number of vigilantes who hid their identities behind masks. This was a departure from the usual procedure in which "citizens' committees" (a term Jackson Holers preferred to the word "vigilantes") operated openly and with the approval of their neighbors. Why these men covered their faces is not known, but they may have sensed that the severity

Charlie "Beaver Tooth" Neil, the artful poacher who wore his snowshoes backwards to mislead game wardens into thinking he had gone in the opposite direction. *W. C. "Slim" Lawrence Collection*.

of the punishment they intended to hand out did not fit the crime and they would be frowned on by others in the valley. Whatever the reason, early one morning in 1901 a sheepherder who had brought his large flock into the Mosquito Creek area was seized at the point of guns by three masked men, who tied him to a tree and whipped him. While this was going on, others shot three hundred of his sheep, killed his horse and dog, then set fire to his camp. Although the herder escaped with his life, he was frightened to within an inch of it, and he quickly went out of the valley, leaving some of his sheep scattered throughout the countryside. Brutal as it was, and far from being even quasi-legal, this action seems to have had the desired effect, for from then on no further attempts to graze sheep in Jackson Hole were reported.

Because Charlie "Beaver Tooth" Neil was not a horse thief or a suspected murderer, he cannot be accorded major league status in the annals of crime in Jackson Hole. He was, however, such an artful poacher whose exploits so delighted everyone, except game wardens, that he became a legend in his time. Year after year, with the full knowledge of all that he was illegally trapping beaver and smuggling their pelts out of the valley, he kept Jackson Holers guessing as to what inventive new scheme he would come up with next to throw the frustrated wardens off his trail. For a while, by wearing his snowshoes backwards when working his traps, he misled the wardens into tracking him in the opposite direction from which he had come—a good stunt, until one day his dog followed him and its pawmarks in the snow revealed the true direction "Beaver Tooth" had gone. Even so, it does not appear that the wardens were able to catch him in the act of poaching. On another occasion, he had his wife appear in the town of Jackson and angrily announce to a game warden that "Beaver Tooth" had struck her and she was leaving him for good. When she told the warden that her husband was about to smuggle a large shipment of pelts out of the valley, he was so grateful for the information that he solicitously loaded Mrs. Neil's luggage on the departing stagecoach. As it turned out, of course, Mrs. Neil's luggage contained the smuggled pelts.

"Beaver Tooth" in no way threatened Jackson Hole's cattle or its elk, so his antics could be laughed at. But the reaction was entirely different when a group of men came into the valley and began slaying elk by the thousands just for the two ivory canine teeth, called tusks, each elk grows in its upper jaw. Then Jackson Holers, perceiving this as a crime against nature as well as against the future of the valley, rose up in wrath. And while the story of the measures they took to rid their country of these predators is a fitting close to an account of "Mountin Law" in Jackson Hole, it more properly belongs within the framework of a more important story—that of the long struggle to save the largest elk herd in the world from the various perils which beset it over many years.

17

The Elk Herd

The shy, graceful and magnificently antlered animal we Americans call an elk is not, strictly speaking, an elk at all, but a wapiti, while the animal we call a moose should be known as an elk. The reason for this confusion is that when the first Europeans came to this continent and saw wapiti, they somehow mistook these light-colored members of the deer family to be a form of moose, an animal known in Germany as "elch" and in Norway as "elg."[1] The Indian word "wapiti" was completely ignored, leaving this animal that is closely related to the red deer of Europe with the misnomer "elk." On the other hand, the Indian word "moose" was applied to the animal the Europeans should have called "elk." By now it is much too late to set this topsy-turvy matter right, and as Olaus Murie, the great naturalist, wrote with resignation, "I suppose the wapiti will continue to be called elk in North America, while in far-away New Zealand the animals that have been introduced from Jackson Hole and Yellowstone are called by their correct North American Indian name, 'wapiti'!"[2]

The elk, like man, did not come into being in the Americas. Evolving in central Asia, herds of the original species drifted in the course of eons until they were dispersed over the upper half of the globe. Some wandered west to the rim of North Africa and into Europe, where they became the red deer, while others ventured east, crossing an early Bering land bridge to become the elk of North America. By the time the first Europeans arrived and mis-named them, elk were spread over the greater part of what would become the United States, although there is no evidence that they penetrated in numbers quite as far east as to Atlantic coastal waters or very deeply into the southern tier of states. One theory holds that they were primarily plains animals until driven into the moun-tains by the advancing frontier. Another suggests that some herds had already made their home in high and wooded places in the Rocky Mountains well before then, a theory borne out to some extent by the journals of the mountain men who, ranging far ahead

Early Stephen Leek photograph of just a small part of the elk herd wintering in Jackson Hole. *S. N. Leek Collection, Western History Research Center, University of Wyoming.*

of the leading edge of civilization, found elk, though apparently not in abundance, in the region of Jackson Hole and Yellowstone. Perhaps for as many as five hundred years the elk have grazed in summer in the high country of Yellowstone, then have sought lower and more sheltered sites when the first heavy snows fell.* Certainly within the memory of man they have, with thousands of them annually migrating down to their favorite winter range, Jackson Hole and its outlying areas.

For years, the elk grazed along the fertile bottom lands, particularly in the vicinity of Flat Creek, where the National Elk Refuge is now located, pawing through the usually shallow snow there to reach the nourishing grasses and wild hay. But then the valley began

* It is generally assumed that elk and moose were in Jackson Hole long before men, even early men, arrived. However, Charles M. Love of the Department of Anthropology and Geology at Western Wyoming College states that in all probability "elk are very recent arrivals from the east, most likely within the last 500 years." To this he adds: "We know from historical accounts and tracings the moose did not arrive before 1865." (Letter to the author, January 30, 1975)

to be settled, so as the long columns of elk returned each fall they found more and more of their grazing grounds turned into cultivated fields from which the hay had been cut and stacked, leaving only stubble. Still, for a number of years there was enough forage in the valley to sustain the herd, and it was only when extreme winters brought abnormal depths of snow, or when the snow became so thickly crusted it could not be pawed through, that serious losses were suffered. These conditions occurred in the winters of 1887 and 1898, and although some ranchers doled out as much hay as they could spare to the starving animals, many thousands perished. Not until somewhat later, however, did the winter feeding of the herd come to be viewed as a critical problem. At the turn of the century, the major concern of Jackson Holers for the preservation of the elk was focused on what they perceived to be human, rather than natural, threats—first the Indians, who were thrown out of the valley; then the sheepmen, who were kept out of the valley; and finally the so-called "tuskers," whose ruthless slaughter of the elk for their canine teeth reached such proportions the residents decided that they, too, had to be dealt with by means of "Mountin Law."

With what has been estimated as upwards of sixty thousand elk wintering in or near Jackson Hole during the early years of settlement, the poaching of an extra bull or cow was not considered the most reprehensible of crimes. It was therefore not unusual for otherwise respectable Jackson Holers to exceed their legal limit of two elk a year, using the meat and hides to feed and clothe their families. But occasional poaching by residents and organized poaching by outsiders were viewed as two quite different matters. When, in the late 1890s, a group of men built hideaway cabins in the northern end of the valley and began killing elk both in large numbers and out of season, selling the meat in Idaho, the acting superintendent of Yellowstone National Park became so incensed he proposed that federal protection of the herd be extended south into Jackson Hole. It was foolish, he pointed out, for army troops to enforce no-hunting regulations while the elk were on their summer range in the park only to have them walk into a hail of bullets when they migrated into the upper reaches of the valley. As with most words of wisdom, they at first went unheeded, and the poaching continued despite efforts by some Jackson Holers to help the few state game wardens carry out the Wyoming law. Others also advocated that federal protection be given the herd when it moved south, but to no avail, and not until 1905 did the Wyoming legislature act on its own, creating the Teton Game Preserve, a tract of almost six hundred thousand acres extending from Yellowstone to Jackson Hole, in which no hunting was allowed. As enlightened as this measure was, in the opinion of many it was doubtful that it could be enforced, because by then a new breed of killers had come into the valley, casehardened men who were not afraid to flaunt the law openly and were not above intimidating both the wardens and the residents in order to kill elk solely for their teeth.

It is odd that Jackson Hole's elk came to be threatened with extinction in the early 1900s for the same reason its beaver had been back in the 1830s, a vogue in what men wore. It is also odd that the vogue was brought about by people who called themselves, of all things, Elks—more specifically, the Benevolent and Protective Order of Elks. Unfortunately for the animals, the two ivory canine teeth, or tusks, which become especially large and well formed in the bulls, were adopted as emblems of the lodge and worn by members in the form of watch fobs, rings and cuff links. Also, unfortunately for the animals, as the fad became more popular the tusks became more valuable, until a good pair brought about twenty-five dollars and an outstanding pair as much as one hundred dollars. At first, this was a windfall for Jackson Holers, for with the largest herd of elk in the world wintering on their doorsteps, residents were assured of four tusks each merely by observing the legal limit of two elk to a hunter. In addition, hundreds and sometimes even thousands of elk died of starvation or natural causes each year, and during one winter a thousand elk were reported to have been killed by wolves. It was therefore simple enough for residents to carry pliers in their pockets and extract the tusks from the jaws of the carcasses to be found here and there. But the windfall was too good to last. Soon Jackson Holers noticed bands of strangers coming into the valley, and shortly thereafter they began to realize that not only was the future of the elk herd being endangered, but their own future as well.

By this time, the elk herd had become an integral part of the lives of the people of Jackson Hole, and not entirely for commercial reasons. While guiding hunters provided the principal source of income for many residents, there were other reasons the herd was valued as something the valley would be much the worse for losing. Some had come to view the elk as a priceless natural wonder, a symbol, like the Tetons themselves, of the unique character of the

A tusker's cabin discovered at the head of Jackson Lake in 1960 by Verba and "Slim" Lawrence. *W. C. "Slim" Lawrence Collection.*

wilderness country in which they made their homes. To others, the elk provided a bridge to the outside world, drawing in hunters from the East, Europe and elsewhere, whose dollars were welcome, to be sure, but whose regular return was also looked forward to as a connection with what was going on "out there." Even those who stood to lose by the presence of the elk, such as ranchers whose haystacks were often raided by the hungry animals, had come to recognize the need to keep the herd intact. One of them, a rancher named James Chambers, expressed this feeling when he said, "These pesky elk have caused us so much grief in the past few years, I almost wish I had never seen one of them, but we have to protect them, even if they are eating us right out of house and barn."[3] Although the tuskers did not know it, the elk had many friends in Jackson Hole.

One by one, Jackson Holers had experiences which made it clear the strangers were not ordinary hunters. Stephen Leek, who lived on Jackson Lake, wrote, "One evening at dusk in early spring I was returning home from Jackson upon the public road when a shot was fired on the mountainside above. Looking up I saw outlined against the twilight sky an elk who staggered and then fell. A man walked up to it and it tried to rise and then lay still. The next day I climbed to the place and found the elk—with only its teeth taken."[4] Another resident, snowshoeing through an isolated part of the valley, came upon the bodies of eighteen bulls with only their tusks missing. And James Chambers, who had been finding more and more carcasses untouched in every way except for the tusks, was almost killed when "A bullet passed right over my head, and an elk dropped dead within a few yards of me."[5] What had been curiosity about the strangers quickly turned to alarm as it was driven home to the people of Jackson Hole that the elk herd was being seriously depleted, especially the larger and more mature bulls.

So heavy was the destruction that one of the tusker gangs is estimated to have killed sixteen hundred elk, while another source estimates that "in one winter tuskers killed more elk and left them to rot than were killed in ten years of normal hunting."[6] To make matters worse, the tuskers became more brutal and more brazen. They drove elk into deep drifts of snow, where they foundered, then pulled out the tusks from the still living animals. What is more, in a bar in the town of Jackson three of them openly boasted they were going "to hang a game warden's hide on the fence."[7] Although the warden walked into the bar and faced them down, the few wardens in the valley were badly outnumbered and the carnage continued until the winter of 1906. Then Jackson Holers, deciding that enough was enough, formed a vigilance committee to deal with the problem in a typically direct, no-nonsense way.

At the committee meeting held in the Clubhouse, a social center in Jackson, Otho Williams voiced the temper of Jackson Holers when he said, "If there is anyone present who is not willing to take hold of the end of a rope, he can get up and leave this meeting."[8] Not a man left. Before the meeting ended, however, cooler heads prevailed and the summary hanging of the tuskers was voted down in favor of issuing an ultimatum ordering them to clear out of the valley within forty-eight hours or be shot.

As bold and full of brag as the tuskers had been, the chilling warning that if they remained in Jackson Hole they would be "left dead in your tracks for the scavengers to devour" made them quickly agree to leave within the allotted time.[9] But first, they loaded a wagon with trophy heads and sent one of their number to Jackson to report the fictitious killing of a game warden in the northern end of the valley. When the settlers fell for the ruse and

Stephen Leek's photographs, such as this taken of dead elk after the winter of 1908–09, brought the plight of the starving Jackson Hole elk to the attention of the American public. *S. N. Leek Collection, Western History Research Center, University of Wyoming.*

rushed there, the tuskers escaped with most of their loot, crossing over the Tetons into Idaho and taking a train to California, from which two of the leaders were later extradited, tried and fined. That was the end of tusking on a large and organized scale. And it also marked the end of "Mountin Law" in Jackson Hole, because no more vigilance committees were formed, the people having apparently decided that the time had come to leave the administration of law and order in the hands of duly appointed officials.

The next year, 1907, the Wyoming legislature made tusking a felony. This, along with more stringent enforcement of game laws and the discontinuance by the Elks of canine teeth as emblems, assured the survival of the herd, or at least assured that it would not be gunned out of existence. But the problem of starvation remained. It soon became evident that with the spread of ranching in the valley there was not enough winter carrying capacity for the elk, who suffered terribly, particularly when heavy snows covered the natural forage to an unusual depth. After severe winters, elk carcasses were to be found by the thousands, and stories from those days recount the plight of the animals in heartrending detail. One settler wrote, "I have walked for a mile on dead elk lying from one to four deep," going on to say that a rancher he knew "pulled 450

Hungry elk raiding a haystack many years ago. *Bruce Porter Collection*.

dead elk off his hay meadow."[10] Another wrote, "Darkening the snow in all directions . . . were pitiful tawny patches that marked where a bull or a cow or a calf had fallen . . . their ribs so visible that you wonder why they haven't broken through the taut skin."[11] Driven beyond fear of man by hunger, the elk knocked down specially built high fences around haystacks, jumped through barn windows in an attempt to eat with the cattle and, in one instance, walked up to a cabin door and ate the bristles off a new broom. So desperate did the animals become that they even invaded the streets of Jackson in search of food. One account says, "Big bulls, ribs showing, eyes feverish, unafraid, forced their way into the stables, became a menace to the citizens. Schoolchildren were kept from school; households were besieged."[12]

The people of Jackson Hole were deeply troubled by the suffering they saw all around them, but there was little they could do to relieve it. While many ranchers generously spread out some hay, there was not nearly enough to meet the need, what with thousands of elk roaming the countryside, each capable of consuming at least seven pounds a day. Moreover, the ranchers themselves were faced with disaster as the hunger-crazed animals ripped into their haystacks and devoured huge amounts of the precious fodder before they could be driven off. One vignette of the damage the elk did is given by Bertha Chambers Gillette in her book *Homesteading with the Elk*, where she tells of her mother breaking into tears as she stood helplessly and watched a herd depart at sunup after having demolished a haystack that had been counted on to see the family's cattle through the winter. The valley had become truly besieged: the residents by the animals they had grown to appreciate as a vital part of their country and their lives, and the elk by the worst killer of all, starvation.*

The turning point in the fate of the elk came in 1909, when the Wyoming legislature appropriated five thousand dollars for the purchase of hay. Although the amount was far too small to feed more than a fraction of the famished animals, it did provide the basis for a winter feeding program, which was gradually increased as Congress became aware of the problem. In 1911, Congress appropriated twenty thousand dollars for feeding purposes, and the following year founded the National Elk Refuge by authorizing the purchase of almost two thousand acres of private meadows on the outskirts of the town of Jackson. To this another thousand acres of public land were added, thereby forming the nucleus of what would eventually become a huge sanctuary to which the elk could return each winter. While this was a milestone in the preservation of the elk (and in the history of American conservation), and although other parcels of land were added from time to time, many years would pass before enough land would be set aside to support the main body of the herd. Until then, hard winters continued to take a toll, but on nowhere near the scale of what had happened before. To all intents and purposes, the herd had been saved from the danger of becoming extinct through mass starvation. Danger from humans, however, continued to be a threat. During World War I, a group advanced the incredibly asinine proposal to kill off the elk and send the meat in cans to the doughboys in France. Fortunately, nothing came of it.

More than any other man, Stephen Leek brought about the government action that saved the elk. And he did it primarily with an

---

* One rancher hung a lantern from the fence around his haystack and found that the light frightened the elk, at least at first. Then, before going to bed one night, he looked out the window and saw the light of the lantern bobbing in the darkness, a spectral glow moving across the fields. What had happened is that a bull elk had hooked the lantern on his antlers, and there it remained all winter as he ranged up and down the valley, becoming locally famous as "the lantern bull."

instrument only then beginning to come into its own as a powerful shaper of public opinion, the camera. One of Jackson Hole's first settlers, Leek arrived in 1888, later married Nick Wilson's daughter and still later built a hunting lodge on Jackson Lake. By 1907, he was in the state legislature, where he is credited with having introduced the bill making tusking a felony, and in the following years he wrote and lectured tirelessly in an effort to call the winter-ravaged conditions of the elk to the attention of the nation. But it was his pictures more than his words that dramatized the plight of the elk and led to the program which saved them. By climbing into haystacks and lying in wait for hours, by dressing in white so his movements against the snow would be less visible and even by painting his camera white, Leek was able to get close enough to shoot some of the most remarkable photographs of elk ever taken. When these appeared in magazines and newspapers across the country, the sight of the pathetic animals so shocked the public that Congress was forced to act, first with an appropriation for hay, then with an appropriation for land and finally to make the herd a ward of the Department of the Interior, which to this day shares the responsibility for managing and feeding the herd with the Game and Fish Commission of Wyoming. This forward-looking man, who saw before others that one of this continent's greatest natural gifts had to be preserved, is now forgotten, yet few more than he deserve a niche in the conservation hall of fame, if one is ever built.

As time went on, the National Elk Refuge was enlarged by bits and pieces, but it was still much too small to provide a satisfactory winter range for all the elk, whose numbers in the mid-1920s were estimated at twenty thousand head. After a few especially bad winters when many died, there again was an outcry about the starving elk of Jackson Hole, and in 1927 the Izaak Walton League raised funds to buy approximately two thousand acres of grazing land adjoining the Refuge. While national publicity was given the herd and its benefactors, no notice was given a young government biologist who arrived in the valley the same year and who, just as Stephen Leek had done earlier, would play the central role in once more saving the elk, this time from a baffling malady then reducing the herd at an alarming rate. Sent down from Alaska, where he had conducted an extensive study of the caribou, Olaus Murie's instructions from the United States Bureau of Biological Survey were to study all aspects of the life of the elk in order to develop a more effective program for their management. In time, this is what

Elk calf suffering from *Necrotic stomatitus*, the disease which until identified by Olaus Murie greatly depleted the elk herd in the 1920s. *Photo by Olaus Murie, February, 1928*.

Stephen Leek feeding elk during the winter of 1919–20. *U.S. Forest Service*.

he did, later publishing the landmark work *The Elk of North America*. But at first his most pressing assignment was to discover why so many elk were dying in a strange way, first taking on a wasted, drooping appearance, then having difficulty breathing, then becoming too weak to stand, until at last they would lie down and die.

Murie followed the elk in all the seasons, to the high country in summer and to various parts of the Refuge in winter, where he performed autopsies on hundreds of the sprawled bodies, patiently recording symptoms and collecting blood and tissue specimens. At last, he verified his theory that the elk were dying of a disease, *Necrotic stomatitis*, caused by a bacillus which invaded the animals when coarse forage or the sharp fibers of willow branches opened lesions in their mouths. He determined that the problem was brought about by both an overcrowded range, which forced the elk to browse farther down on branches than they would normally do, and the feeding of foxtail hay, a variety with unusually sharp awns. A new form of hay was substituted immediately, but the other part of the solution—the expansion of the Refuge so the elk could spread out and graze on only natural forage—was longer in coming. Once it did, through government purchases and private gifts that by 1935 had increased the Refuge to its present size of 23,754 acres, the elk prospered.

Olaus Murie was an unusual man. Not only a first-rate scientist and one of this country's foremost naturalists, he was also an excellent writer and artist. His fondness for the animals he studied comes through these words he later wrote describing his delight, while he was still trying to solve the mystery, when spring came and those elk not afflicted with the disease began their migration out of the valley.

> *After a winter of living with the wapiti through their dark days— watching them die, examining them, working in snow and blizzard and below-zero cold, trudging home across the fields night after night with cold and bloody hands and a few more unpleasant data in my notebook—you can imagine my joy at the spring release of the survivors out onto the greening hillsides, up through the aspen groves, and on north to first verdure and new smooth red-brown coats and the endless freedom of the summer world.*[13]

Today the elk of Jackson Hole have little to fear, except in autumn when the guns of the hunters begin booming in the hills. In some seasons more than six thousand have been killed, a statistic

Margaret and Olaus Murie. *Photo by Phyllis Stevie.*

which standing by itself could lead one to think the elk are again being ravaged to the point of oblivion. But this is not the case. With the herd sometimes totaling nearly fifteen thousand animals, an annual thinning is necessary to keep them from multiplying at such a rate they would soon exceed not only the natural feeding capacity of the Refuge, where from seven to eight thousand usually gather, but also the natural feeding capacity of the widely scattered canyons and bottom lands in and around the valley, where the balance of the herd winters. And even when the snow becomes too deep or too thickly crusted for them to reach the natural forage, the elk no longer starve, for alfalfa pellets are spread out in the Refuge and at several other feeding stations in the area. Having survived wolves, tuskers, starvation and disease, the elk herd of Jackson Hole is now well protected and well fed, its future secure.

Years ago, Donald Hough wrote, "The elk herd is the greatest single thing about the valley," and in many ways he was right, although the statement should be amended to include the Tetons as well.[14] Nonetheless, the elk are so much a part of the life and consciousness of Jackson Hole their importance cannot be adequately described, other than to say that it is impossible to imagine Jackson Hole being Jackson Hole without them. They also happen to be, oddly enough, the source of funds for the local Boy Scout troop. Every spring, after the male elk have shed their antlers (they quickly regrow another pair), the boys are allowed to enter the Refuge and pick them up by the truckload. They are then sold at public auction in the town square of Jackson, the highest bidders often being gentlemen from the Orient, where the antlers in powdered form are highly valued as an aphrodisiac. Of all the curiosities about Jackson Hole, few are more curious than that the Boy Scouts, although innocently enough, traffic in love potions, and that some of the fallen antlers of the elk are returned each year to Asia, the land from which so many millennia ago these animals the Indians called wapiti came.

18
The Angry Years

As early as 1898, the director of the United States Geological Survey recommended that Jackson Hole either be added to Yellowstone National Park or be made a separate park, but nothing came of it. By the time the subject was broached again, a large part of the valley was settled and privately owned, thereby posing a special problem that until then no other national park had had to face. As a result, Jackson Hole became the battleground on which was contested for more than thirty years what has been called "one of the most remarkable conservation fights of the twentieth century."[1] Remarkable it was, and bitter, too, because before it was over the people of the valley were pitted against one another, commercial interests were pitted against the then still thin ranks of conservationists, the Forest Service was pitted against the National Park Service, states' righters were pitted against the federal government and the greater part of the American press was pitted against President Franklin D. Roosevelt.

In 1916, when the National Park Service was first established as a division of the Department of the Interior, Stephen Mather, who had made his fortune promoting Twenty Mule Team Borax and had "an itch for public service," was chosen to be its director.[2] He, in turn, chose as one of his assistants a dynamic young man named Horace Albright, who before his career was over would leave as lasting a personal imprint as any man on the nation's parks and the policies governing them. In July of 1916, these two made an overnight trip south from Yellowstone to take their first look at the Tetons and Jackson Hole, and what they saw so impressed them they decided on the spot that both the mountains and the valley should be added to Yellowstone National Park. What they did not see was the opposition their plan would later run into from many different sources, including the Department of Agriculture's Forest Service, which in 1908 had been placed in charge of the Teton National Forest, embracing not only large timber lands around Jackson Hole, but also the Tetons themselves.

Mather and Albright were not long in enlisting others in their cause, notably Wyoming Senator Frank Mondell, who in 1918 introduced a bill in Congress to extend Yellowstone Park's boundaries south to include the Tetons and all the land reaching down to the northern end of Jackson Hole. The bill passed the House of Representatives and looked as though it would breeze through the Senate, but it was unexpectedly blocked there by Senator John Nugent of Idaho, whose sheep-raising constituents feared that the new park would not allow them to continue grazing their flocks on the western side of the Tetons, as was permitted by the Forest Service.*

The following year, Albright became the first National Park Service superintendent of Yellowstone Park (until then administered by the War Department), and Mondell reintroduced his bill in an amended form both he and Albright thought would appease the Idaho sheepmen. To encourage support for the bill, Albright appeared on a summer evening in the town of Jackson before a group of about one hundred people, mostly dude ranchers, cattlemen and Forest Service employees. By this time, he and Mather had perfected a more or less canned speech they delivered to residents of areas being considered for national park status, the substance of which was that everyone would profit from the inflow of tourists and the improvement of roads the establishment of a park would bring. Usually, the speech was well received, but now it boomeranged. To Albright's shocked surprise, he was "almost hooted off the platform."[3]

The dude ranchers, led by Struthers Burt, who was both a dude rancher and a nationally known writer, lashed out at the thought of their valley being opened to hordes of tourists in automobiles, demanding accommodations in fancy hotels. It would, they said, destroy the frontier atmosphere and drive away the kind of people who enjoyed vacationing on dude ranches. The cattlemen also angrily opposed the plan, questioning the sincerity of the promise that grazing rights in the valley, then granted by the Forest Service, would be continued by the new park. Although the Forest Service employees sat in silence, not joining in the attacks, they also disap-

---

* Historically, the two services have had differing philosophies as to how public lands should be managed. The National Park Service is committed to conservation and purely recreational use, exclusive of hunting. The Forest Service tends to believe in multiple use, with its lands open to recreation of all kinds, as well as to commercial interests, on a permit basis, for logging, mining, oil and gas drilling, hydroelectric power and the grazing of sheep and cattle.

In 1920, Jackson was the first community in the United States to elect an all-female slate of town officials. *Teton County Chapter, Wyoming State Historical Society.*

proved, fearing the loss of their jobs if the Park Service were to take over a large part of the lands for which they were responsible. When the meeting ended after midnight, the new superintendent of Yellowstone Park was so battered that the rancher who drove him to his place to spend the night compared the ride to "taking Jess Willard home," a reference to the recent boxing match in which Jack Dempsey had knocked out the former champion in the third round.[4] Faced with this incident in Jackson Hole and growing opposition to the park idea elsewhere across the state, Senator Mondell decided that it would be best for his political career to withdraw his bill.

The "Roaring Twenties" fully lived up to their name in the town of Jackson, where despite Prohibition and state laws against gambling, a drink was always to be had and the sound of dice chattering, roulette balls clicking and cards being slapped on tables could clearly be heard coming from back rooms.* But while life was lively

* Even the good ladies of Jackson did not seem to mind the drinking and gambling, for when in 1920 the town voters put into office the first all-female slate ever elected by any municipality in the country, the new officials devoted their attention to more important matters, such as the improvement of streets and the acquisition of land for a cemetery. What is more, they did such a good job they were returned to office in the next election.

in Jackson, the issue of extending Yellowstone Park south into Jackson Hole quieted down. Albright continued to cherish his dream, only now he changed his tactics, moving from an outspoken and aggressive role to a behind-the-scenes position, where he patiently cultivated important state officials and influential men in the valley, hoping to convince them as he had already convinced the editor of the *Saturday Evening Post* that "the best part of Yellowstone Park is not yet in the park."[5] However, it was not so much his efforts that caused a number of Jackson Holers to revise their thinking about the future of their country as it was a series of separate and unrelated developments which began when a severe drought hit the West.

At the time the drought drove up prices for winter hay, the boom market created for beef by World War I collapsed, so by the early 1920s the prosperous cattlemen of just a few years earlier were on the edge of bankruptcy. As Albright said later, now "They wanted to sell their places. They wanted to sell them very badly."[6] Still another reason to think twice about what the future might hold in store arose when, contrary to the wishes of many Jackson Holers, tourists began to invade their valley, inspiring some local entrepreneurs to erect gasoline stations, cheap overnight cabins and hot dog stands along the road at the base of the Tetons, particularly near Jenny Lake at the foot of the Grand Teton itself. This shabby commercialism was bad enough, but it was yet another development that so enraged Struthers Burt and other dude ranchers that they decided to fight to protect Jackson Hole from further exploitation, and in this fight they discovered their most steadfast allies to be Horace Albright and the National Park Service.

In the early 1920s, a private group made a secret filing at the capitol in Cheyenne to obtain permission to dam Jenny Lake and nearby Leigh Lake, two of the loveliest lakes in all of Jackson Hole, with a plan in mind to sell the water in Idaho. When Struthers Burt became aware of the scheme, he began to expose it as a threat both to the water supply of northwestern Wyoming and to the basic topography of the valley itself. As unsightly as tourist cabins and hot dog stands might be, they could be torn down if and when the time came, but concrete dams, dredged channels cut through the countryside and artificially enlarged lakes containing thousands of trees killed by the raised waters would scar the face of the landscape forever. Quietly, but effectively, Horace Albright supported the campaign of Burt and other dude ranchers, bringing National Park Service pressure to bear, with the result that the Wyoming

State Engineer finally refused to give the private interests permission to go ahead. The lakes were saved and Horace Albright had at last made some friends in Jackson Hole.

By now Struthers Burt had moved a long way from the hostile position he had taken against the park proposal when Horace Albright first presented it. So fearful had he become of what the exploiters might try next that he wrote, "I am afraid for my own country unless some help is given it—some wise direction. It is too beautiful and now too famous. Sometimes I dream of it unhappily."[7] There were others who shared his foreboding, a few of whom gathered under the kerosene lamps of a store in Jackson and discussed ways the still primitive character of the valley might be preserved. Out of these concerns came what has since been acclaimed an historic meeting in the destiny of Jackson Hole. On a July evening in 1923, in Maud Noble's cabin on the banks of the Snake River in the village of Moose, Albright listened to a proposal advanced by Burt and four others to have Jackson Hole set aside as a national recreation area under the protection of the federal government (but not as a national park), where hunting, dude ranching and grazing would be continued on a limited basis. From rim to rim, the valley was to be a "museum on the hoof—native wildlife, cattle, wranglers, all living for a brief time each summer the life of the early West," with the funds to finance it coming from private donors who had visited and enjoyed dude ranches in Jackson Hole.[8] It was a novel idea, reflecting the changing attitude of some Jackson Holers, but it proved to be impractical. When two of the men spent several months soliciting contributions, they were able to raise only a few thousand dollars.

There things stood until the summer of 1925, when it was revealed that the Forest Service was planning to issue permits for logging on the shores of Jackson Lake and for the opening of several mines elsewhere in the valley. This disturbing news, coupled with the growing feeling of more and more residents that Jackson Hole's best chances for survival in its natural state were as a recreational area, led Pierce Cunningham and Si Ferrin to circulate a petition calling for either Wyoming or the federal government to set the valley aside "for the education and enjoyment of the Nation as a whole."[9] The petition was signed by ninety-seven property owners, many of whom, ironically, would later vehemently oppose a plan designed to do exactly what they had requested.

A bronze plaque on Maud Noble's cabin in Moose commemorates the meeting held there in 1923 in words implying that this was

Rodeo on the Elbo Ranch near Jenny Lake in the 1920s. The grandstand in the background was one of the unsightly structures which prompted John D. Rockefeller, Jr., to begin land purchases. *Teton County Chapter, Wyoming State Historical Society.*

when the tide turned in the struggle to save Jackson Hole. Actually, if any plaque should be mounted anywhere to commemorate the turn of the tide, it should be on a bluff overlooking the Snake River, and the date it should bear is 1926. In July of that year, when John D. Rockefeller, Jr., his wife and sons Laurance, Winthrop and David visited Yellowstone National Park, they were taken by Horace Albright down to Jackson Hole for their first look at the Tetons. From a vantage point above Jackson Lake, watching the mountains as the sun moved into the west and a moose browsed in a marsh nearby, Rockefeller was overwhelmed by what he later described as "quite the grandest and most spectacular mountains I have ever seen . . . a picture of ever-changing beauty which is to me beyond compare."[10] As a contrast, the next day the party drove down the road on the west side of the Snake River to Jenny Lake, where the construction of tourist facilities had mushroomed. Now, in addition to gasoline stations, cheap cabins and hot dog stands, the visual blight included a dance hall, a billboard advertising a local ranch as the "Hollywood Cowboy's Home," the rusting bodies of junked automobiles and a ramshackle rodeo arena complete with bucking chutes, stables and a grandstand.

This ugly clutter shocked Rockefeller, and he was even more shocked when Albright pointed out that because all of the land was private more of the same kind of clutter could be expected to spring up as an increasing number of tourists came into Jackson Hole. Albright later recalled Rockefeller quietly asking how much it would cost to purchase these properties, to which he replied that he did not know but would find out. Then, on their way out of the valley, they stopped on a bluff above the Snake River, and as the Rockefeller family looked out upon the Tetons and the sweep of the valley, the thirty-six-year-old superintendent of Yellowstone Park told the fifty-two-year-old philanthropist of his dream of somehow, someday bringing the Tetons and Jackson Hole under the wing of the National Park Service. Rockefeller made no comment and the subject was not mentioned again during the balance of the family's stay in Yellowstone. Albright could not even be sure that Rockefeller had paid any attention.

Rockefeller had been listening, all right. It was Albright who may not have paid close enough attention to Rockefeller's words. By late fall, a map of the privately owned lands west of the Snake River had been drawn at Albright's request, along with a cost-of-purchase estimate amounting to about $250,000. When Albright presented the papers in New York, Rockefeller glanced at the map and said, "Mr. Albright, you haven't given me what I want," explaining that he was thinking of buying up all the land on *both* sides of the Snake River and turning it over to the National Park Service.[11] Albright was staggered, but recovered to say he would get the necessary information to Rockefeller as soon as possible.

In February of 1927, Albright forwarded new maps and estimates showing that there were about 400 landowners in the valley holding somewhat more than 100,000 acres at a market value estimated to be approximately $1,000,000. These were such large numbers that Albright worried about what would happen if Rockefeller decided to go ahead with the venture and word leaked out as to both its sponsor and its purpose. Fearing this would send asking prices beyond reach and trigger an outburst from those who were still antagonistic to the idea of a national park in Jackson Hole, he therefore in his covering letter advanced a plan for acquiring the land in secrecy. No one was to know that Rockefeller was in any way connected with the purchases, nor was anyone to be told what the ultimate disposition of the land was to be. The mechanism he suggested to achieve this was a dummy corporation whose employees were to be kept in the dark as to its true objective, and he concluded his letter with these words: "I think if it [acquisition of land for the park] could be consummated, it would go down in history as the greatest conservation project of its kind ever undertaken."[12] Although Albright did not realize it at the time, the secrecy he advocated would within a few years come back to plague the reticent multimillionaire who was becoming his friend.

Rockefeller studied the proposal and early in 1927 gave it his approval.* Except for having his aides inform several important officials in Washington of his plans, he went along with Albright's advice to proceed in secrecy. In fact, so carefully did he mask his identity that even Harold Fabian, who was retained as counsel to organize the Snake River Land Company, did not know for whom or for what purpose he was working. Nor did the man who was hired as the company's purchasing agent, a former supervisor of the Teton National Forest now turned Jackson banker, Robert Miller, who back in pioneer days had loaned hay to the newly-arrived and hard-pressed Wilson family at a very high rate of interest. Although as president of the bank he had inside information about mortgages and the value of properties, Miller also had such an antipathy to the National Park Service and Horace Albright that he would later become one of Rockefeller's most adamant foes.

As soon as Miller began buying up properties, so many rumors spread about the Snake River Land Company and its motives that Rockefeller had Wyoming's governor and congressional delegation informed in confidence as to what it was all about. But no one in Jackson Hole was told anything, leading to even more wild rumors and speculations, including one that the Mormon Church was surreptitiously trying to obtain control of the valley. Meanwhile, the earlier bill to annex the Tetons to Yellowstone Park was resurrected in Congress and a Senate subcommittee hearing on the bill was held in Jackson. At the hearing, an overwhelming majority of the valley residents who attended voiced their approval of park status for the mountains, at the same time making it known that they preferred them to be kept separate from Yellowstone Park.

Backed by Wyoming Senator John Kendrick, the bill creating Grand Teton National Park was passed early in 1929, not long after

---

* The year 1927 was eventful in Jackson Hole. Rockefeller decided to buy up land for the future expansion of the park; the Izaak Walton League gave 1,760 acres to the National Elk Refuge; and the natural dam created by the Sheep Mountain landslide two years earlier broke, releasing the water of the lake it had formed to flood the lower valley and wash away the up-and-coming town of Kelly, drowning six people.

Guil Huff atop his house floating in the lake which began to form when a huge section of Sheep Mountain slid into the Gros Ventre River in 1925. *U.S. Forest Service*.

The town of Kelly was washed away and six people were drowned when the natural dam created by the Sheep Mountain landslide broke in 1927. *U.S. Forest Service*.

Horace Albright had been called back to Washington and named Director of the National Park Service. While speeches were made and dedication ceremonies were duly performed to celebrate the new park, the larger question of what was to become of Jackson Hole itself remained unanswered, because little of the endangered valley floor other than the six small lakes at the foot of the Tetons had been included. All that had been accomplished was to transfer the eastern side of most of the Tetons from the Forest Service to the National Park Service, which though not pleasing to the Forest Service or its supporters such as Robert Miller, caused no uproar.

It is not altogether clear why Miller suddenly resigned from the Snake River Land Company on the last day of 1929. Some say the company had become dissatisfied with his performance on the grounds that he had concentrated his purchasing efforts on the eastern side of the valley, where his bank held many mortgages. Some have even suggested that he used the threat of foreclosure to force a number of owners to sell, and in other cases offered unrealistically low bids for the ranches of those who were his enemies. But these charges appear to have grown out of a dislike for the man himself rather than from any evidence of improper action on his part. What is more likely is that Miller left the company because he had come to suspect it was part of a plan to add Jackson Hole to the new Grand Teton National Park, which Albright was known to favor and he was against. Whatever the reason, shortly after Miller resigned it was publicly disclosed that John D. Rockefeller, Jr., was the Snake River Land Company's largest stockholder and the land was being bought to be given to the federal government.

The revelation that Rockefeller was behind the mysterious land purchases, with Albright and the National Park Service in league with him, split the valley down the middle. Whatever rationality had attended the controversy to this point now died, and emotion took over. Friends and neighbors lined up in two bitterly opposed camps which would hurl charges and countercharges, innuendoes and distortions back and forth for years and years. So heated did the issue become that some people even stopped speaking to each other, and hostesses had to make up their guest lists carefully to avoid pitched battles at their dinner tables. On the one side, for the most part, the businessmen of Jackson supported the plan to expand the park as a boon to the valley's economy; the dude ranchers supported it as the only way to preserve Jackson Hole in its wilderness state; and the local newspaper, the *Jackson's Hole Courier*, while

Horace Albright speaking at the dedication of Grand Teton National Park in 1929. *National Park Service, Grand Teton National Park.*

trying not to offend half its subscribers, supported it as best for the area's future. On the other side, for the most part, cattlemen damned the proposed expansion of the park as a diabolical plot to deny them grazing privileges; sportsmen damned it as an underhanded way to curtail hunting; Forest Service employees damned it as another move by the National Park Service to take over still more of their lands; and some property owners who had already sold their places, now that they knew they had sold to a Rockefeller, damned it as a cunning trick by which they had been cheated. Caught up in the furor, even many of those residents who had earlier signed the petition to have Jackson Hole set aside "for the education and enjoyment of the Nation as a whole," which is what a national park is all about, abruptly reversed themselves and joined the opposition.

While at this distance in time it is difficult to understand fully why the anti-park forces became so violent in their denunciation of the National Park Service, Horace Albright and John D. Rockefeller, Jr., the reaction seems to have stemmed largely from four underlying fears, the first two of a general and traditional nature, the other two quite specific. There was the fear of most Westerners,

Jackson Hole's Representative Newspaper

THE GRAND T

Published Weekly by the Grand Teton Publishing Co.

JACKSON, WYOMING

VOLUME 1

TUESDAY, MAY 24, 1932

FEUDAL LAWS NOW IN FORCE IN JACKSON HOLE; ROCKEFELLER, JR., REQUIRES RENDITION OF FEUDAL SERVICE BEFORE GIVING GRANTS AND PRIVILEGES.

As a superior the Rockefeller interests hold thirty-five thousand acres of our valuable farming lands in the Jackson Hole Valley, now returned to nature, improvements destroyed and taxable values lost in the maze of the past.

For the use of this land and privileges for grazing thereon, and the lands are here and there, surrounded by public domain, on which rights are as yet privileged, he NOW REQUIRES GRATUITOUS DONATIONS AND CERTAIN SERVICES OF THE CATTLE MEN, OR A PART OF THEM, AS A PART OF THEIR FEALTY, FOR THE USE OF THIS LAND FOR GRAZING PURPOSES.

THE ROCKEFELLER INTERESTS, THE NATIONAL PARK SERVICE, AND THE BIG CATTLE MEN OF THE VALLEY, THIS IS WHAT WE PROPOSE TO SKIN.

It is a current report that at a meeting in Spring Gulch last week at which a number of Park Extensionists were present and participating that a local representative advised that from now on the Rockefeller lands were being protected from all grazing privileges unless and until, it was agreed that the use of the same depended upon RENDERING FEALTY TO THE ROCKEFELLER CROWN OF WEALTH AND AGGRESSION.

As presented, the certain few cattle

Your Interests Are in Jackson

The gabby spellbinder having something to sell on C. O. D. orders and $1 down is with us again.

He talks you into buying his goods, all C. O. D., higher in price and less in value than your local merchant has on his shelves. Your little wad, saved for emergencies, succumbs to the smooth, oily tongue of the non-resident agent who collects afterward. Let us ask who gave you a few groceries last winter when you and the kids were actually hungry?

It wasn't some stranger was it? No! It was the local merchant who stretched his credit to help you out.

Are you the fellow who sent your money down to Montgomery Ward for your supplies last fall?

Let us tell you something that you will understand in the future. Times have not started to get bad. Next year will be just one hundred per cent worse for you than this last year. People who went down in

The Question is, Y or No

Just what interests are back Leslie Miller, who has announced candidacy in the coming primary the nomination for governor we not know! Did he promise O'Neil that he would keep out of race before Tom announced himself WE SAY HE DID.

We have Tom O'Neil's word for His word is good with us. The pushers in Cheyenne and elsewhere who in one breath rave against Republican party making endo ments for political expediency, form against it, and holler "organ tion," are as fine a body of fixer this state has produced since 1918, year of the fusion. We say now that some of those old ones now in the same limelight as the The only time this bunch ever a good licking was when George Beck of Cody took away from the State for Champ Clark for pi

Headline from *The Grand Teton*, May 24, 1932, reflects the extent of that newspaper's hostility to John D. Rockefeller, Jr. *Teton County Library.*

many of whom firmly believed in states' rights, of the federal government and its encroachment on their lives. There was the fear of most Westerners of the so-called "Eastern establishment," especially as typified by men of great wealth. There was the fear of most ranchers that their herds would no longer be allowed to graze on government lands. And there was the fear of most residents of Teton County that the tax revenues to be lost if the private properties became federally owned would cripple their local government. Soon all of these fears were being played on by a new newspaper in Jackson, whose editorial views not surprisingly reflected the views of Robert Miller.

"FEUDAL LAWS NOW IN FORCE IN JACKSON HOLE; ROCKEFELLER, JR., REQUIRES RENDITION OF FEUDAL SERVICE BEFORE GIVING GRANTS AND PRIVILEGES."[13] Although the headline was far from accurate, it does accurately convey the caliber of journalism practiced by *The Grand Teton* and its editor, William Simpson, a former native of the valley who had been encouraged and, it is said, even backed financially by the incensed Robert Miller to return and start the new paper as a rival to the *Jackson's Hole Courier*. Stridently opposed to the "unholy plan for taking the Jackson valley for National Parks," Simpson promptly dubbed the Snake River Land Company's Harold Fabian "The Weasel," shortened the name of the company to "The Snakes" and accused the *Courier* of being "the mouthpiece of the predatory Rockefeller interests."[14] As for Albright and the already existing Grand Teton National Park, he "and his crowd strong-armed it from the state" while Rockefeller's secret agents "BROW-BEAT and THREATENED RESIDENTS of the valley with CON-DEMNATION PROCEEDINGS against their land unless they sold to Snake River Land Company at SNAKE RIVER PRICES."[15] Simpson was as free with his facts as he was with his use of capitals. Congress, not Albright and his "crowd," had created Grand Teton National Park from existing federal lands, and "The Snakes," even if they had wanted to, had no power of any kind to condemn properties. While small details such as these did not bother Simpson, the many charges of misdoings, especially when Rockefeller's name was mentioned, received national attention and troubled Wyoming's two senators to the point of calling for a Senate inquiry into the Snake River Land Company.

By the time a Senate subcommittee held hearings in Jackson in 1933, Rockefeller had bought or had agreed to buy slightly over 35,000 acres for slightly more than $1,400,000 from 320 different landowners. Despite this large number of transactions, in no instance was it found that any browbeating or threatening had taken place. To the contrary, it was established that fair and even generous prices had been offered, with many testifying that they had received more for their land than they had expected. The major complaint at this time and long thereafter was that by acting in secrecy Rockefeller had conspired to cheat the landowners "out of their heritage," a highly emotional reaction which did not take into account the fact that had it been made known that Rockefeller money was behind the Snake River Land Company asking prices would have become prohibitive.[16] As a result of the hearings, the Senate investigators and newspaper reporters from the East, who had traveled across the continent on the promise they would uncover a scandal to "eclipse Teapot Dome," went home empty-handed.*[17]

* For a moment at the start of the hearings, a Jackson Hole resident who had sold his land to the Snake River Land Company led the investigators and newsmen to think they were on to something big. When asked whether there had been any coercion at the time he sold out, he replied that there certainly had been. But then he added, "I coerced them until they bought my property." (*Jackson Hole News*, Grand Teton National Park Special 25th Anniversary Issue, p. 9)

In 1934, a bill was drafted in Congress which attempted to placate both factions. In broad terms, it would have accepted Rockefeller's lands, would have permitted cattle grazing to continue and would have compensated Teton County for its lost tax revenues. Looking back, the bill made sense, but by this time attitudes had been so set in concrete it was probably impossible for any bill to have passed. Nor were the diehards against park expansion the only ones to blame. Several national conservation groups lobbied strongly against it on the highly technical grounds that the planned inclusion in the park of Jackson Lake, a reservoir, would "violate national park standards."[18] Horace Albright could only bemoan the inability of idealists to understand practical problems, observing, "It is a pity that conservation is always being thwarted by its own friends."[19]

In 1938, a staunch states' righter named Frank Horton was elected to Congress from Wyoming, and no sooner was he there than he introduced a bill that went far beyond anything proposed before—the outright abolition of Grand Teton National Park. Too unreasonable even for other staunch states' righters, the bill was defeated, but it was a barometer of the intensity of feeling that had been aroused throughout Wyoming, particularly on the score of allowing the properties Rockefeller had purchased to be turned over to the National Park Service and become tax-exempt. From then on into the early 1940s, the Wyoming delegation to Congress was able to block all legislation for park expansion, and it appeared that the long stalemate would go on forever. And perhaps it would have, except for a letter John D. Rockefeller, Jr., wrote the Secretary of the Interior, Harold Ickes.

By November of 1942, it had become evident that it was easier for a camel to go through the eye of a needle than for a rich man to donate land to the national park system. His patience finally worn thin by the constant bickering and name-calling of almost a decade and a half, balked at every turn in his wish to give his countrymen a gift for the future, Rockefeller wrote Ickes to inform him that he was planning to divest himself of the Jackson Hole properties one way or another within a year. This and a follow-up letter spurred Ickes to persuade President Roosevelt to activate a plan long considered by the National Park Service. It was a drastic step which when taken absolutely infuriated Congress, states' righters, most of the residents of Wyoming, hundreds of newspapers across the country and almost everyone else already upset by what they considered Roosevelt's high-handed ways. Whereas only Congress was

Original entrance to Grand Teton National Park. *National Park Service, Grand Teton National Park.*

empowered to create a national park, the President, using his executive authority, could create a national monument, and this is what Roosevelt did in March of 1943. By issuing a proclamation establishing the Jackson Hole National Monument, he formed a new preserve consisting of approximately 200,000 acres, drawn largely from the Teton National Forest, other federal lands in the valley and Rockefeller's holdings. If what had gone before was fireworks, now real bombs began to burst.

Members of Congress blasted the proclamation as a subterfuge to undermine and usurp their powers, with one senator calling it "a foul, sneaking Pearl Harbor blow."[20] Editorials tore into it as still another example of Roosevelt riding roughshod over the other branches of government, likening it to his earlier attempt to pack the Supreme Court. Columnist Westbrook Pegler apoplectically equated it with Hitler's annexation of Austria. The governors of six western states condemned it as an unconscionable assault on the sovereign rights of states. The head of the powerful Wyoming Stock Growers Association, carried away by his own rhetoric, detected the "cloven hoof of our most ruthless bureaucrat" (Ickes) in the proclamation, comparing it somewhat fuzzily to the Boston Tea Party.[21] And one Jackson Hole lady, expressing a sense of personal ownership of the landscape not uncommon to many people in the valley then and now, exclaimed, "We GAVE them the Tetons! What *more* do they want?"[22] Roosevelt had stirred up a hornet's nest and, according to one observer, had made Wyomingites "as grumpy as a bear with a sore ear and as immune to reason."[23] The description appears to have been as apt as it was colorful, because one Wyomingite, the governor himself, was so immune to reason he wrote an open letter to the President threatening to call out the police to "evict from the proposed Jackson Hole Monument any federal official who attempts to assume authority."*[24]

Roosevelt's signature on the proclamation was barely dry when Wyoming Congressman Frank Barrett introduced a bill to abolish the Jackson Hole National Monument, reject Rockefeller's properties and restore the lands taken from the Teton National Forest to the Forest Service. Such was the temper of Congress that there was a good chance it would pass, for many members of the Senate and House felt that Roosevelt had gone too far and should be taught a lesson. Even as hearings were being held on Barrett's bill, Wyoming Senator Joseph O'Mahoney used a familiar congressional tactic to hamstring the National Park Service from assuming control of the new lands by attaching a rider to the Interior Department's annual appropriations bill forbidding the use of any of the funds for the monument's administration. Meanwhile, as all this was going on, out in Wyoming a group of Jackson Holers, mostly cattlemen, became too impatient to wait for the outcome of these parliamentary maneuvers. On a morning in May, they gathered at the Elks' Club in Jackson, carrying guns, and cheered speeches rallying them to march on the monument and force a showdown with the federal government for their rights, even if it might lead to bloodshed.

Despite a guarantee given by Secretary Ickes to honor all cattle rights-of-way and grazing privileges in the new monument, the cattlemen chose to believe that when they drove their herds north for summer grazing they would be met at the monument's boundary by armed federal authorities and turned back. This was a fantasy of their own creation, because local National Park Service offi-

---

* While the reaction to the establishment of the monument was almost entirely negative, there were a few approving voices to be heard. The *Caspar Tribune-Herald* reminded its readers that prior to Rockefeller's purchases the road through the valley had been on its way to becoming "a long lane of unsightly structures that would mar the primitive beauty of the area." And a former Wyoming governor, Leslie Miller, expressed gratitude to Rockefeller for his foresight, saying that if the opposition to the monument won out, "Wyoming will hang her head in shame." (T. A. Larson, *History of Wyoming*, pp. 500–501)

Wallace Beery, the Hollywood actor who participated in the protest march on the Jackson Hole National Monument in 1943. *Teton County Chapter, Wyoming State Historical Society.*

cials had repeatedly assured them they had as free access as ever to these lands. But the fantasy became more and more real in their minds, until they finally decided to strap on their guns and defy the federal government by driving six hundred and fifty yearling Herefords across the monument. Wallace Beery, the gravel-throated Hollywood actor who had made a Western movie in Jackson Hole and had built a summer home in the valley, now joined their ranks. On the morning the men met at the Elks' Club while their wives tended the assembled Herefords on a ranch north of Jackson, Beery appeared theatrically astride a white horse, wearing the cowboy hat he had worn in the movie and with a .30-.30 Winchester in a rifle sheath on his saddle. So caught up was he in his role that as he added his voice to those of the other speechmakers he is said to have ordered the group to "Shoot to kill!"[25]

Up to this point, everything had gone according to plan as the men at the Elks' Club checked their weapons and expressed their strong feelings against the monument before herding the cattle on their do-or-die march. Farther up the valley, however, the cattle became so restless the wives either could not hold them in place or decided to start the drive on their own, and before they knew it they had crossed the southern boundary of the monument and were on their way upcountry. When the word got back to town, Wallace Beery and the others threw their guns and several cases of beer into cars and raced north, still convinced a fight was to come. To their disappointment, it turned out the issue they had created in their minds was no issue at all. Not a single federal official was anywhere in sight. "So," as Donald Hough wrote, "all concerned now sat down on the bank of a small creek marking the boundary of the Monument, and threw empty beer cans across it, each toss accompanied by loud imprecations directed at the Government of the United States, as personified by the Monument. Then they went home."[26]

In 1944, the Barrett Bill to abolish the Jackson Hole National Monument was voted through the House of Representatives by a comfortable margin and through the Senate unanimously. President Roosevelt then killed it with a pocket veto, evoking still another outcry about dictatorial methods. But in a message explaining why he had taken the action, he paved the way for an end to the years of infighting which by now had almost everyone exhausted. He recommended that Congress pass legislation to compensate Teton County for lost tax revenues; he reaffirmed the Interior Department's guarantee of continued grazing privileges; he held out the carrot of overall financial gain to the region when World War II ended and tourist travel resumed; and he added, apparently to calm the fears of those in Jackson Hole who had not sold their properties, "No lands have been or can be confiscated; no citizens have been or can be dispossessed."[27] His words should have done much to conciliate the anti-monument forces, but the more rabid among them were not yet finished.

Early in 1947, Congressman Barrett reintroduced his bill to abolish the monument with confidence it would pass. What he had not allowed for were the conservationists, who had grown stronger and more militant, as quickly became evident when the Sierra Club, the Izaak Walton League, the Wilderness Society, the Boone and Crockett Club, the Camp Fire Club of America and others made their voices heard. Horace Albright, no longer in government service, also joined in, mustering a powerhouse of friends and acquaintances to express their distaste for the bill—among others, former

President Herbert Hoover, whom he had taken fishing on Yellowstone Lake in 1927; Governor Thomas Dewey of New York, for whom he had voted in the presidential election of 1944; and Governor Earl Warren of California, an old friend from college days. With opposition as prestigious as this, the Barrett Bill died in the Rules Committee and to all intents and purposes the thirty-year war was at an end. All that remained to be done was to work out the terms of the peace.

Governor Lester Hunt of Wyoming soon expressed the changing mood of many of his constituents when he said to Struthers Burt, "My God, how I'd like to see this constant controversy stop."[28] Senator O'Mahoney also let it be known that he was for a settlement of some kind, and even Congressman Barrett began to come around. Then, when Hunt was elected to the Senate in 1948, the last barriers came down. Quiet negotiations began between Wyoming's congressional delegation, the National Park Service and the Jackson Hole Preserve, a corporation Rockefeller had formed to administer the lands he had bought until they could be deeded to the government. Gradually, a compromise was hammered out to the satisfaction of all parties. Although a relatively small amount of land in the southeastern part of the valley was to be turned over to the Forest Service, by far the greater part of the monument's lands were to be added to Grand Teton National Park. In return, Teton County was to be reimbursed for tax losses over a period of several decades, and grazing rights were to be honored for the lifetime of existing leaseholders and their heirs who were living at the time. Interestingly, the elk herd posed the thorniest problem, because it was against National Park Service policy to permit hunting within any of its parks, yet it was necessary for hunting to continue in order to keep the herd at the proper size to prevent the recurrence of starvation conditions. On this issue each side refused to budge until an adroit concession was made whereby the park would annually deputize hunters as temporary park rangers to reduce the excess elk. With this concession, it was all over. The bill sponsored by O'Mahoney and Hunt sailed through Congress and was signed by President Harry Truman on September 14, 1950.

Today few would argue that the creation and later expansion of Grand Teton National Park was best for both Jackson Hole and the nation. All it takes is a drive from Jackson up toward the park to see how right it was. On still private land bordering the highway, gasoline stations, camper parks, concessions offering trail rides,

Mr. and Mrs. John D. Rockefeller, Jr., picnicking in Grand Teton National Park in 1931. *National Park Service, Grand Teton National Park*.

hamburger stands and places selling fireworks assail the eye—a visual reminder of the kind of Coney Island the entire valley could have become if John D. Rockefeller, Jr., had chosen to remain aloof. Yet, such is human nature that if a man is rich, even if he uses his riches in a good cause, he is as often vilified as praised. Certainly it was true of this man, who although he conducted himself scrupulously throughout the long struggle, was frequently smeared and slandered. To balance the scales somewhat, perhaps it is only fair to quote Horace Albright, who in later years, when recalling some of the dark days the National Park Service had gone through in its efforts to save many of the natural wonders of this land, wrote, "We have had conscientious, perceptive men, who have quietly stepped in at critical times and turned the tide when everything seemed to be going against us. Mr. Rockefeller is such a friend of our heritage."[29] For that matter, so were men such as Struthers Burt and Albright himself. But for them and all the others who cared, one of the world's most beautiful valleys would have been lost.

19

Latter-Day Mavericks

From the days of the mountain men to the present, Jackson Hole has hosted a long cavalcade of individuals who, by any standards, would stand out in a crowd. Some have been full-fledged eccentrics, others rough-hewn nonconformists and still others just people who lived their lives in primary colors, but they all found a haven here, a friendly environment for their independent ways. And although the controversy over Grand Teton National Park for a time put a dent in the valley's tradition of tolerance for divergent views, it did not break it. Much of the animosity was directed at outside forces, particularly the federal government, which were suspected of trying to take the valley's future out of local hands and manipulate it from a distance. Within the valley, despite heated exchanges on the political and economic issues, there was little recrimination against those who sold, or did not sell, their properties as they saw fit. Both sides admired the spunk of Geraldine Lucas, a spirited lady who had homesteaded her land and had climbed the Grand Teton at the age of fifty-nine, when she flatly refused to sell, taunting the Snake River Land Company's agent with an impossibly steep price. "You stack up those silver dollars as high as the Grand Teton," she told him, "and I might talk to you."[1]

Many years ago, Donald Hough wrote that when American society began to become more complicated and competitive, "As queer a collection of halfwits, apostles, remittance men, social outcasts, certified public accountants, broken aristocrats, chronic drunks, [and] last-ditch women haters as ever floated into the same backwater now discovered the ramparts of the Tetons . . . Each new arrival in turn took one look around, saw he was among friends, and threw down his pack."[2] While the picture Hough drew was greatly exaggerated, his words did and still do contain a large kernel of truth. For a community its size, Jackson Hole has attracted an unusual number of people of widely assorted backgrounds who were not afraid to step beyond the accepted norms of social behavior and live their lives as they chose. By no means is this to say that the valley has been a Mecca for crackpots, although it has had its share, but rather that it has long offered a most congenial climate for free spirits, a number of whom have become part of the local legendry.

Among the first settlers, there was "Uncle Jack" Davis, the recluse described previously who preferred the company of birds and beasts to that of men and women. For all of his idiosyncrasies, including the unheard-of heresy of being a vegetarian in game-rich Jackson Hole, he was warmly regarded by the other residents, and no one ever suggested that he be "put away."

Close on his heels another vivid personality arrived in 1892, when Bill Menor took up land along the Snake River at present-day Moose and started the first ferry. Bill was a natural grouch with a natural flair for profanity who enjoyed being both mean and profane to those he did not like, sometimes even refusing to ferry them over the river, although there was no other way across for many miles north or south. At the same time, if he did like someone he could be more than openhanded with his home-fermented huckleberry wine, an act of generosity that left many recipients less than grateful, for it was so potent it could, as Charles Russell once said of a similar lethal brew, "make a humming-bird spit in a rattlesnake's eye."[3]

Bill's brother Holiday, who joined him in the valley in 1905, was also an irascible man with an even greater talent for cussing, beginning and ending almost every sentence with the expletive "Holy Saviour!"—with far more earthy expressions interspersed throughout. On one occasion, he delivered what may have been the longest and most inspired outpouring of profanity ever heard in the town of Jackson. Just after buying a new suit and hat, he was walking to the Crabtree Hotel when a woman accidentally threw a pan of dishwater on him from the upper floor of the Clubhouse, a community social center. Continuing to the hotel, he held an audience spellbound as he raged on and on about what had happened, an abbreviated version of his monologue going something like this: "Holy Saviour! An asterisk man gets asterisk dressed up once in seventeen asterisk years and an asterisk woman has to climb up above him and throw asterisk dishwater all over him. Why the asterisk couldn't it have been an asterisk minute earlier or an asterisk minute later? Holy Saviour, yes!"[4]

Each of these bachelor brothers was so strong-willed and quick-tempered it was inevitable they would have a falling-out. When it came, Holiday built a cabin across a channel of the Snake from

Early settler "Uncle Jack" Davis, Jackson Hole's version of Saint Francis and its first vegetarian. *Jackson Hole Museum*.

Bill's place, and for two years they did not exchange a single word, although they were frequently seen shaking their fists at each other. Finally reconciled, they went on venting their spleens at those whose ways displeased them and the world in general, not caring a whit what others thought of their pungent language and brusque manners—and most of the people of the valley liked them all the more for it.

For some reason or other, Easterners have been prominent among those who added splashes of color to the valley. One of

In center, Bill and Holiday Menor, the strong-willed
bachelor brothers who operated the ferry at Moose.
National Park Service, Grand Teton National Park.

John Dodge, lover of poetry and mules, was one of
Jackson Hole's most colorful eccentrics. *Jackson Hole
Museum*.

them was John Dodge, Jackson Hole's foremost "character" during the early decades of this century. A man of many parts—Harvard graduate, one-time laboratory assistant of William James, student of poetry, flutist and lover of mules—Dodge lived by himself in a log cabin on the Snake River. There, to keep his fire going without having to cut and carry wood, he would shove a twenty-foot length of lodgepole pine through the window into the front of the stove, then push it farther into the stove as it burned down. His method of plowing was equally unorthodox. Riding on a sulky plow, he would start the mules, then open a book of poetry and read aloud to them as they wandered aimlessly about the field, carving it into strange, random designs. When asked why he did not plow in normal, straight furrows as others did, he replied, quite logically, that in his view of things it really did not matter how the field got plowed as long as it got plowed.

Dodge was also fond of burros, or at least he was until several he knew behaved in a manner he considered highly dishonorable. In warm weather, he liked to cook his breakfast on a campfire outside his cabin, meanwhile playing his flute and feeding flapjacks to a neighbor's burros who made it a practice to join him. But one morning he went into the cabin to get something and returned to find that the burros had eaten the sheet music of a favorite waltz, a breach of hospitality for which he never forgave them. Dodge's neighbors, on the other hand, were very forgiving of the bizarre things he did. A shy man, he once got out of his bath to answer the door wearing nothing but a bucket over his head, an incident that shocked few and delighted many.

When his wealthy sister from the East paid him a visit and found him living in a log cabin in a wilderness, she was appalled and asked, "What do you see in this godforsaken place?" Pointing to the magnificent Tetons rising to scrape the clouds, he tried to answer the question which over the years has been asked by so many who cannot comprehend why some people are attracted to and held by this remote corner of Wyoming. "Ye gods, Carrie," he said, "what more does a man want when he has all that?"[5] Carrie had no idea of what he was talking about, but his friends and neighbors understood. John Dodge had found not only a beautiful country, but one so big there was plenty of room for his eccentricities.

Although Struthers Burt can by no means be called an eccentric, he was a maverick who broke away from the herd, which in his case was composed largely of Princeton classmates and friends from the Mainline of Philadelphia. After attending Oxford and Heidelberg and teaching English at his alma mater, Burt went west and eventually became a successful dude rancher in Jackson Hole. The transition was not easy, however, especially since he had the misfortune to spend his apprenticeship as the partner of Louis Joy, who several years earlier, in 1908, had started the first dude ranch in the valley.

In order to fill the ranch with guests, at the beginning of each season Joy would induce an Easterner to buy in as a partner and promote the ranch to his friends and acquaintances back home. Then, when the guests had arrived, Joy would employ all sorts of diabolical tricks designed to make the partner appear to be hopelessly ignorant and inept, until the partner, thinking he was losing his mind, would finally abandon both the ranch and his investment, leaving Joy with the spoils of the psychological war. Burt's higher education in no way prepared him to deal with a confidence game such as this, but he somehow escaped with both his sanity and his bankroll, and soon started the Bar BC Ranch near Moose.

Burt was a maverick in more ways than one. Not only an Easterner turned dude rancher, he was also a convert to conservation at a time when the cause was new and its supporters were viewed with a certain amount of suspicion. Moreover, he did something else which is sometimes viewed with suspicion—he wrote novels and short stories, and wrote them so well they were published and acclaimed nationally. But with it all, he became one of Jackson Hole's most popular and respected figures, a man who was himself respectful of the foibles of others, as evidenced by his close friendship with John Dodge and the Menor brothers (in fact, it was he who brought the feuding brothers back together). There was, however, one kind of person he could not stand and whom he described when he distilled his many years of outdoor experiences with a wide variety of people, Easterners and Westerners alike, in these words: "I do not fear silken people in rough countries—silken men or silken women. What I fear is the big so-called 'regular' fellow; the hundred per center who worships his bathtub and his automobile. I want either one of two classes when I am in a tight or uncomfortable place, the very simple man or woman or the very civilized ones. The tough blade does not break, neither does the rapier."[6]

Struthers Burt, the Princeton graduate and Philadelphia "Mainliner" who became a dude rancher in Jackson Hole. *Photo taken by Mildred Capron in 1951.*

Ed Benson first came to Jackson Hole in 1919 to hunt elk and was so taken with the valley he returned with his family and became a resident. Looking around to see what he could do to make a living, he concluded that what the town of Jackson needed was electricity, so he built a house through the basement of which a branch of Cache Creek flowed to turn two small turbines. Soon Jackson had electricity and the state of Wyoming had one of the most perplexing problems ever to confront any Game and Fish Commission.

Finding that the trout of Cache Creek gathered in the pool in his basement, during the winter Ed would excuse himself when company came, take his fishing pole and go downstairs, shortly to return to the amazement of his guests with fresh trout for dinner. When this was brought to the attention of the Game and Fish Commission, Ed was accused of fishing out of season, a charge he boldly countered by ordering the state "to keep their silly trout out of his basement."[7] Then, blatantly defying the authorities, he cut a hole in the kitchen floor above the basement, lengthened his line and brought the flapping fish directly to the frying pan. Again accused of breaking the law, Ed now told the state to keep the confounded fish out of his kitchen, citing their presence in the upstairs part of his house as an invasion of his constitutional right to privacy.

No one knew what to do, so no one did anything. Ed went on serving fresh trout, a man admired with amusement throughout the valley for standing up for his "rights."

A highly publicized member of the international set, the heiress of a huge newspaper fortune and a Polish countess by marriage, Cissy Patterson should have been completely out of place in "cow country." Instead, she became one of Jackson Hole's best liked dudes and part-time residents. After divorcing the count, she came to Jackson Hole in search of peace and quiet, both of which she found. She also found something else that drew her back to the valley as long as she lived. "I have seen taller mountains and larger lakes," she once told a friend, "but the people here I love."[8] The feeling was mutual. The unconventional, outspoken Countess of Flat Creek, as she was called by the people of the valley because her ranch lay near the headwaters of that stream, hit it off with almost everyone.

Part of the lore of Jackson Hole is that Cissy was one of the few women who could begin to hold a candle to the Menor brothers in the art of cussing. As to her credentials, Clay Seaton, the driver of the stagecoach that carried people in and out of the valley over Teton Pass, and himself no slouch as a cusser, once said that Cissy was the only one, man or woman, he ever let talk to his horses when they needed talking to. "I owe her much," he said with admiration. "She didn't teach me all I knew in talking to horses, but she sure as hell gave me a few wonderful new ideas."[9]

In an era when the concept of the liberated woman still lay far in the future, one might think that Cissy's independent ways would have been looked on with disapproval by the residents of a remote community in the high Rockies. And perhaps a few did disapprove.

Cissy Patterson, the "Countess of Flat Creek." *Courtesy Felicia Magruder*.

By and large, however, Jackson Holers liked Cissy for being the woman she was, unafraid to live and speak as she saw fit.

In 1948, when she knew she was dying, Cissy asked for her private railroad car to be prepared to take her to Jackson Hole. But it was too late. She never made it back to the place and people she loved so much, and where she is remembered to this day, not with awe but with affection, as the Countess of Flat Creek.

Donald Hough once related a small incident that goes a long way toward summing up the free and easy, live-and-let-live atmosphere of Jackson Hole. Himself still another maverick from the outside world, Hough was stranded with his wife and son in the town of Jackson in the 1920s when he lost all of his money at a roulette table, and he ended up staying for years, also becoming enamored of the valley and its people. One of his first acquaintances was a clerk in the hardware store, who came to dinner at the Houghs dressed in a black coat, striped trousers, a tie with a pearl stickpin and spats. Because Hough was dressed only in a flannel shirt and a pair of hunting pants, there was a moment of embarrassment. Then the clerk cut the Gordian knot by saying, "You dress that way because it's a novelty and a change from what you are used to. I dress this way for the same reason. We are both right."[10]

"We are both right." What a superb simple sentence that was, not only solving the trivial problem of the moment, but by and large expressing what tolerance for others' differences is all about.

The tradition of respect, even admiration, for individualism is still very much alive in Jackson Hole. Unlike many other communities, large and small, where the pressures to conform are intense, here to be a maverick is not to be a pariah. As a result, the valley has attracted a wide diversity of people with a wide diversity of interests and values. In addition to a more-than-average number of outright eccentrics and colorful nonconformists, the ranks include many other less flamboyant people who have nonetheless chosen to break away from their herds and "do their own thing"—artists, writers and craftsmen striving to express themselves; doctors, lawyers and businessmen who have thrown over lucrative urban livelihoods in order to enjoy their families at a less hectic pace; well-educated young men and women who would rather struggle to make a living in a lovely and still wild country than go to work for a giant corporation; retirees who refuse to spend their declining years surrounded by contemporaries talking about nothing but golf and their physical ailments; even celebrities and millionaires who have cast their lot in favor of a simpler, less conventional life. For them all, the valley provides an environment rarer than one of just clean air and pure water. It is an environment which fosters those who, like the mountain men generations earlier, have the courage to live their lives as they wish and the forbearance to let others do the same. And it is a part of Jackson Hole's heritage every bit as priceless as the Tetons and the elk herd.

A trail ride setting out from the Triangle X Ranch. *Courtesy Louise Turner Bertschy*.

20

The Present, A Postscript

Just as there is a tradition of tolerance in Jackson Hole, there is also a tradition of independence. Illustrative of it, Wyomingites like to tell the story of an Englishman in the 1880s who rode up to a ranch and inquired of the foreman whether his master was in. The answer was that the s.o.b. hadn't been born yet. Whether true or not, the story expresses the fierce pride most Westerners still take in being independent, of standing on their own, with no man allowed to call himself their master, and it is an attitude very prevalent in Jackson Hole to this day. Coupled with this attitude, there is an innate distrust of big government, a fear that not only are its social and economic programs sapping individual initiative, but that it is also becoming the biggest master of all. Early in 1977, this fear was voiced at the polls in Jackson Hole when an overwhelming majority of voters rejected a proposal to accept federal funds to build a modern swimming complex. Those who were in favor of the proposal argued that it would cost the community nothing, pointing out that if the money were not spent here it would be spent elsewhere. On the other hand, those who were opposed felt that as a matter of principle the money should not be taken just because it was available, and they further perceived that what appeared to be a gift would probably become a burden as maintenance costs, to be paid from local taxes, rose each year. Without knowing they did so when they turned down the federal funds, the voters of Jackson Hole were following the advice of a former valley cowboy named Jack Davis, who once said, "Don't never accept no gift what eats."[1]

While this spurning of a proffered gift from the federal government is refreshing and attests to the fact that what are often called old-fashioned values are still very much alive in Jackson Hole, life in the valley has undergone and is continuing to undergo great changes. Because of the pressures brought about by the tremendous number of visitors who come to see and ski the Tetons each year (approximately four million in 1977), as well as by a permanent population expanding at a rate many find alarming, the people of Jackson Hole are once again worried about the future of their valley. And with good reason, for problems previously thought to be exclusive to large cities across the United States are now raising their heads here, especially in the town of Jackson, in the form of inadequate housing, insufficient waste disposal, seasonal unemployment, traffic congestion and even a degree of crime. In addition, in and around Jackson commercialism appears to be running rampant as more motels, pizza parlors, gasoline stations and souvenir shops spring up for each new tourist season. But what many view as potentially the largest problem of all lies outside of Jackson in the surrounding countryside, particularly farther to the north in the valley proper, where substantial holdings of private land still exist in an undeveloped state. It is the fear of those who are mindful of what happened near Jenny Lake in the 1920s that without effective land-use controls these properties may also be developed in an unseemly way. In their eyes, the specter of helter-skelter residential and commercial construction within sight of the Tetons themselves has not, after all, been laid to rest.

Because less than three percent of the land in Teton County is privately owned, with the balance in the hands of the federal and state governments, the cause for concern may appear to be exaggerated. However, the seemingly small three percent amounts to about 70,000 acres, many of which overlook, border on or are actually within the boundaries of Grand Teton National Park and therefore highly visible. If, through lack of foresight, these lands are allowed to become the sites of large condominiums, cluster housing and even commercial enterprises, then this unique landscape will indeed be marred, and the long struggle which was waged over so many years to protect the natural wilderness beauty of Jackson Hole will have suffered a setback.

But this is not likely to happen, for unlike the 1920s and 1930s, when the residents of Jackson Hole were bitterly divided among themselves as to which direction the valley's future should take, today they are more or less of one mind—or at least as much so as is possible in any community of independent-thinking, outspoken people. Recently, a public opinion survey revealed that by far the greater proportion of the valley's residents are strongly in favor of more stringent zoning ordinances and building codes, and strongly opposed to unlimited growth. Still more recently, the commissioners of Teton County instituted a comprehensive plan designed to control the use of land and preserve scenic areas, and the National Park Service announced a policy prohibiting the further development of private lands existing within its boundaries. As might be expected, both actions have caused controversy, but not so much on the issue of whether their ultimate goals are generally good as on the specific ways in which they will be implemented. While both actions will probably continue to be criticized and perhaps even contested for some time to come, it now appears that Jackson Holers by and large agree in principle that the beauty of the land the Tetons look down upon must not be endangered.*

Although Jackson Hole has not remained immune from many of the problems of our time, there are few, if any, other places those who know it would rather visit or live. On the other hand, there are few, if any, other places those who do not know Jackson Hole seem to have more misconceptions about. Hence, the all too familiar question asked by those who have never visited the valley: "What in the world do you do with yourselves out there?" The question automatically presupposes that just because Jackson Hole is surrounded by wilderness and is still sparsely populated (huge Teton County has only about 9,000 people in all), it is a social and intellectual desert where, after the Tetons have been seen, the most stimulating thing left to do is watch horses switching their tails at flies. But what a surprise those who ask the question are in for when they see this country for themselves. Once they recover from being stunned by the sheer grandeur and magnitude of the landscape, they are almost invariably astonished by the valley's variety and vitality of life, its remarkable blend of culture and sophistication with rugged outdoor activities. In many ways, as they discover, Jackson Hole may be the most cosmopolitan community of its size in the United States.

On the streets of Jackson, newcomers are surprised to find working cowboys brushing elbows with socialites, a bucking-bronco rodeo taking place just up the road from a polo match and saloons with an old-time flavor vibrating to the beat of Western music while not all that far away a summer symphony orchestra performs Mozart. And they are further surprised when they learn that this still relatively inaccessible pocket in the high Rockies also offers many fine art and crafts galleries, several first-rate small museums, two live summer theaters, an excellent library, two well-edited

---

* As this book goes to press, still another step has been taken to preserve the scenic and ecological integrity of Jackson Hole. A bill has been introduced in Congress to permit the purchase of scenic easements from private landowners, who while retaining their land would sell off their right to develop it in ways that might jeopardize the natural beauty of the area. Whether or not the bill passes, it reflects the growing determination on the part of many to call a halt to further encroachments on the Jackson Hole landscape.

Staying aboard a bucking bronco at the Jackson rodeo. *Photo by Michal Sellett in "The Jackson Hole News."*

Sunday afternoon at the Jackson Hole Polo Club. *Photo by Steve Beedle in the "Jackson Hole Guide."*

A performance by the Jackson Hole summer symphony orchestra. *Photo by Roger LaVake.*

Resident artist Conrad Schwiering painting the Tetons. *Photo by Elizabeth McCabe in the "Jackson Hole Guide."*

Big game hunting camp in a snowstorm. *Photo by John Turner.*

newspapers, a beautifully produced local magazine, lively year-round nightspots complete with professional entertainment and a wide selection of good restaurants and shops. A New York or San Francisco it may not be, but Jackson is far from being a backwater cow town.

Newcomers are also surprised by the vibrancy of the valley's social life, although perhaps they would not be if they understood that the art of having a good time is still another carefully cultivated local tradition. For generations, the people of this country where distances are great, winters long and neighbors far apart have used the slightest pretext for getting together to have a dance, a party, a supper, a picnic or some other kind of social gathering. Back in the 1930s, one of the favorite pretexts was a fire, or even a false alarm, after which the volunteer firemen and onlookers alike would repair to the Cowboy Bar in Jackson to discuss the event over a few drinks. Often, before anyone knew it, a party would be in progress that would last for hours, if not days. In fact, Olaus Murie said that one false alarm led to a party at the Cowboy Bar which started on a Saturday afternoon and did not end until early the following Tuesday morning. It has also been said that years ago the famous "cocktail hour" in Jackson Hole began around Labor Day and went on until around Thanksgiving, when the serious partying began, which could continue "until March or until jail, whichever comes first."[2] And while the people of Jackson Hole today are much more moderate, they still take a back seat to no one in knowing how to get together and have fun. Not long ago, a visitor commented that he had never seen a place where so many friendly people could have such a good time merely at the sound of an ice cube dropping into a glass, or at the sound of picnic sandwiches being packed into a saddlebag.

As for outdoor life, the range of activities to be found in Jackson Hole, summer and winter, would be hard to duplicate elsewhere. Here one can enjoy some of North America's finest hunting and fishing, downhill and cross-country skiing, mountain climbing and camping, horseback riding and backpacking, even boating in the form of canoeing, kayaking or simply rubber-raft floating the waters of the Snake River and its tributaries. Golf, tennis and, as mentioned earlier, even polo are played here, and for those so boldly inclined there is hang-gliding. About the only sport Jackson Hole does not offer is swimming in a large, federally-financed pool, the local voters having expressed themselves quite forcefully on that issue. All in all, indoors or out, social or athletic, in terms of culture or entertainment, there are few activities Jackson Hole does not offer along with its diversity of active, talented and free-spirited people. It is therefore not surprising that so many who know the valley return year after year, with a growing number so taken with it they want to make their homes here.

But above and beyond all these attractions, what one must always come back to are the Tetons, that sky-piercing backdrop against which the history of Jackson Hole has been acted out. Like the sea, they are vast, primeval, incredibly beautiful and, as man reckons time, eternal. For at least eight million years, they have towered above one of the wildest and most spectacular regions on this planet, and there is no reason to believe they will not continue to do so for millions of years to come. For at least ten thousand years, they have drawn humans to them, and there is also no reason to believe they will not continue to do so for thousands of years to come. And just as we today know so little about the Early Hunters who once stood at the feet of these mighty mountains when the last glaciers of the Ice Age still lingered in their canyons, those who come here in the distant future will know little about the men and women whose lives were lived out in the mountains' shadows from the time of John Colter to the present. A thousand years from now, a few ancient artifacts may be unearthed—a mountain man's beaver trap, an early settler's plow, a cowboy's spurs, a tourist's license plate—but these strange clues will mean little to a race who by then will have journeyed to the stars. The only thing they will know for certain about all of these people from the far-off past is that they, like themselves, were drawn to the land of the Tetons.

Notes

Quotation page
[1] Hamilton Basso, "There's a Lot of Room in Wyoming," *Holiday*, vol. 10 (August 1951) p. 39.

Preface
[1] Struthers Burt, *The Diary of a Dude-Wrangler*, p. 28.

Acknowledgments
[1] Donald Hough, *The Cocktail Hour in Jackson Hole*, pp. 194–195.

Chapter 1
[1] Struthers Burt, *The Diary of a Dude-Wrangler*, p. 31.
[2] Bernard DeVoto, *Across the Wide Missouri*, p. 49.
[3] Bernard DeVoto, *The Year of Decision: 1846*, p. 163.
[4] Fritiof Fryxell, *The Tetons: Interpretations of a Mountain Landscape*, p. 41.
[5] Margaret and Olaus Murie, *Wapiti Wilderness*, p. 125.

Chapter 2
[1] The information on which this chapter is based came principally from George Gamow's *A Planet Called Earth*, Fritiof Fryxell's *The Tetons: Interpretations of a Mountain Landscape*, John D. Love's and John C. Reed's *Creation of the Teton Landscape* and the text on the reverse side of the U.S. Geological Survey's 1971 map of Grand Teton National Park.

Chapter 3
[1] Gary Wright, "Valley of the Ancients," *Teton: The Magazine of Jackson Hole*, vol. 8, p. 15.
[2] Much of the information in this chapter, particularly that having to do with the Athapaskan-speaking people and the abandonment of Jackson Hole by the Indians, is derived from *The People of the High Country: Jackson Hole Before the Settlers*, by Dr. Gary Wright, who kindly allowed me to read his work in manuscript form.

Chapter 4
[1] Reuben Gold Thwaites, ed., *Original Journals of the Lewis and Clark Expedition, 1804–1806*, vol. 5, p. 146.
[2] Ibid., vol. 5, p. 341.
[3] Richard Oglesby, *Manuel Lisa and the Opening of the Missouri Fur Trade*, p. 41.

Chapter 5
[1] Washington Irving, *The Adventures of Captain Bonneville, U.S.A.*, p. 173.
[2] Frances Fuller Victor, *The River of the West*, pp. 79–80.

[3]   Burton Harris, *John Colter*, p. 82.

[4]   Ibid., p. 15.

[5]   Ibid., p. 125.

[6]   Merlin K. Potts, "The Discovery of Jackson Hole and the Yellowstone," *Campfire Tales of Jackson Hole*, p. 8.

[7]   Reuben Gold Thwaites, ed., *Original Journals of the Lewis and Clark Expedition, 1804–1806*, vol. 2, p. 383.

[8]   Harris, *John Colter*, p. 97.

[9]   Hiram Martin Chittenden, *The American Fur Trade of the Far West*, vol. 2, fn. p. 715.

Chapter 6

[1]   Stanley Vestal, *Jim Bridger*, p. 274.

[2]   Francis Parkman, *The Oregon Trail*, p. 111.

[3]   Washington Irving, *Astoria*, p. 257.

[4]   Ibid., pp. 265–266.

Chapter 7

[1]   Dale L. Morgan, *Jedediah Smith and the Opening of the West*, p. 19.

[2]   Don Berry, *A Majority of Scoundrels*, p. 83.

[3]   Ibid., p. 364.

[4]   Bernard DeVoto, *The Course of Empire*, p. 538.

[5]   Frances Fuller Victor, *The River of the West*, p. 111.

[6]   Berry, *A Majority of Scoundrels*, p. 299.

[7]   Osborne Russell, *Journal of a Trapper*, p. 19.

[8]   Victor, *The River of the West*, p. 187.

Chapter 8

[1]   Don Berry, *A Majority of Scoundrels*, p. 319.

[2]   T. D. Bonner, ed., *The Life and Adventures of James P. Beckwourth, Mountaineer, Scout, and Pioneer, and Chief of the Crow Nation of Indians*, p. 99.

[3]   Ibid., p. 95.

[4]   Elinor Wilson, *Jim Beckwourth*, p. 169.

[5]   Ibid., p. 126.

[6]   Frances Fuller Victor, *The River of the West*, p. 448.

[7]   Ibid., p. 449.

[8]   Stanley Vestal, *Jim Bridger*, p. 216.

Chapter 9

[1]   Nathaniel Pitt Langford, "Ascent of Mount Hayden," *Scribner's Monthly*, vol. 6 (June 1873) p. 135.

[2]   C. G. Coutant, *History of Wyoming*, p. 711.

[3]   J. Cecil Alter, *Jim Bridger*, p. 282.

[4]   Ibid., p. 289.

[5]   Ibid.

[6]   Ibid.

[7]   Stanley Vestal, *Jim Bridger*, pp. 205–206.

[8]   Hiram Martin Chittenden, *The Yellowstone National Park*, pp. 55–56.

[9]   Aubrey Haines, *The Yellowstone Story*, vol. 1, p. 77.

Chapter 10

1   Elijah Nicholas ("Uncle Nick") Wilson's story of his youth was originally published in 1910 under the title *Among the Shoshones*. It was later reissued, with some minor alterations in the text, as *The White Indian Boy*. This particular quotation comes from *The White Indian Boy*, p. 10.

2   Wilson, *Among the Shoshones*, p. 32.

3   Wilson, *The White Indian Boy*, p. 50.

4   Wilson, *Among the Shoshones*, p. 31.

5   Ibid., p. 218.

6   Ibid., pp. 43–44.

7   Ibid., p. 41.

8   Ibid., p. 124.

9   Ibid., p. 137.

10   Ibid.

11   Fred Reinfeld, *Pony Express*, p. 9.

12   Wilson, *Among the Shoshones*, p. 160.

13   Ibid., p. 220.

14   Ibid., p. 247.

Chapter 11

1   Orrin H. and Lorraine G. Bonney, *Bonney's Guide: Grand Teton National Park and Jackson's Hole*, p. 108.

Chapter 12

1   William Henry Jackson, *Time Exposure*, p. 187.

2   The Earl of Dunraven, *The Great Divide*, p. 17.

3   Nathaniel Pitt Langford, "Ascent of Mount Hayden," *Scribner's Monthly*, vol. 6 (June 1873) p. 135.

4   Elizabeth Arnold Stone, *Uinta County*, pp. 243–244.

5   Nathaniel Pitt Langford, *The Discovery of Yellowstone Park*, fn. pp. 52–53.

6   Nolie Mumey, *The Teton Mountains*, pp. 23–24.

Chapter 13

1   Orrin H. and Lorraine Bonney, *Battle Drums and Geysers*, p. 25.

2   Ibid., p. 22.

3   Ibid., pp. xxiv–xxv.

4   Ibid., p. 155.

5   Ibid., p. 154.

6   Ibid., p. 547.

7   Ibid., p. 549.

8   From Doane's journal.

9   Information obtained in an interview with Emil Stip Wolff in Jackson Hole, August 5, 1975. According to Mr. Wolff, Doane's men told his father that prior to the end of the expedition the lieutenant spoke of donating the unnamed boat to a museum. As a joke among themselves, they said that if he had done so he probably would have first named it for himself. Mr. Wolff also recalls his father saying on a number of occasions that Doane's men thought he was "crazy."

10   From Doane's journal.

11   Sources, in order of quotation:

Bonney and Bonney, *Battle Drums and Geysers*, p. 141.

Ibid., p. xviii, from the Foreword by George B. Hartzog, Jr.

Merlin K. Potts, "The Doane Expedition of 1876–77," *Campfire Tales of Jackson Hole*, p. 37.

[12]   Frank Calkins, *Jackson Hole*, p. 107.

Chapter 14

[1]   Freeman Tilden, *Following the Frontier with F. Jay Haynes*, p. 117.

[2]   From the press releases of Lt. Col. Michael Sheridan and Lt. Col. James Gregory, which were later published in a portfolio entitled *Journey through the Yellowstone Park and Northwestern Wyoming, 1883*. One copy is in the Western Americana Collection of the Yale University Library, from which a microfilm of the contents was obtained.

[3]   Hiram Martin Chittenden, *The Yellowstone National Park*, p. 93.

[4]   Several requests made of the Library of Congress to provide a microfilm of *The Rajah, or the Great Sporting Excursion of 1883* were to no avail, although not because of any lack of cooperation on the part of the library. The one remaining copy of the burlesque has vanished from the stacks, and despite a special search has not been found. I have therefore relied on Frank Calkins' *Jackson Hole* for quotations from the anonymous "Unc Dunkam."

[5]   Ibid.

[6]   Ibid.

[7]   Sheridan and Gregory, *Journey Through the Yellowstone Park and Northwestern Wyoming, 1883*.

[8]   Ibid.

[9]   Tilden, *Following the Frontier with F. Jay Haynes*, p. 138.

[10]   From *The Rajah*.

[11]   Ansel Adams and Nancy Newhall, *The Tetons and the Yellowstone*, p. 71.

Chapter 15

[1]   Struthers Burt, *The Diary of a Dude-Wrangler*, p. 111.

[2]   Bruce Le Roy, *H. M. Chittenden*, p. 59.

[3]   Frank Calkins, *Jackson Hole*, p. 143.

[4]   Burt, *The Diary of a Dude-Wrangler*, p. 266.

[5]   Ibid., p. 271.

[6]   Ibid.

[7]   *New York Times*, July 27, 1895.

[8]   D. M. Browning, "Indian Disturbances in 'Jackson Hole' Country, Wyoming, 1895," *Annals of Wyoming*, vol. 16, no. 1, p. 22.

[9]   Ibid., pp. 25–26.

[10]   Ibid., p. 17.

[11]   Ibid., p. 26.

[12]   Ibid.

[13]   Elizabeth Arnold Stone, *Uinta County*, pp. 236–237.

[14]   William L. Simpson Collection in the Western History Research Center at the University of Wyoming.

[15]   Ibid.

[16]   Ibid.

[17]   Ibid.

[18] Freeman Tilden, *Following the Frontier with F. Jay Haynes*, p. 227.
[19] Ibid., p. 240.
[20] Burt, *The Diary of a Dude-Wrangler*, p. 114.

Chapter 16
[1] Elizabeth Arnold Stone, *Uinta County*, p. 231.
[2] B. W. Driggs, *History of Teton Valley, Idaho*, p. 126.
[3] Fritiof Fryxell, "The Story of Deadman's Bar," *Campfire Tales of Jackson Hole*, p. 41.
[4] "Writings of Richard 'Beaver Dick' Leigh" in the Western History Research Center at the University of Wyoming.
[5] Struthers Burt, *The Diary of a Dude-Wrangler*, p. 295.
[6] Raold Fryxell, "The Affair at Cunningham's Ranch," *Campfire Tales of Jackson Hole*, p. 45.
[7] Ibid., p. 46.
[8] Elizabeth Wied Hayden, "Shoot Out at Cunningham's Cabin," *Teton: The Magazine of Jackson Hole*, vol. 8, p. 31.
[9] Elizabeth Wied Hayden, *From Trapper to Tourist in Jackson Hole*, p. 26.

Chapter 17
[1] Margaret and Olaus Murie, *Wapiti Wilderness*, p. 33.
[2] Ibid., p. 34.
[3] Bertha Chambers Gillette, *Homesteading with the Elk*, p. 159.
[4] Frank Calkins, *Jackson Hole*, p. 134.
[5] Gillette, *Homesteading with the Elk*, p. 157.
[6] Elizabeth Wied Hayden, "Driving Out the Tuskers," *Teton: The Magazine of Jackson Hole* (Winter-Spring 1971) p. 22.
[7] Calkins, *Jackson Hole*, p. 135.
[8] Hayden, "Driving Out the Tuskers," p. 36.
[9] Gillette, *Homesteading with the Elk*, p. 161.
[10] Calkins, *Jackson Hole*, pp. 208–209.
[11] Struthers Burt, *The Diary of a Dude-Wrangler*, p. 127.
[12] Donald Hough, *Snow Above Town*, p. 199.
[13] Murie and Murie, *Wapiti Wilderness*, p. 139.
[14] Hough, *Snow Above Town*, p. 196.

Chapter 18
[1] Donald C. Swain, *Wilderness Defender*, p. x.
[2] Ibid., p. 35. When Woodrow Wilson appointed a member of the Department of the Interior to the Federal Reserve Board, he told the Secretary of the Interior to go out and "find another millionaire with an itch for public service," which the Secretary did by recruiting Mather.
[3] Ibid., p. 117.
[4] Ibid.
[5] Ibid., p. 129.
[6] *Jackson Hole News*, Grand Teton National Park Special 25th Anniversary Issue (September 1975) p. 2.
[7] Struthers Burt, *The Diary of a Dude-Wrangler*, p. 331.
[8] Ansel Adams and Nancy Newhall, *The Tetons and the Yellowstone*, p. 87.

[9]   David J. Saylor, *Jackson Hole, Wyoming*, p. 172.

[10]   Nancy Newhall, *A Contribution to the Heritage of Every American*, p. x, from the Prologue by Fairfield Osborn.

[11]   Swain, *Wilderness Defender*, p. 160.

[12]   Ibid., p. 161.

[13]   *Jackson Hole News*, 25th Anniversary Issue, p. 5.

[14]   Ibid., pp. 2, 4, 8.

[15]   Ibid., p. 8.

[16]   Swain, *Wilderness Defender*, p. 253.

[17]   *Jackson Hole News*, 25th Anniversary Issue, p. 4.

[18]   Swain, *Wilderness Defender*, p. 252.

[19]   Ibid., pp. 252–253.

[20]   Saylor, *Jackson Hole, Wyoming*, p. 203.

[21]   T. A. Larson, *History of Wyoming*, p. 500.

[22]   Margaret and Olaus Murie, *Wapiti Wilderness*, p. 123.

[23]   Swain, *Wilderness Defender*, p. 268.

[24]   *Jackson Hole News*, 25th Anniversary Issue, p. 11.

[25]   Donald Hough, *The Cocktail Hour in Jackson Hole*, p. 241.

[26]   Ibid.

[27]   *Jackson Hole News*, 25th Anniversary Issue, p. 11.

[28]   Swain, *Wilderness Defender*, p. 280.

[29]   Newhall, *A Contribution to the Heritage of Every American*, p. 175.

Chapter 19

[1]   Orrin H. and Lorraine G. Bonney, *Bonney's Guide: Grand Teton National Park and Jackson's Hole*, pp. 82–83.

[2]   Donald Hough, *Snow Above Town*, p. 19.

[3]   Edgar Beecher Bronson, *Reminiscences of a Ranchman*, p. 310.

[4]   Frances Judge, "The Story of Menor's Ferry," *Campfire Tales of Jackson Hole*, p. 57.

[5]   Bonney and Bonney, *Bonney's Guide*, p. 115.

[6]   Struthers Burt, *The Diary of a Dude-Wrangler*, pp. 129–130.

[7]   Donald Hough, *The Cocktail Hour in Jackson Hole*, p. 191.

[8]   Ibid., p. 156.

[9]   Ibid.

[10]   Hough, *Snow Above Town*, p. 73.

Chapter 20

[1]   Wendell and Mary Ellen Wilson, *The Teton Valley Ranch Wrangler* (May 1975).

[2]   Donald Hough, *The Cocktail Hour in Jackson Hole*, p. 13.

Bibliography

Adams, Ansel and Newhall, Nancy. *The Tetons and the Yellowstone*. Redwood City, Calif.: 5 Associates, 1970.

Alter, J. Cecil. *Jim Bridger*. Norman: University of Oklahoma Press, 1962.

Bakeless, John. *Lewis and Clark, Partners in Discovery*. New York: William Morrow & Company, 1947.

Bancroft, Hubert Howe. *History of Nevada, Colorado, and Wyoming: 1540–1888*. San Francisco: The History Company, 1890.

Barry, Nielson J. "John Colter's Map of 1814," *Wyoming Annals*, vol. 10, no. 3 (July 1938).

Beal, Merrill D. *The Story of Man in Yellowstone*. Caldwell, Idaho: The Caxton Printers, Ltd., 1949.

Berry, Don. *A Majority of Scoundrels*. New York: Harper & Brothers, 1961.

Bonner, T. D., ed. *The Life and Adventures of James P. Beckwourth, Mountaineer, Scout, and Pioneer, and Chief of the Crow Nation of Indians*. New York: Alfred A. Knopf, 1931. (First published by Harper & Brothers in 1856.)

Bonney, Orrin H. and Lorraine G. *Bonney's Guide: Grand Teton National Park and Jackson's Hole*. Houston: Published by the authors, 1972.

———— *Battle Drums and Geysers*. Chicago: The Swallow Press, Inc., 1970.

Bronson, Edgar Beecher. *Reminiscences of a Ranchman*. Lincoln: University of Nebraska Press, 1962. (First published in 1908; revised edition published by A. C. McClurg & Co. in 1910.)

Browning, D. M. "Indian Disturbances in 'Jackson Hole' Country, Wyoming, 1895," *Annals of Wyoming*, vol. 16, no. 1 (January 1944). (Report made in 1895 by the Commissioner of Indian Affairs.)

Burt, Struthers. *The Diary of a Dude-Wrangler*. New York: Charles Scribner's Sons, 1924.

Calkins, Frank. *Jackson Hole*. New York: Alfred A. Knopf, 1973.

Camp, Charles L., ed. *James Clyman, Frontiersman: The Adventures of a Trapper and Covered-Wagon Emigrant as Told in His Own Reminiscences and Diaries*. Portland, Oregon: The Champoeg Press, 1960.

Carrighar, Sally. *One Day at Teton Marsh*. New York: Alfred A. Knopf, 1967.

Carson, Christopher. *Kit Carson's Autobiography*. Lincoln: University of Nebraska Press, 1966. Edited by Milo Milton Quaife.

Carter, Harvey Louis. *'Dear Old Kit': The Historical Christopher Carson*. Norman: University of Oklahoma Press, 1968.

Ceram, C. W. *The First American: A Story of North American Archaeology*. New York: Harcourt Brace Jovanovich, Inc., 1971.

Chittenden, Hiram Martin. *The American Fur Trade of the Far West*, 2 vols. Stanford, Calif.: Academic Reprints, 1954. (First published by F. P. Harper in 1902.)

———— *The Yellowstone National Park*. Norman: University of Oklahoma Press, 1964. Edited by Richard A. Bartlett. (First published by Robert Clarke Company in 1895.)

Clark, Ella E. *Indian Legends from the Northern Rockies.* Norman: University of Oklahoma Press, 1966.

Coutant, C. G. *History of Wyoming.* Laramie, Wyo.: Chaplin, Spafford & Mathison Printers, 1899.

DeVoto, Bernard. *The Year of Decision: 1846.* Boston: Houghton Mifflin Company, 1942. Sentry Edition.

———— *Across the Wide Missouri*. Boston: Houghton Mifflin Company, 1947. Sentry Edition.

———— *The Course of Empire*. Boston: Houghton Mifflin Company, 1952.

———— ed. *The Journals of Lewis and Clark*. Boston: Houghton Mifflin Company, 1953.

Doane, Gustavus Cheney. Lieutenant Doane's reconstructed journal of his expedition on the Snake River in 1876, a typescript copy of which is in the library of Grand Teton National Park.

Driggs, B. W. *History of Teton Valley, Idaho*. Rexburg, Idaho: Eastern Idaho Publishing Company, 1970. (First published in 1926.)

Dunraven, The Earl of. *The Great Divide*. Lincoln: University of Nebraska Press, 1967. (First published in London by Chatto & Windus in 1876.)

Dunwiddie, Peter W. "The Nature of the Relationship between the Blackfeet Indians and the Men of the Fur Trade," *Annals of Wyoming*, vol. 46, no. 1 (Spring 1974).

Ewers, John C. *The Blackfeet: Raiders on the Northwestern Plains*. Norman: University of Oklahoma Press, 1958.

Fabian, Josephine. *The Jackson's Hole Story*. Salt Lake City: Sam Weller's Zion's Book Store, 1972.

Ferris, Warren A. *Life in the Rocky Mountains*. Denver: The Old West Publishing Co., 1940. Edited by P. C. Phillips. (First published in serial form in 1843 and 1844.)

Fryxell, Fritiof. *The Tetons: Interpretations of a Mountain Landscape*. Berkeley: University of California Press, 1938.

———— "The Story of Deadman's Bar," *Campfire Tales of Jackson Hole*. Moose, Wyo.: Grand Teton Natural History Association, 1960.

———— "Prospector of Jackson Hole," *Campfire Tales of Jackson Hole*. Moose, Wyo.: Grand Teton Natural History Association, 1960.

Fryxell, Roald. "The Affair at Cunningham's Ranch," *Campfire Tales of Jackson Hole*. Moose, Wyo.: Grand Teton Natural History Association, 1960.

Gamow, George. *A Planet Called Earth*. New York: The Viking Press, 1963.

Gillette, Bertha Chambers. *Homesteading with the Elk*. Salt Lake City: Utah Printing Company, 1967.

Guthrie, A. B., Jr. *The Big Sky*. New York: William Sloane Associates, 1947.

———— *The Way West*. Houghton Mifflin Company, 1949.

Hafen, LeRoy R., ed. *The Mountain Men and the Fur Trade of the Far West*, 10 vols. Glendale, Calif.: The Arthur H. Clark Company, 1965–1972.

———— and Ghent, W. J. *Broken Hand: The Life Story of Thomas Fitzpatrick, Chief of the Mountain Men*. Denver: The Old West Publishing Company, 1931.

Haines, Aubrey L. *The Yellowstone Story: A History of Our First National Park*, 2 vols. Boulder: Yellowstone Library and Museum Association in cooperation with Colorado Associated University Press, 1977.

Harris, Burton. *John Colter, His Years in the Rockies*. New York: Charles Scribner's Sons, 1952.

Hayden, Elizabeth Wied. *From Trapper to Tourist in Jackson Hole*. Jackson, Wyo.: 1969. (No publisher given.)

—— "Shoot Out at Cunningham's Cabin," *Teton: The Magazine of Jackson Hole*, vol. 8 (1975–1976).

Haynes, Jack Ellis. "The Expedition of President Chester A. Arthur to Yellowstone National Park in 1883," *Annals of Wyoming*, vol. 14, no. 1.

Hough, Donald. *Snow Above Town*. New York: W. W. Norton & Company, 1943.

—— *The Cocktail Hour in Jackson Hole*. New York: W. W. Norton & Company, 1956.

Hyde, George E. *Indians of the High Plains: From the Prehistoric Period to the Coming of the Europeans*. Norman: University of Oklahoma Press, 1959.

Irving, Washington. *Astoria*. Norman: University of Oklahoma Press, 1964. Edited by Edgeley W. Todd. (First published in 1836.)

—— *The Adventures of Captain Bonneville, U.S.A.* Norman: University of Oklahoma Press, 1961. Edited by Edgeley W. Todd. (First published in 1837.)

Jackson Hole News, Grand Teton National Park Special 25th Anniversary Issue (September 1975).

Jackson, William Henry. *Time Exposure*. New York: Cooper Square Publishers, Inc., 1970.

—— "First Photographing of the Tetons," an address prepared for the dedication of Grand Teton National Park.

Judge, Frances. "The Story of Menor's Ferry," *Campfire Tales of Jackson Hole*. Moose, Wyo.: Grand Teton Natural History Association, 1960.

King, Bucky. "When Hospitality Fostered an Industry," *In Wyoming* (October–November 1975).

Krakel, Dean, II. *Season of the Elk*. Kansas City, Mo.: The Lowell Press in cooperation with the National Cowboy Hall of Fame and Western Heritage Center, Oklahoma City, 1976.

Langford, Nathaniel Pitt. *The Discovery of Yellowstone Park*. Lincoln: University of Nebraska Press, 1972. (Reproduced from the edition of 1905.)

—— "Ascent of Mount Hayden," *Scribner's Monthly*, vol. 6 (June, 1873).

Larson, T. A. *History of Wyoming*. Lincoln: University of Nebraska Press, 1965.

Leigh, Richard. "Writings of Richard 'Beaver Dick' Leigh." Original diaries and letters in the Western History Research Center at the University of Wyoming.

Le Roy, Bruce. *H. M. Chittenden: A Western Epic, Being a Selection from His Unpublished Journals, Diaries and Reports*. Tacoma: Washington State Historical Society, 1961.

Leydet, François. "Jackson Hole: Good-bye to the Old Days?" *National Geographic*, vol. 150, no. 6 (December 1976).

Livingston, Kathryn. "Jackson Hole: America's Most Spectacular Hideaway," *Town & Country* (February 1976).

Love, John D. and Reed, John C., Jr. *Creation of the Teton Landscape*. Moose, Wyo.: Grand Teton Natural History Association, 1971.

Mattes, Merrill J. "Jackson Hole, Crossroads of the Western Fur Trade, 1807–1829," *Pacific Northwest Quarterly*, vol. 37, no. 2 (1946).

———— "Jackson Hole, Crossroads of the Western Fur Trade, 1830–1840," *Pacific Northwest Quarterly*, vol. 39, no. 1 (1948).

———— *Colter's Hell & Jackson's Hole*. Yellowstone Library and Museum Association and Grand Teton Natural History Association, 1962.

Morgan, Dale L. *Jedediah Smith and the Opening of the West*. Lincoln: University of Nebraska Press, 1964. (First published by Bobbs-Merrill Company in 1953.)

Muench, David and Pike, Donald G. *Rendezvous Country*. Palo Alto, Calif.: American West Publishing Company, 1975.

Mumey, Nolie. *The Teton Mountains: Their History and Tradition*. Denver: The Artcraft Press, 1947.

Murie, Margaret and Olaus. *Wapiti Wilderness*. New York: Alfred A. Knopf, 1969.

Murie, Olaus. *The Elk of North America*. Harrisburg, Pa., and Washington, D.C.: The Stackpole Company and the Wildlife Management Institute, 1951.

Nelson, Fern K. *Soda for the Sourdoughs*. Jackson, Wyo.: Grand Teton Printing and Publishing, 1973.

Newhall, Nancy. *A Contribution to the Heritage of Every American: The Conservation Activities of John D. Rockefeller, Jr.* New York: Alfred A. Knopf, 1957.

Oglesby, Richard Edward. *Manuel Lisa and the Opening of the Missouri Fur Trade*. Norman: University of Oklahoma Press, 1963.

Ortenburger, Leigh N. "The Hayden Survey Expedition of 1872," *Naturalist* (Spring 1976).

Parkman, Francis. *The Oregon Trail*. New York: New American Library, 1950. (First published in 1849.)

Paul, Elliott. *Desperate Scenery*. New York: Random House, 1954.

Peirce, Neal R. *The Mountain States of America*. New York: W. W. Norton & Company, Inc., 1972.

Phillips, Paul Chrisler, with concluding chapters by J. W. Smurr. *The Fur Trade*, 2 vols. Norman: University of Oklahoma Press, 1961.

Porter, Mae Reed and Davenport, Odessa. *Scotsman in Buckskin*. New York: Hastings House, 1963.

Potts, Merlin K. "John Colter: The Discovery of Jackson Hole and the Yellowstone," *Campfire Tales of Jackson Hole*. Moose, Wyo.: Grand Teton Natural History Association, 1960.

———— "The Mountain Men in Jackson Hole," *Campfire Tales of Jackson Hole*. Moose, Wyo.: Grand Teton Natural History Association, 1960.

———— "The Doane Expedition of 1876–77," *Campfire Tales of Jackson Hole*. Moose, Wyo.: Grand Teton Natural History Association, 1960.

Reinfeld, Fred. *Pony Express*. Lincoln: University of Nebraska Press, 1973. (First published by the Macmillan Company in 1966.)

Righter, Robert W. "The Brief, Hectic Life of Jackson Hole National Monument," *The American West*, vol. 13, no. 6 (November–December 1976).

Russell, Osborne. *Journal of a Trapper*. Lincoln: University of Nebraska Press, 1965. Edited by Aubrey L. Haines. (First published by the Oregon Historical Society in 1955.)

Ruxton, George Frederick. *Life in the Far West*. Glorieta, N.M.: The Rio Grande Press, Inc., 1972. (First published in 1848.)

Saylor, David J. *Jackson Hole, Wyoming*. Norman: University of Oklahoma Press, 1970.

Settle, Raymond W. and Mary Lund. *Saddles and Spurs: The Pony Express Saga*. Lincoln: University of Nebraska Press, 1972. (First published by the Stackpole Company in 1955.)

Simpson, William L. Collection of his papers in the Western History Research Center at the University of Wyoming.

Stone, Elizabeth Arnold. *Uinta County: Its Place in History*. Laramie, Wyo.: The Laramie Printing Company, 1924.

Sunder, John E. *Bill Sublette, Mountain Man*. Norman: University of Oklahoma Press, 1959.

Swain, Donald C. *Wilderness Defender: Horace M. Albright and Conservation*. Chicago: University of Chicago Press, 1970.

Thwaites, Reuben Gold, ed. *Original Journals of the Lewis and Clark Expedition, 1804–1806*, 8 vols. New York: Arno Press, 1969. (First published by Dodd, Mead & Company in 1904–1905.)

Tilden, Freeman. *Following the Frontier with F. Jay Haynes*. New York: Alfred A. Knopf. 1964.

Tobie, Harvey Elmer. *No Man Like Joe: The Life and Times of Joe Meek*. Portland: Oregon Historical Society, 1949.

Trenholm, Virginia Cole and Carley, Maurine. *The Shoshonis: Sentinels of the Rockies*. Norman: University of Oklahoma Press, 1964.

Vestal, Stanley. *Jim Bridger*. Lincoln: University of Nebraska Press, 1970. (First published by William Morrow & Company in 1946.)

———*Joe Meek, The Merry Mountain Man*. Lincoln: University of Nebraska Press, 1963. (First published by Caxton Printers, Ltd., in 1952.)

Victor, Frances Fuller. *The River of the West*. Oakland, Calif.: Brooks-Sterling Company, 1974. (First published in 1870.)

Wakefield, Robert. *Schwiering and the West*. Aberdeen, S.D.: North Plains Press, 1973.

Wedel, Waldo R. *Prehistoric Man on the Great Plains*. Norman: University of Oklahoma Press, 1961.

Wilkins, Thurman. *Thomas Moran: Artist of the Mountains*. Norman: University of Oklahoma Press, 1966.

Wilson, Elijah Nicholas. *Among the Shoshones*. Salt Lake City: Skelton Publishing Company, 1910.

———, in collaboration with Howard R. Driggs. *The White Indian Boy*. Yonkers-on-Hudson, N.Y.: World Book Company, 1919.

Wilson, Wendell and Mary Ellen. *The Teton Valley Ranch Wrangler*. Jackson Hole (May 1975).

Wister, Fanny Kemble, ed. *Owen Wister Out West: His Journals and Letters*. Chicago: University of Chicago Press, 1958.

Wister, Owen. *The Virginian*. New York: The Macmillan Company, 1902.

Wright, Gary. "Valley of the Ancients," *Teton: The Magazine of Jackson Hole*, vol. 8 (1975–1976).

——— "The Coming of the People," *Naturalist* (Spring 1976).

——— *The People of the High Country: Jackson Hole Before the Settlers. (Manuscript)*

Index